"Stunningly original . . . By breaking every rule of tl something unique and sublime: a beautiful chronicle of a life as yet unfinished . . . a shining and sincere miracle of a book." —*NPR*

"Searing . . . rendered in vivid, painful, and regularly funny reminiscence. But more than anything else, this bildungsroman is a wry document of American class strata." —*O, The Oprah Magazine*

"Gorgeously written and uncommonly insightful." —*People*

"Magnificent . . . at turns exuberant, humorous, unsentimental, imaginative, keen. . . . The locus of the book is [Gerald's] extraordinary journey. . . . Along the way, he learns plenty about his country, the elites who run it and the underclass subject to their rule. He often relays his insight with indelible aphorism. . . . His life, and this memoir, serve as proof of his prodigious talents, of the truth that, for the gifted like him, struggles . . . can yield something miraculous." —*The New York Times Book Review*

"Gerald writes a powerful commentary on race in America simply by telling his life story." —*Entertainment Weekly*

"Undeniably inspirational." —*Vanity Fair*

"Infuriating and deeply moving . . . It's a rare memoirist who does not just recall, but inhabits the past, who understands that memory is a pliable thing, a means to, not the end of, a story . . . There's a bit of Barbara Kingsolver in this, a bit of James Baldwin . . . urgent, lyrical [and] timely." —*The Texas Observer*

"Compulsively readable. . . . Gerald's staccato prose and peripatetic storytelling combine the cadences of the Bible with an urgency reminiscent of James Baldwin." —*BookPage*

"A beautifully written cautionary tale about the toll taken by society even on those like [Gerald] fortunate enough to defy the tremendous odds against their success." —*Vulture*

"A memoir of lacerating honesty and self-awareness, a book that lets you feel how badly the author needed to write it . . . *There Will Be No Miracles Here* is a portrait of a man looking for what's real, within and for himself. It's also a testament to the power of written words and the role they play in personal transformation. Reading Gerald's book is to see the author come alive, and to look in wonder at the process." —*The Dallas Morning News*

"A vital missive to these cracked-up times . . . Gerald nimbly avoids the twin perils of self-pity and romanticism, with writing that is muscular and direct." —*Out*

"[Gerald] takes on the important work of exposing the damage done to America, especially its black population, by the failure to confront the myths, half-truths, and lies at the foundation of the success stories that the nation worships." —*The Atlantic*

"An extraordinary portrait of what it means to live on both the bottom and the top of American life." —Anand Giridharadas

"Somehow Casey Gerald has pulled off the most urgently political, most deeply personal, and most engagingly spiritual statement of our time by just looking outside his window and inside himself. Extraordinary." —Marlon James

"A deeply spiritual memoir about growing up black, poor, and gay in evangelical Texas; Gerald has become a superstar as a TED talker and MBA powerhouse, but this book is quiet and reflective, a document of fearless humility." —*The Boston Globe*

"[A] compelling look at how the elite maintain their status at the expense of others."
—*Paste*

"From the first line of this astonishing book, we know we are in for a trip we've never gone on before in memoir. The book braids, un-braids, and re-braids threads of the personal, the political, and the philosophical, in a voice that is ironically comedic and at the same time wholly sincere. *There Will Be No Miracles Here* is a glowing literary event." —Kiese Laymon

"A formally inventive and lyrical memoir about boyhood, blackness, masculinity, faith, privilege, and the search for self that investigates the idea of the American dream, and how the myth of ascension—including the author's own—is what can ultimately undo us." —*Poets & Writers Magazine*

"Casey Gerald's book is urgent, mesmeric, soaring, desperately serious, wounded, and, at times, slyly, brilliantly comic. The world he creates is vivid, the invocation of the personal and the political sharp and knowing. The style is flawless, the pace perfectly judged. Electrifying." —Colm Tóibín

"This is the book for all of us who have juggled double (and triple, and quadruple) consciousnesses, and for those of us who have prayed to false gods and passed as false selves. Casey Gerald leads us through blackness and boyhood, love and masculinity, faith and privilege, on his journey toward the only self who could write these fierce and luminous pages. This book is fire." —Danzy Senna

"Gerald pulls no punches in telling his extraordinary story, which he relates with unsparing truth, no small amount of feeling, and a complete lack of sentimentality. Painful lessons dart in and pummel his unsuspecting self, and scenes of startling intensity are often pierced—and pieced back together—by light and humor . . . Richly layered writing on poverty, progress, race, belief, and the actual American Dream."
—*Booklist* (starred review)

"Hardly a by-the-numbers memoir, this is a powerful book marked by the author's refreshingly complicated and insightful storytelling."
—*Kirkus Reviews* (starred review)

"A wide-ranging, hard-to-define memoir of family, identity, and belonging."
—*Library Journal*

CASEY GERALD

THERE WILL BE NO MIRACLES HERE

Riverhead Books   New York

RIVERHEAD BOOKS
An imprint of Penguin Random House LLC
penguinrandomhouse.com

First Riverhead hardcover edition: October 2018
Riverhead hardcover ISBN: 9780735214200
First Riverhead trade paperback edition: October 2019
Riverhead trade paperback ISBN: 9780735214224

Printed in the United States of America

Book design by Lauren Kolm

Some names and identifying characteristics have been
changed to protect the privacy of the individuals described.

Penguin is committed to publishing works of quality and integrity.
In that spirit, we are proud to offer this book to our readers;
however, the story, the experiences, and the words
are the author's alone.

THERE
WILL
BE NO
MIRACLES
HERE

I do not want the world to end.

Nobody asked me, though. *Boy you're too young to have an opinion!* They cry and cry each time I offer up a couple cents. Maybe so. Maybe. But if twelve is too young to think, it sure as hell is too young to die.

I guess it won't be *death.* I will simply *disappear,* in the twinkling of an eye, right around midnight on the last night of this world, 31 December 1999, when Jesus Christ returns to set His kingdom up for good and for good reason. Things have really gone to shit since He's been gone. Ever since He got Himself killed for trying to help the weak and poor and scorned around Judea, and since He fled back home to lick His wounds, to spend two thousand years in exile, and since His buddies spread a story in His stead to men and women everywhere, some of whom were so inspired that they, too, wound up hung and shot and flayed for similar transgressions— and *still,* somehow, it seems each day, there are more poor, more weak, more scorned among the earth, myself included, which is why the Son of man is on His way to pick me up.

Just a minute!

Got to find my shoes somewhere in this house where all my space is borrowed, temporary. A little corner of somebody else's closet. Their bed.

Their bathroom sink. Their dinner table. A stranger in the country of my kin, but that's all right. There are many mansions over there and plenty room for me. *Here I come . . .* out the door and down the sidewalk to the long and boxy town car where Clarice sits waiting. She will disappear as well. Must be why her head is bare, why those thick gray curls are washed and set but unadorned, ready for her crown reserved in layaway. Or does she wear no hat tonight simply because it's Friday? I don't know for sure. Don't know anything for sure when it comes to her, my father's mother, or when it comes to my own mother, wherever she is—or when it comes to anybody else who played some role in making this world what it has been for these twelve years. But that's all right, too. He knows it all. *We're on our way.*

The gravel parking lot is nearly full, not even ten o'clock yet. I see a few cars trampling the grass along the wall of naked trees that separates the neighborhood from the church grounds, as my father's father intended. God rest his soul, wherever it resides. He left the church to his offspring. Left the town car to his widow. Left instructions that she keep her parking space up front so we don't have to search at all, just roll right in. *We're here.*

In the sanctuary, someone saved a seat for her. *Scoot over some,* I ask them with my eyes and they scoot, since I'm with her and I'm small. Much bigger than I was when I first entered this sanctuary as a thought of my parents'. Place still looks the same, just like every other sanctuary to me, except for all the red. Woolly fabric, dried-blood red, covers every inch of the floor and the seat of each wooden pew and each armless, high-back chair in the pulpit. There's even a strip of it stitched on the robes worn by the choir members who will sing tonight one final time. Singing now, in fact.

Behind their choir stand is the empty pool, filled once a month for baptisms. They say it takes only one dip in that water and you'll be set for life, *after*life. *They* say a lot of things that ain't the truth, so I went back a second time, right after my twelfth birthday this past January, to be sure. I also decided, a few months ago, to read the Bible on my own—three or four pages a day. But that early stuff was boring and the clock was ticking, so to speak, so I moved on to a timely novel, *Left Behind*, and made it through enough of that to warn you: Never read it. Believe me. Since then, I've tried to talk to God a lot more and to sin a lot less. Had a hard time doing either.

According to the clock nailed to the back wall above the audiovisual control room, where tonight's service is being recorded for some reason, we have only an hour. Whoever is left behind to watch will probably not see me, crunched between old women, but they will see that the place is packed, hardly an empty seat. I could tell you all about the many gathered, who they are, where they come from. But none of that matters anymore. The only thing that counts tonight is where they are *going*, and that's none of my business, being a child and all. Besides, I have my own eternity to worry about.

Outside, beyond this sanctuary, are other worries—at least, that's what I heard on television. Some worry the computers will revolt at midnight, unable to comprehend the year 2000. Each machine's rebellion will spark some small catastrophe: Planes, unable to find their way, will fling themselves down to earth—darkened earth, since streetlights will not heed commands to glow past midnight. Dams and sewers will surrender to the water's long-held wish to flow all over the place, all over the people, who will not be warned because the telephones will not connect them to each other anymore. They will have only themselves. Won't even have money, except whatever cash is on hand, since bank accounts will reset to 1900, when everybody was broke. They will be broke again tonight, and hungry, too, as many grocery shelves have been emptied. *Oh, sinnerman.* The worst is yet to come. Plagues. Riots. An atom bomb or two on accident, and more: a lake of fire where each sinnerman and sinnerwoman and sinnerchild (twelve years and older) will swim, ablaze, forever and ever. I might be down there with them if I have not made the right decisions these twelve years, but there's still time: ten minutes, says our pastor, who's calling us down to the altar so we can pray until midnight comes, until He comes. *Let's go.*

Now we're crowded together in the altar space and in the aisles. Some are sweating—nerves as much as heat. The pastor is sweating most of all, as he should. Seems to me that every time he's laid his hands on some sick parishioner, they've wound up sicker. A few have even died. That can't be a good sign for him, nor for those relying on his intercession, which I'm not. I have seen enough to doubt the holy men, and so I've memorized my own private prayer.

Lord, please take me with You when You come.

That is all I have to ask of God, and I will get my answer soon. It's 11:57 (had to peek back at the clock). Close my eyes, focus on my silent incantation, *Lord, please take me when You come*, listen to the people shout and moan. Louder. Higher. Now the organ's running strong—can you hear it? Feel the sweaty palms grip firm and the eyes clench tight down here at the altar, where one will be taken and one will be left, where wheat and chaff will be torn apart, and the glory will be revealed. *Lord, please take me when you come* in this din of end-time noise, the heat now stifling beneath low-hanging lights, and—*in the precious name of Jesus . . . Amen!* The pastor shouts. It's over.

There's a hand still holding mine—Clarice's, I see, when my eyes refocus. On the clock I see it's after midnight. And around the sanctuary I see no fewer bodies. Has He come and left us all? No one seems too worried. Same *Happy New Year!* hugs as always, same hymn before the benediction. Outside are the same cars in the gravel parking lot and in the grass, cranking up just fine. No snow. No fire. Not a flicker from the streetlights as Clarice drives away from the church. No panic in the voices on the radio. Above our heads, the planes are flying on, carrying everyone where they hope to go tonight. I'm carried to my mother's mother's house.

Inside, I see that everyone who was missing in the last millennium is still gone. Everybody else is here, awake, boiling black-eyed peas. *Hey y'all* ... I just want a slice of cake, smuggle it to the room in back where I keep a mattress. On the tiny television, its bunny ears wrapped in aluminum foil, Peter Jennings is right where he is supposed to be, on channel 8, where he will stay for twenty-three hours and ten minutes, to coach the world through its demise. If I understand Mr. Jennings correctly, it has been over for a long time in other places. He speaks to Diane Sawyer in New York, where, somehow, an extra hour has already passed. Charlie Gibson is in London. Barbara Walters, Paris. I like and trust them both a good deal and it seems that they will soon witness the first morning after what was meant to be the final night. I don't understand. Screen cuts to Connie Chung live in Las Vegas, surely high on the list of the damned. Midnight. Fireworks. Kisses. Nothing else. Peter Jennings has never lied to me, and so I have to accept that *I* got something wrong, that *I* am a fool or worse. I mean, how exactly would Jesus have kept coming back again and again, based on the different time zones? Hadn't thought of that. Now that I do, now that it dawns on me how big a joke I am, how sick I made myself with dread and even hope—well, there's nothing left to do but cry. It *is* over. I'm still here.

I am *still* here, nearly twenty years later, and will let twelve-year-old me rest now. He had a rough night. Surely would have cried, sitting there at the edge of his mattress, if he had been the type of boy who cried. But he wasn't, anymore. And he did not want the world to end. His world had already ended. He wanted to be *rescued*—the Rapture had seemed an elegant solution: instantaneous escape for him, damnation for his enemies, robes and slippers, plenty food to eat, *and God shall wipe away all tears; and there shall be no more death, neither sorrow, nor crying, neither shall there be any more pain.* Yes. He wanted some of that. But midnight struck and the Son of man did not appear, so in the place of Paradise, he had to find a kingdom of this world.

Well, really all that he—all that *I*—hoped to find was somewhere to call home and some money, US dollars preferably, and, at some point, a spot on the varsity football squad and, soon after that, a beautiful boy to sneak off with on prom night. Nothing more or less than what was offered in the movies. Maybe a little more. I admit that, aside from those basic desires, I also longed for something to believe in. That was greedy. My mistake. I had not learned that *the search for belief is very likely the most violent known to man, not infrequently ending in death or derangement*, but I did learn and I now know. The search has not yet killed me, though I am a bit deranged—and *that* may be the best that I have been in all these years. For I have been so many things along my curious journey: a poor boy, a nigger, a Yale man, a Harvard man, a faggot, a Christian, a crack baby (alleged), the spawn of Satan, the Second Coming, Casey. I have been left once or twice. Been found, too. And every time I turned around, the world began to end again—it's even ending right this minute, I hear. *Three cheers for the end of the world*, if you ask me.

You see, it could be said that I, from my starting place in the valley of *the least of these*, made it to the mountaintop. Not that I set out to do so. Just was afraid and open-minded. Anyway, I'm back. I have not returned with empty hands. No. I have come with urgent news: we must find another mountain, if not another world, to call our own.

And if *they* say this is an unreasonable, impossible thing to request, I will tell them of a village that I heard of not too long ago. The village, somewhere in France, sometime in the seventeenth century, became the site of frequent miracles, according to the peasants there, who were so struck by symptoms of the supernatural that they put down their plows. This, of course, pissed off the local officials. They tried to reason with the peasants, to quell the mass hysteria, to no avail. At last, the officials sought an intervention from the highest power in the land, who sent them back with a sign. An *actual* sign, which was erected in the village square for all to see. It read:

THERE WILL BE NO MIRACLES HERE
BY ORDER OF THE KING

Mine, then, is the story of a peasant boy and the king (or a few presidents) and, with luck, God and His miracles or lack thereof.

PART ONE

**Write the things which
thou hast seen.**

The Apocalypse of John
Revelation 1:19

chapter ONE

There had been much better days, I promise. At least one. Let me paint a picture—or tell you about one that I still own because I stole it.

The family stands together in a lush Ohio field with a sprinkle of leaves at their feet, and trees, some dying, towering behind them, a small red barn with white lattice beside them. The man, the father, tall like those trees, brown like the bark, is smiling. His mustache wraps around his wide mouth, big teeth. His head is square and strong and on straight, his hair low and wavy. His white shirt and light blue jeans are starched. His hands are larger than most men's hands, better than most men's hands at certain things, which is why they made him famous for some years, some years ago. He clasps these hands around a little girl, eight or nine years old: the daughter. They seem to shield her heart, also covered by a thick black sweater with many colored patches. She looks like she's got good home training: stands at attention, arms at her sides, feet together, no space between the knees. A portrait-perfect smile, cheeks shiny and plump and bronze. There is a thin white ribbon in her black hair—a ribbon likely tied and hair likely pressed by the woman in the portrait: the mother, who stands by the man. Their elbows touch. She holds her head highest of all. She has the biggest smile of all, red lipstick. She has the biggest hair of all—burnt blonde, parted on the right side, billowing out and down in curls, falling on the shoulders of her white lace blouse. She wears no rings. She rests her hands, nearly balled into fists, skin the shade of sand-castles, on the shoulders of a little boy: the son. Somebody failed to train this boy or else he did not listen. His little legs are turned to the side. His blue jeans are crooked, too. His left arm floats up, away—he may be trying to wriggle away from his mother, or he may believe his arms are airplane wings. Hard to tell. Unclear, also, why his head leans over, nearly parallel to the ground. Because it is so big or because he is so happy? Those en-thused eyebrows, the twinkles in his eyes (that might just be a glare on the photograph), a smile so intense that his dimples look like craters on a small brown moon. Maybe God was sticking His pointer fingers in the boy's cheeks. Maybe he was just born that way. Who knows? All we know from this artifact is that this family took one pretty picture together on one fine fall day in 1991 or '92. That they stood together and wore crisp blue jeans and clean white blouses. That they smiled, heads straight or crooked.

See the family. Savor them. Soon, they will be destroyed. They will destroy each other. They will destroy themselves. The world or fate or mysteries untold will destroy them in a little while, for the boy needs to travel most of this journey alone—and if he does not *need* to (which, as the boy, would be my argument), then he *will* anyway.

Not yet.

For now, he's got joy in his cheeks and his mother's hands on his shoul-ders and his sister at his side and his father running the whole show as he was wont to do. He was Rod Gerald, after all.

As a high school quarterback growing up in South Dallas, Rod Gerald pos-sessed two of the fastest legs and two of the steadiest hands in America. They were traits that made him the envy of football players and the prize coveted by big-time college recruiters. Even the legendary Woody Hayes swooped down to South Oak Cliff from Columbus, Ohio, where he presided over one of the

best-oiled, most proficient, and successful football factories in the nation.
Hayes wanted Gerald throwing the football for Ohio State University, and he
dropped a few $100 bills in the collection plate of Gerald's preacher father to
drive home his point.

Woody got his money's worth, I'd say: convinced that eighteen-year-old boy to leave his mother and his father and his three older brothers and three younger sisters and all the girls who had been shouting his nickname—*Crow!*—from the stands and reading his stage name—*Rod Gerald* (his name was Roderic)—in newspapers since the eighth grade and go to Columbus and cleave to Woody Hayes and become one flesh or nearly with Ohio State football. The journey would cost him at least one of his lives, but for a time, beginning in 1975, it gave him a new one, a better one. His new life made him the second black quarterback in Ohio State's history, took his exploits from the pages of the *Dallas Morning News* to the *Columbus Dispatch* and *Sports Illustrated* and the *Washington Post*, which announced his new nickname: *The Magician, because he vanishes in front of tacklers' eyes.* And on New Year's Day 1977, by magic if not miracle, the boy became a legend. In the first quarter of the Orange Bowl, with Ohio State losing 10–0 to Colorado, Woody called Rod Gerald from the bench, where he had sat out five games with a broken back, and asked him, barely healed, to fix the mess. The boy complied: dazzled 65,537 pairs of eyes in the stands and however many more tuned in to NBC to see the 27–10 Buckeye victory. Was named the game's Most Valuable Player. Number 8 in your programs, number 1 in your hearts. For a time.

Many things transpired in the next decade. Four I can prove: in May 1982 Roderic married Debra West, who as a little girl had also visited his preacher father to be baptized and thereafter to hear him preach. In September 1982, almost too many months early, the newlyweds brought a daughter, Natashia, into the world. In January 1987, on Epiphany, I was born. In March of that same year, Woody Hayes died. Before he passed on,

Mr. Hayes had convinced his quarterback to return to Columbus and finish the degree that, for reasons we will understand soon enough, had been aborted.

I also know that Rod Gerald earned his diploma in 1989, if only because I've looked at the graduation photo many times, if only because I'm in it. And I know that sometime between then and the aforementioned day in '91 or '92, Rod Gerald became a local legend once again: coach of the Dublin High basketball team, coach of the Mifflin High football team, code enforcement officer for the city of Columbus. The same Rod Gerald that you might recognize at the Horseshoe on game day, who might be the answer to your Buckeye trivia question, whose name might be on your Ohio State throwback jersey—and for these reasons, the same Rod Gerald who was, by 1993 or '94, a real pain in my ass.

You see, a great man is an inconvenience as a father, in part because every boy wants to be a man (until it happens), *his own* man, and that is hard enough to do without everybody calling you the *son* of somebody. I envied, in a way, the boys I'd come to know who had been told so often by so many, *Your daddy ain't shit* . . . because for all the things that I could and did and will say about mine, I could not say that he wasn't shit. He was the greatest man that I had ever known, and *his* daddy, whom we'll get to, was the greatest man that *he* had ever known and this was, most likely, the root of all the evil inside each of us. It was also the reason I threatened to kill myself one night in 1994, I'm almost sure. You'd think I would remember the exact date and motive, but all I have left is a clear memory of the method, strangulation, and my final words: *I guess I'll have to kill myself to get some freedom around here!*

I ran through the den to my bedroom, past the only memento displayed in our apartment, a scarlet felt banner with gray script that read *Rod Gerald 1977 Orange Bowl MVP*, and began to wrap the long black cord of my Sega Genesis controller around my little neck as fast as I could, though not fast enough, because Daddy caught me before I got my freedom and commenced to give me, instead, his long black belt.

He won that skirmish and almost every other, as he was Rod Gerald, a winner. And when he wasn't forcing me to stay alive and I wasn't trying to overthrow him, which only happened once or twice, he seemed to have all the patience in the world for me. Showed me, for example, how to make the bunny ears with my shoelaces and how, instead of tripping a boy in peewee football practice, to put my helmet in the boy's chest and wrap my arms around his waist and drive my legs until his back was on the ground. *Knock his dick in the dirt, Scooter.* Such was the kind of wisdom my second-grade teacher hoped Rod Gerald would offer to her class for Buckeye Day 1994.

On Buckeye Day, kids at Prairie Norton Elementary School, and no doubt kids all the way up in Cleveland and down in Cincinnati, learned to consecrate themselves to Ohio State. We wore necklaces made of buckeye nuts and Buckeye T-shirts, and the lesson plan was adjusted to teach Ohio State football instead of cursive or whatever else they taught in elementary school in those days. An actual Buckeye's presence would be divine. I asked Daddy when he got home from work and he said what he often said about things he was going to say no to: *We'll see, Scooter.* We saw.

He instead sent one of the VHS tapes of Ohio State football that were stacked under the television in our living room—only one of which I had seen, and only then for a few short seconds because when I pressed *play* I was met with the grainy image of a long-haired, bare-shouldered woman violently sucking what I was almost sure was a penis, except that it was far too large to be real. Mama, from the kitchen, had cried out with that noise she made that sounded like a muffler backfiring—*ugh, Roderic!*—and rushed over to switch off the TV. I hurried into my room without asking any questions. Let her off the hook. I figure that's why she didn't fuss when I was caught with the back massager in my underwear a few months later.

We had that kind of understanding, my mother and me, even though I did not understand so many things about her. Didn't understand, for example, why she went to a beauty convention for a whole year, and why she and Daddy sent me and Tashia to Dallas that year instead of bringing us along to cheer her on or just hang out. You hardly ever understand the most important things until it's too late for the understanding to do anybody any good. Since I was only five at that time, I reasoned that my mother was beautiful enough to need a year or more to convene re: her beauty and that was *okay* as long as it didn't take forever, which it didn't. Tashia and I went right back to Columbus and Mama was still beautiful and I didn't ask any questions then, either, because I was six and then seven and had other things to think about—and besides, my mother never made any sense to me and that's what I liked about her.

Every other adult seemed desperately committed to making sense. They were all headed somewhere in a hurry, and on their way they always had to tell me that I didn't have my shirt on right or that I needed to lotion my ashy knees, that I was talking too much, too loud, or not correctly, that I had better stay out of their high heels, that I needed to put on deodorant, that I had to either come inside or go outside but *choose* because I was wasting the air-conditioning and running up the electric bill.

Mama was the only person I knew who didn't do any of the stupid stuff grown people were doing all the time. She didn't wear clothes around the house if she didn't want to (in part because she stood before the bathroom mirror for hours each day), and she didn't eat her vegetables, and she didn't laugh at jokes if she didn't understand them, but sometimes laughed when no joke had been told. She gave me bologna for breakfast, and melted cheese and sugar on my toast instead of spreading jelly, and told me *Take some Tylenol, baby!* when I said I had a stomachache. And when I split my eyebrow open flipping in the bed she didn't scold me, just laid my bleeding head in her lap to feed me peanut butter on our way to the hospital. And when I almost drove her car into the front door of the Drug Emporium, she yelled at the security guards instead of me. And when Daddy said I could not listen to Boyz II Men, she went and bought the tape herself. I'm not saying she was perfect, just that I sure benefited from her imperfections. Maybe that's what magic is: a useful mistake. Otherwise it's just a bad decision, which is what I thought my daddy made with the tape he sent for Buckeye Day.

I was sitting in Ms. Baughman's dark room in pure bliss, swinging my little legs—not because I was finally witnessing Ohio State football but because the greatest days of primary school involved a metal cart with a TV on top and a VCR on the shelf below—when Ms. Baughman stopped the tape and turned on the lights. *Man, what if somebody dubbed over the football game with that woman?*

It wasn't that. Ms. Baughman had stopped the tape early because the footage Daddy had chosen to send was of the 1978 Gator Bowl match between Ohio State and Clemson, which had also ended prematurely. Seconds after Ohio State's quarterback (the one who replaced Rod Gerald) threw a ball directly into the arms of a Clemson linebacker to seal a Buckeye defeat, Woody Hayes retaliated by punching said linebacker in the throat as he ran to the Ohio State sideline. *You SOB, I just lost my job!* Woody was reported to have yelled at that poor boy from Clemson, who for all the money in the world would not have bet that his place in college football history would be secured by taking a sucker punch from an old man. Woody's career was, in fact, over. So was Buckeye Day.

Ms. Baughman tried to wrap the fiasco in a noble message nobody was listening to:

See, kids, we have to keep our tempers under control, right?

Yes, Ms. Baughman! as we swung our feet or dug in our noses or searched for some residue of Fruit Roll-Ups in our book bags.

I could do all types of psychoanalysis to try to figure out why Daddy sent that tape instead of coming to my class. Maybe he couldn't leave work. Maybe it seemed a clever way to get back at Woody, who had cost him *his* job as starting quarterback. Maybe he was simply tired of being Rod Gerald. He'd already attempted to offload the name to me, and would have succeeded had my sister not already been, at four, the wisest person in the family.

Daddy's idea was that I become Roderic Alan Gerald, Jr. My mother protested, since she wanted me to carry her name instead: Debra Ann would become De'Brian, in keeping with the 1980s trend of naming kids with no thought to the price they would later pay in school, job searches, or self-esteem. At a stalemate, they turned to Tashia, who offered: *Call him Casey.* She borrowed the name from a soap opera character, Dr. Casey, a woman. I don't know what she was trying to say.

Tashia got her wish and rightly so. I had been her baby as much as Mama's and Daddy's, my aunties told me. When I asked what was wrong with Tashia's back, why she had a brace that she was supposed to wear but didn't, they reminded me it was my fault. I had been so big—*chile, you were so BIG*—that Tashia, still in pigtails, newly robbed of two front teeth, had to lean—*chile, she was almost leaning on the floor!*—just to keep me balanced on her hip. My jowls were fat and my eyes drooped, but my grip was firm like I'd been holding on to my sister since before I even existed. In the pre-thoughts of our mother's womb I had known her, had found her message left behind for me: *Don't worry, I'll be waiting for you.* I don't mean to say she was born just to serve my needs—I really am working to be a good feminist, which is very serious business—but that if she had not been born I would not have my name and she might not have those rods in her back to keep her spine from breaking and we would not have learned so soon to hold on to what we had even if it was too heavy.

By Buckeye Day 1994, Tashia seemed eager to let me go or at least not speak to me much, even though we lived under the same roof and shared first a let-out couch and then a waterbed and then, finally, a room with twin beds that Daddy came to sit on every night and pat us to sleep. And so I had to imagine what she was like through other people. Some days I thought she was Brandy Norwood—a wholesome girl with skin the color of the chunks in Blue Bell buttered pecan ice cream, sitting in a swing in the park with dookie braids singing to a boy:

I want to be down
I want to be down with you

Other days I thought she was Lauryn Hill in *Sister Act 2*—same skin, same braids, same voice in sometime-service to God, same funky attitude with the authorities, even her father, her favorite person in the world. She was his favorite, too, except for one weekend morning when, lying on Daddy's chest to read his daily planner, I watched him take out a ballpoint pen, put a tiny blue star next to the date, and write, mouthing the words just so I could hear: *Casey will be more successful than his sister, because he listens.*

She must have really pissed him off that day. But a day often comes when a girl stops taking shit from anybody, and I'm glad hers had arrived. Otherwise I would have been sitting up dead at the hands of my neighbor-friend's younger brother, who was the only white person to ever call me *nigger* to my face, or the American Indian boy a few doors down whose fingernails were almost as long as his hair, which I tried to pull once, before he slashed me. Would have been, in other words, a casualty of the Thumbleweed Drive Race Wars of 1994.

These battles broke out every few months. I'd be leaning against the back of Daddy's black Ford Probe, scratching the paint off, or walking from Ms. Wonderlich's apartment across the way with a stale sprinkled sugar cookie in my hand, or digging for a rock that had some gold inside, and I'd hear the cry:

Race war!!!!!!!!!!!!!

The fleck of paint flits away, the sugar cookie is crushed under a shoe, the empty rock is folded into my fist, and I call for Tashia, just like the In-dian boy calls for his sister, and the white boy calls for his big brother, and we run, all of us, to a spot that the universe has preordained as the place of bloodletting, where we will pay for the sins of our fathers and forget that we are friends and ignore the fact—if only for a short moment of suspense in that time of day when you no longer have to shield your eyes to watch the sun—that, aside from Tashia and the little Indian, nobody knew how to fight.

Tashia knew it all: what my name should be, how to fight, how to sing, that I liked her best friend's sister without me even saying a word. And I assumed she knew why, one day in 1995, Daddy packed up all the family's stuff and said that we were going back to Dallas. Going *home*.

chapter **T W O**

I remember rain.

I can see it: Kentucky rain, the rocks cry out on us as we pass through. *Hosanna, hosanna,* rain. The procession home, the road, the Via Dolorosa. Tennessee: the crooked ways still bent, the valley not exalted, the road will wind and give us rain. *Hallelujah!* A song of rain and blindness: we're coming home.

Can the whole sky be water and the hills hide us in the mist and all you hear is the march of rain up the hood and down the window and under the wheel and on the world behind. I don't know home, but I know rain.

Daddy, I can't see.

Me either, Scooter. Nobody can see in this rain. But all you have to do is keep your eye on that white line. Look.

There is a world that exists, maybe in another time or on another star, but I know it's there, and I'm holding the back of the driver's seat so I can see the white line guide our tires through the rain. I would put this pen down. I would close my bank account and give my monies to the poor. I would ask the Lord to still my voice so I never say another word if I could only sit there in the storm and watch that line again, forever.

Instead I watched Daddy drive across the Trinity River—though it's also possible I was asleep in the car. Whatever the case, I have seen a great deal of America since, and have learned that you can't understand a place if you don't understand its water. Dallas ain't any different, which is why some people simply say *he's from the other side of the Trinity River* and thus explain my whole existence or so they think but are, in part, quite right. Most cities have railroad tracks to separate poor colored people from other citizens. In Dallas, there's a whole goddamn river between us. Nothing moves in the Trinity River, aside from toxic waste. Very few things or people move across it for long: folks south of the river cross it via freeways that usher them to work or a nice shopping mall. Those north of the river cross it to get out of town—to Waco or San Antone or hell maybe all the way to Mexico. Anywhere but Oak Cliff, our destination. I bet Daddy would have kept on driving to Mexico, too, if he had known what plans Oak Cliff had for him. But either he did not know or he had strange priorities and so he drove into the driveway that would come to be The Driveway of my life in many ways, the crumbling concrete driveway of my mother's mother's house.

The house had been her husband Cleo's house, since he was the man and he had the money, thanks to Ross Perot, who might have been the 42nd president of the United States if he hadn't told the truth so much. Mr. Perot had hired Cleo, long before I was born, to train the Perot horses and landscape the Perot properties—which Cleo did so well that he was later able to open his own landscaping company and build his own horse barn about a five-minute drive or twenty-minute horse ride away from the house he bought on the south side of the Trinity River before it was a sad thing to do, a house he last saw hours before his death in 1991 (sixty-two years old; massive heart attack), by which time the landscaping company was bankrupt, the horse barn was rotting, and his widow was working as a domestic on the north side of the Trinity River to supplement the social security check that would come each month in lieu of an inheritance.

THERE WILL BE NO MIRACLES HERE

Still, Dorothy carried on Cleo's legacy: kept that small two-bedroom house clean, kept the ivy trestles pruned and the hedges trimmed, kept hope alive for the garage door until it fell off the hinges. She continued hosting parties—*get-togethers*—as the couple had been doing since the sixties, when Cleo and his brother opened The Atmosphere, one of the hottest nightclubs in Dallas for a short while, but long enough for Bobby Blue Bland to make a brief appearance, which ended when Cleo saw Bobby try to dance with Dorothy. Perhaps since Cleo was no longer around, Bobby Blue Bland was still the star of Dorothy's get-togethers, still calling for somebody, maybe her, to

Shine on your love light
Let it shine on me

Which didn't have nothing to do with God, as far as I could tell—all those old men and old women howling at each other like they were still down in the country, jigging in the living room, bumping into each other in the short hallway, stepping out onto the back porch for a smoke, spilling their toddies on the little children, smushing the faces of the little children in their big old bosoms.

Dorothy—let's call her Granny, be respectful—also carried on the legacy that I most remembered Cleo for: she, like her favorite granddaughter, refused to take shit from anybody, especially from me.

I should say, before I make my case against this woman, that one of the many reversals we, you and I, will experience together will be Granny's transformation into a saint, perhaps the only saint in this whole story. In the meantime I shall heap great clumps of dirt on her reputation, which will not surprise her in the least, since she knew (or so she said) from the day I was born that I was either the spawn of Satan or the actual Antichrist or, if nothing else, had a lot of the devil inside of me (which, in a way, was prophetic). We had been confirmed in our views of each other back in 1992, on Halloween.

The sun had long gone down. I'll say it was ten o'clock just for kicks, though I'm pretty sure I could not tell the time at five. I know Granny was asleep on the couch in the living room—a satin magnolia-colored Victorian kind of thing, with wooden claws for legs, scratched and chipped over the years. I believe I was lying on a pallet or a little mattress on the floor in her room because that's where I slept most nights, since when I shared Granny's bed she fussed so much each time I turned over or fidgeted that I learned to sleep on my stomach, stiff as the embalmed, all night. That, as you can imagine, was not fun, so at some point I settled for the floor and was there, around ten o'clock, when the doorbell rang.

Trick or treat!

I had not gone trick-or-treating that Halloween, since my mother's baby sister, Shon, was the only person who took me anywhere, and she did not believe in the occult. I had seen Halloween on television, though, had heard about it at school, and it sounded like one hell of a good time for all involved, part of the fun being the moment you hear the doorbell ring then hear a voice shout *trick or treat!* then rush to the door to give candy and joy to whoever stands on your front porch, even if it's after nine o'clock, even if the trick-or-treaters are two haggard grown men in old coats instead of costumes, which I saw through the window.

Just a minute!

Man, I tell you what, I was so excited to bless these trick-or-treaters, I probably would have tripped over something if I didn't always walk so carefully on my tiptoes. I slid out of my sleeping place and made it to within a few steps of the front door before Granny raised her head.

Don't you open that door.

At five, nothing too bad had happened to me yet—my birth, which I had forgotten; a beesting at four; a few whippings—so this, refusing to open the door for trick-or-treaters, was the most unconscionable act I had witnessed in my life.

But Granny! They just want some candy!

She lifted her head a little more, nightcap on, glasses now on, watching me.

Casey, I don't care what they want. Get away from that door ... you hear?!

I heard what she said. Felt it, really. If you have ever been in a crowded restaurant minding your business when, suddenly, a far-off waiter drops a tray of dishes, and the sound of disaster rings out, a hush falls over the restaurant, and you feel ashamed, strangely, for the waiter and for yourself—if you have heard and felt that, then you have heard and felt Dorothy West's voice when she hollers like she hollered at me on Halloween 1992. So yeah, I heard her. But I did not understand. All these people wanted was a little treat for Halloween, somebody to open the door with a smile and a Baby Ruth or something to replace the nothing in their buckets or lives. I kept my eyes on Granny but took another step toward the door, my little arm beginning to rise.

Casey! She shot up like Thomas A. Edison himself had run the world's best electricity through her bones. *What did I say?!? Got—*

Granny was up from the couch now, lunging toward the kitchen door—*lunging for what?* I wondered—I jumped back from the door but did not run until I saw that she had lunged for the giant corn broom of Damocles that she smashed roaches with and was now lunging for my *narrow tail*, about to smash me like she smashed those roaches who never hurt nobody, coming after me with that broom like she was Jesse Owens's sister or something, chasing me like I was a goddamn cockroach instead of a boy trying to give some joy to a few strangers on the porch, but I was a lot faster than a roach and just as nimble, at least more nimble than this old woman with that nasty broom, and so I hollered and ran and she chased me and I kept running—even at five, I could usually run for as long as I needed to—and she kept chasing me until she couldn't anymore, until she got tired and gave up and dropped the broom and looked at me like she wanted me roach-dead and I looked at her from halfway behind a door and knew that she was finished and wrong and mean and she knew that I was the devil and quick and we both knew that there would be no candy and no joy for the trick-or-treaters or us or anybody else in the world, that night.

A quarter century later, I still get sick to my stomach when I think about how those men must have felt, left out in the cold like that on Halloween. And I bet I felt a little ill when we walked into her house again three years later—and relieved when we left soon after. It may have been that very same day, or a month down the line, but it was soon enough that it did not seem to take too long to come: the day my father's father delivered us.

Come on ride with me, Scooter. Papa's outside.

In those days I did not hesitate to ride anywhere with hardly anybody, especially my daddy, and so I ran to get my shoes and by such time as I found them he was already lurching across Dorothy's lawn, leaning, smiling, head tilted into the sun like a man for whom the light was not a threat. He scurried across one lane of Old Ox Road and then the median and then reached a ruby-red Rolls-Royce parked on the other side.

I finally made it there myself, climbed into the backseat, and clicked my dusty seat belt. Daddy settled in at the left hand of his father, Cornelius Howard Gerald, whom he called Daddy and whose grandchildren and sometimes his wife called Papa. Papa's body took up the entire driver's seat. His hands smothered the bony steering wheel. He glanced back at me, big eyes behind brown aviator shades. His voice rumbled like your hand in a bowl of pinto beans—

Roderic.

Hey Daddy . . .

Is that Casey?

He knew it was me, but this was how all old people greeted children—
is that so-and-so that I already know it is?

Yes it's me, fool! I shouted with my mouth closed. I knew very well that
I was not to speak unless spoken to directly, so just sat there and waited to
be verified.

Yes sir, sure is. Negro's getting big, ain't he?

He he he . . . my lawd!

Papa was, in fact, going blind, but his vision was still good enough to
drive that Rolls-Royce and to see eight-year-old me and to look at my
daddy in such a way that he became a bigger man than I had known him to
be and a smaller boy than I was myself. I don't mean that as an insult, by
the way. George W. Bush is the only man I have ever met who was as devoted to his father as my daddy was to his daddy, as willing to do whatever
was required to please the man. One son set his sights on the White House.
The other set his sights on Home. Both should have set their sights elsewhere. But Cornelius wanted his boy close by and here we were, at the
dawn of our demise, with joy.

We made three stops that day.

The first was to Wingfield's, its name in big red marquee letters outside and inside, dim and smoky, stools caked in grease and burgers spilling
over paper plates. A man rushed to the counter.

Afternoon, Pastor Gerald! What can I getcha?

I'd never had a burger that big or been in a restaurant that dirty, so after a few bites, I was glad when my father said *C'mon Scooter,* and we left.

The second stop was across the street at what looked to be a small
junkyard or an abandoned filling station. This was Papa's body shop. He
and Daddy got out to *handle some business.* Who knows what happened
in there.

The last stop was nearby on Marsalis Avenue, the full length of which
you can drive in about twenty minutes, starting at Dealey Plaza, where

John F. Kennedy was shot, and ending at the front gates of Laurel Land cemetery. Papa parked the Rolls-Royce on a small side street, outside a squat white brick home with a mangy front yard and tired fence in the back. He went to the front door, which was hidden from our view. A woman stepped out onto the low concrete patio in either her nightclothes or the saddest day clothes of all time, her head wrapped in a scarf and one hand over her eyes.

This is where we're gonna live, Scooter, Daddy said.

Dang, I thought. Perhaps he thought the same thing, too, but dared not speak it either, having not talked back to his Daddy, that I know of, in nearly forty years.

You may wonder why the old man bossed his boy around so easily, why the Wingfield's man was so quick to offer whatever he desired, why the few dusty body shop attendants hopped to it when he arrived, why that sad old woman did not protest when she was informed that moving time had come—why, in this neighborhood on *the other side of the Trinity River* that everyone who could leave had left, there was an old man, nearly blind, driving a ruby-red Rolls-Royce. The simple answer (and the true one) is that this man had joined, at the age of sixteen, the greatest business in America: the business of saving souls. He'd found a vocation that could help him up off the dirt floor he'd been sleeping on since 1928, and once he got up he kept going: up the road from Dawson to Dallas by '51, out of other pastors' pulpits by '67, when he founded Community First Baptist, *the church that cares about you,* and, when that edifice overflowed, to the Community First Baptist Church Extension on Westmoreland Road in '75, in a nicer section of Oak Cliff and on a plot three times the size, making Cornelius the first black pastor in the city to shepherd two locations, and making his son's historic journey to Columbus only the second-most important thing to happen in the family that year.

Within twenty years Cornelius would have over a thousand members and dozens of *sons in the ministry* who pastored thousands more; within twenty-five years he'd be dead; and within thirty years both locations would be abandoned—the original because it was no longer appealing, Westmoreland because the bank took it. But in the meantime, Cornelius was king of the hill. He knew it. Everybody else knew it, too. And if his wife forgot, he'd knock her teeth out. If his children forgot, he'd push them through a screen door. If his congregation forgot... Well, to this day I have not witnessed a single member entertain the notion that he was not the best among them.

Still, even after doing a lot of work to become a better person, I don't understand why anybody would pack up all their stuff and their family and move to the other pole of America just to be close to somebody, father or legend or not. Why they, as my daddy did, would give up coaching high school teams and enforcing city codes and, instead, make a new living driving daycare vans for one of his daddy's parishioners. He and Papa didn't seem to have any big plans, other than hanging out—the son taking his old man's car to get cleaned, ordering a slab of ribs for the old man's dinner, or sitting under the giant shade tree that towered in the front yard of the house Cornelius and Clarice had built in Lancaster, which is now called a suburb but at that time was just the country.

So many afternoons and evenings and some mornings, too, they would sit there together, saying nothing. If something was said it was usually Papa doing the saying—telling a story, often a joke. And Daddy would rear his head back and open his mouth like he was about to guzzle a quart of oil and laugh so hard that tears would meander down at least one cheek by the time he was done.

Daddy especially loved when Papa asked a question.

Roderic . . . you know the three most dangerous things in the world?

What, Daddy? (Already warming the laugh and tears.)

A white man with a high-powered rifle. A Mexican with a driver's license. And a nigger with some authority.

Ack ack ack!

He he he. Papa always laughed this way, like a Michael Jackson leg kick.

I enjoyed hanging with them well enough, but what I cared most about at the time was that the cost of Daddy's new life of devotion was the life that I had built for myself. Of course I was only eight, so had not done anything at all aside from *live* the way I naturally lived, but simply doing that created, on its own, a life that I didn't find too difficult to navigate, aside from a threatened suicide every now and then. This new way of living was not very delicious to me, a *nobody* in a family big on *somebodys*, the silent son of a legend who had suddenly been downgraded to the supplicant son of another legend, who informed me that we were all sons and daughters of the Legend, God, to whom we had to submit our present lives and the ones to come. That was news to me. I hadn't had any problems with God in Ohio, mostly because I hadn't been thinking about Him and did not get the sense that He was thinking about me. Now We were supposed to be on Each Other's minds nonstop, and that seemed a bit much.

What did I get in return for all this? The third grade, for one, where the sixth-grade girl I thought I loved paid me no mind, the boy I sat next to hated me—*man where you from OHIO?? man you need to go back*—and the chicken pox made me miss a week of class, which led to my first B and one of my last whippings, since Daddy later made it known that he decided never to hit me again once he *started using*.

And I received, in exchange for my friends in Ohio, thirty first cousins, with clusters of every age group, mine already dominated by Papa's sidekicks, Luke and BB, who would in time become like siblings, by which time I didn't have much else. Until then I was just a thirty-first wheel. When I opened my mouth, the cousins laughed—*oooh you white grandmother grandfather pass the Grey Poupon*—and when I walked outside on my tiptoes—*oooh you walk like a little girl!*—the older boy cousins would turn to each other and raise an eyebrow—*I'ono dawg that lil nigga got some sugar in him.* Sure, I did love sugar a great deal, perhaps too much, but I knew very few kids who didn't. Besides, I just didn't want to get my feet dirty. They didn't care.

In addition to all this adoration, I received my own bedroom for the first time, which only made it easier for my sister to get away from me. She, being a normal teenager with a magnetic personality just like her Daddy, disappeared into an abyss of great fun and phone chats and dates with the captain of the South Oak Cliff football team. At least once she disappeared into the night through her bedroom window. I was no snitch, so never told the authorities, in part because before long there were no authorities to tell.

And yet: I was not alone.

One night, sometime after K104 ran its last loop of Missy's "Supa Dupa Fly," after Fox 4 aired *The Simpsons* and *Married . . . with Children,* and after I closed my blinds to watch *America's Most Wanted*—I always closed the blinds because I knew fugitives would see me watching the show and know that I knew they were on the loose and kill me before I had a chance to turn them in and collect my reward—angels appeared on my bedroom walls.

I was lying in bed on my side and, all of a sudden, I saw rows of angels rising up my wall. They were small for angels, about the size of three roaches, which is what I thought they were at first. They glowed with something of a pink haze, not the clean white aura you'd expect. They were identical, all lined up in perfect straight rows, all moving slowly up and to the right. Each angel was holding something, or else had both arms folded over its chest like you do when you're riding down a big slide at a water park. Each looked at me, silent. Not the way the *Mona Lisa* seems to be looking at you regardless of where you stand in the museum but like they were looking right at me as they floated up my walls. I did not kick my legs, which I often did to get to sleep. I did not feel the need to say anything to them or anybody. And I was not afraid.

When I think of that night, I think of a friend, Joshua, who went to

Peru a few years ago to try ayahuasca. Once he'd taken it in, he hiked and sat on the side of a mountain by himself, and saw a red flower a few paces away, standing all alone. The flower took on the voice of God— it *was* God—and God said to Joshua through the red flower: *I hope you understand.*

For five months after meeting Red Flower God on that mountain in Peru, Joshua woke at dawn most days and wished he had died in his sleep. We'd meet for breakfast and his eyes would have little red marks in them from the morning crying, even though Josh was a very tough and very funny kid. I thought, *This is how hard it is to handle God's presence for real and how impossible it is to really understand.* Joshua and I and the whole world would rather die than understand, rather be deaf than have to hear for ourselves the voice of God. So I'm glad I just got a band of angels that night because they didn't say anything and I didn't have to understand and I wasn't afraid and I wasn't alone anymore. I felt at the time that the angels were there to protect me. I wonder now whether they were trying to tear ass out of that house.

Whatever the case, I wasn't alone because, aside from the angels, I had my mother.

Across the hallway from my bedroom was the only working bathroom in the house, and every day, whenever I needed to find her, Mama would be standing before the mirror there, putting her face on. If it was early, she wouldn't have on many clothes, sometimes none. No matter how hot it was, the back of her thigh always felt like she'd just removed an ice pack. Crowded on the sink would be three or four round disks with pancake-colored powder on one side and a dirty mirror on the other, white foam triangles stained with mud, and two lipsticks—one a deep red that she left all over Styrofoam cups, and one fuchsia, which, combined with her big crinkly burnt-blonde hair, made her look like a high-yellow "I Wanna Dance with Somebody" Whitney Houston.

By evening, an hour or so before she made dinner or ordered Little Caesars, Mama would have on at least a robe, and would pull a black tube from her bag for the grand finale, when she'd lean into the mirror and tilt her head back, keeping one eye on her reflection and the other in the top of her eyelid to apply one . . . two . . . three swipes of the brush.

What's that, Mama?

This is Mama's mascara, Man.

Huh? I could never fully make out what she said when she put this stuff on, since she always pulled her mouth tight like she was placing the last bolt in the Brooklyn Bridge and didn't want to kill a million people by losing focus.

Mascara, baby. Mascara.

Ah, okay.

When I wasn't watching this from the toilet, we'd talk. Well, I'd talk, and she'd offer giggles and *uh-huh*s in return. Every now and then I had an idea I wanted to share, the first of which came to me when Daddy's friend Charlie Brown visited. I had never seen Charlie Brown before and haven't seen nor heard from him since, but he spent one night with us, leaving parked outside a white spaceship the length of three or four parking spots. He called the spaceship an eighteen-wheeler and called himself Truck Driver. Charlie Brown said he had seen the whole country, and that he slept whenever he wanted to, on a bed in the back of the spaceship's main cabin. When he wanted to bathe, which he didn't have to do every day, he just eased off the road and went into a big gas station to wash off and buy a soda pop. Charlie Brown made enough money to live just fine and even to send his little boy Power Rangers action figures. Before he left us, Charlie Brown let me sit in the captain's seat of his spaceship, and even though I was small I could see over all the cars and some of the houses and could imagine what it would be like to ride that spaceship and look down over all the land for the rest of my life. I decided then that I, too, would be a truck driver.

The first person I told about my plan was Auntie O, my mother's oldest sister and my godmother, whose chest was so fantastic you could sleep on her during church without leaning far, who always carried Juicy Fruit in her purse, a romance novel in her backseat, and a vodka-grapefruit toddy in her hand, and whose face was so flawless, perfectly painted with shimmer and color, that she never let anyone kiss her directly. She had been Miss North Texas State (or something close) in her twenties and, lacking any banner to carry around in middle age, decided to put her name on the license plate of her gold Honda: *O West.*

Auntie O, I'm gonna be a truck driver when I grow up.

Chile (she held *chile* longer than anyone else in the family), *"going to be,"* not *"gonna be." And, honey, uh-uh, truck driver? We don't do that.*

Oh.

Sitting on the toilet the next day, I told Mama that I wasn't going to be a truck driver anymore because Auntie O said I couldn't.

What? Mama always bit off the end of her *t*'s like a hi-hat. *Baby, O don't know nothing. How's she gone tell you what you can't do when you grow up? Uh-uh.*

She was more upset than I had been, just as she was whenever anybody did or said anything to me that wasn't to her liking, regardless of my fault in the matter. And so I figured that she'd heard enough of my complaints over the third grade, one being the creepy Community First deacon who drove me there and back each day, when I woke one morning to find her face already put on, her first Benson & Hedges Menthol Light already smoked, her coffee mug already lined with red lip prints, and the keys to her Mitsubishi Eclipse in her hand. *Gone and get ready, Man, I'm taking you to school.*

going to school

Get in the car. You'll have to get in the back this is a two-door and she lets me sit in the front but sit behind me because you'll have more room and there's a hump in the middle so you can't sit there sorry. Mama really can't sing but that doesn't stop her and her driving is shaky but that doesn't stop her. I have my own fake wheel on my side and I can do what I want. We're off who knows what's on the radio I don't but I know I can change the station anything you want to hear? K104 is on there's a song that plays every morning that is *everything.*

I love school.

When I wake up early in the morning, I say oooh.

Tonight K104 will play Ginuwine and you can call Cat Daddy for his Confession Sessions but in the morning we'll all believe that school is the greatest thing to happen to us the song is just that good.

We're gonna take the road that loops around the city and separates my sinner family from my saint family whichever is which who knows I don't but I'm just gonna sit up here and watch the trees zoom by ain't it strange how these trees creep up from far away real slow almost floating in place and then when they get close enough to see our face they're zooming by like a bat out of hell. The white line my daddy told me to watch in the rain does the same thing—so many patient dashes up ahead then a panicked streak running under our car waving bye-bye behind us. Can you feel that? It's no care no worry no nothing. Hold on a minute.

Mama which way are we going today?

We're on the right road but we're turning in the wrong place I mean we're turning into the other side of the street and there are cars over there that's not where we want to go even though I don't know much of nothing.

Mama.

Why won't she answer me?

Mama!

I'm in the floor. I look up at her. Her arms are so stiff she's jerking the steering wheel like it's hurting her she's got her head pushed back against her seat does your neck hurt why won't she open those big eyes and look at me why does it sound like she's swallowing something that won't go down *Gone down water stop making my mama try so hard* her face is so bunched up did she smell something bad does her stomach hurt is she dead can you see what's wrong with her? And our car's all messed up dang that man looks mad his car's all messed up too he's getting out he's mad he's coming over somebody else from another car is coming over why do they look so mad and now like they saw something they didn't want to see stop looking at my mama like that c'mon wake up we gotta go she's gone she's turned off she's not studying me she's got her own thing going on and didn't even tell me about it guess I just gotta sit here not gonna cry with these people all in my business didn't plan on my mama being dead but dead people don't move around like that she's a fish got pulled out the tank too soon and got some super strength in her fin arms. Now they're knocking on the window *Let her rest! Not talking to strangers!* Mama c'mon get up she's not jerking not pushing her pretty head in the seat no more can't go no further hold on she's coming back somebody put some water in her mouth while she was gone she's got a strand of blonde hair stuck in her shining white tooth but now she moves. Here she is. Mascara smeared a little bit I wish she didn't cry in front of these people. *Casey—Casey—*she just took a little stroll just needed a catnap*—What happened?—I'm fine—What?* All out of my control now some woman's opened the door she's got my mama some man thinks he's my daddy *Get your hands off me!* But I don't say it got to respect adults I really want to be out of the middle of the street all these people looking at me like I got a problem this is embarrassing why did you do this Mama just sat up and left like that and messed up the car I don't know nothing no numbers how to drive what's wrong with you no school today.

chapter THREE

I bet the third grade would have been a hell of a lot more compelling if someone there, the janitor or crossing guard even, could have taught me how to help my mother—which, prior to being driven into three lanes of oncoming traffic, I did not think necessary.

First I would have needed to know how to slide her foot from gas to brake mid-drive and turn the wheel so we could coast into a parking lot or crash into something cushiony, a ditch maybe. I would have also needed to know how to tell a *seizure*, a burst of electrical activity in the brain, from *death*, the end of electrical activity in the brain. I might have surmised then, though probably not, that Mama's brain had done this before, a few moments before she acquired that scar on her shin. Blacked out in the bathroom, holding a mirror, she told me once I finally asked.

Perhaps I would have then put two and two together to reckon that all this bathrooming was part of a clever ploy to avoid her regular activities, if not everyone entirely. But that would have required some other knowledge I did not have at that time: what exactly *bipolar* meant, which sounded like a decent thing to have, since *bi* meant "two" and I had been taught or assumed that more was better. I also assumed, wrongly, that *bipolar* and *manic depression* were different things, since I'd overheard both terms from my mother's mouth and others' behind her back, though never said to me directly. If I had been spoken to I might have asked, or at least wondered, how manic depression was different from regular depression, which seemed bad enough on its own without somebody calling you a maniac, which is what I figured *manic* implied. They didn't tell me nothing, though, and I didn't ask, and I did not yet have the Internet to find out on my own why, for example, Mama was able to cry for less obvious reasons than anyone I knew, longer and more freely, and laugh for less obvious reasons, too. That these and other gifts, these imperfections that had been so good to me, were actually burdens. That she'd become a burden to herself and others back in 1992 and went, therefore, perhaps against her will, to a *facility*, not a beauty convention. And yet this visit must have been a waste of time for all involved, since nobody seemed any more able to help her and seemed even less interested, now that I think about it. But instead of yelling at her or calling her crazy or telling her she needed to get out of bed and *do something*, anybody who had a problem with her could have just asked me to figure it all out and I would have gladly done so, after some basic training and a reprieve from third grade. People always underestimate the power of children and that is probably why the world is so messed up right now.

Anyway, all I knew that morning was not much, which I am happy to blame on the fact that I was eight years old, but I wasn't all right and holy, either. I was embarrassed to be stuck in the middle of the street and I was also upset that Mama let those strangers see her, face undone, strapped onto a stretcher and placed into an ambulance in broad daylight. Aside from that, I was thrilled to escape school for a day and I bet I smiled when Shon arrived on the scene, earrings dangling, with her shredded jean jacket and her half-blonde half-black bob, smacking her gum.

Hey, Man, you alright?

Shon didn't demand honorifics—I didn't have to call her ma'am or auntie—she didn't listen to Bobby Bland like Granny, or Kenny G like

Aunt Ronnie (my mother's older sister, who was like Christmas Eve all the time). Shon listened to Prince, even though she had to come home and pray after seeing him in concert. She was the one who taught me to tie my shoes, who drove me up the street to fetch my lunch kit after I threw it at an older boy and ran, who took me to Six Flags every year, where she left me with Auntie O to ride the kiddie rides because she didn't have time to be boring. And though she was a serious lover of Christ—she told me never to touch the horoscope rolls at the grocery store because that was the occult—Shon made reading the Bible every night cool because the one she gave me had a white leather cover and gold embossed lettering.

Mmhmm, I'm fine. And off we went.

And before long, maybe that evening or the next day, Mama was fine, too. Back in the bathroom, smiling again, smoking. Only unconscious when she went to sleep at night, which was no big problem because she let me know—*night Man love you night night Mama love you too.* Her car was ruined, sure, but that was also not a problem: behind a wooden fence on wheels out at his country home in Lancaster, Papa had a cavalcade of once-luxury cars, even a Lincoln limousine now filled with wasp's nests. From these dry bones his baby son freely chose the final three cars of our family.

The first was a Deuce-and-a-Quarter the color of brussels sprouts, which Daddy drove only once because it wouldn't start again. He parked it in the stale garage attached to our house, and he and his friends spoke of the Deuce-and-a-Quarter like I'd someday hear a Yale tour guide speak of the Gutenberg Bible.

The second car, which Papa delivered with real pride—*Now take care of this one, Roderic*—was a 1975 periwinkle-blue Cadillac DeVille. The car was so long that its wings hung out the back of most driveways, so wide that I could lay my full body across the backseat, and so old that when I did, I would sit up with periwinkle-blue dirt all over my clothes, smelling like a home that should have been condemned by the city.

Somehow, my mother and father decided it was a good idea to pick me up from school in this car. My elementary school, Robert L. Thornton, where Cleo and Dorothy had sent their children, sat at the top of a hill, up the street from Granny's house, and I could see, from Thornton's front steps, at least a block downslope in either direction. When I spotted the DeVille, I fixed my gaze far beyond it, since I believed at the time that I could be invisible if I *looked* invisible, which only required avoiding eye contact with anybody who was looking at me.

Scooter!

My technique wasn't perfect yet. I ignored Mama's shouts from the passenger seat.

Scooter?

Kept walking.

Scooter!

I could not get by.

Oh hey, Auntie!

Not the end of the world for my classmates to know that I was related to people who drove cars like this, as long as they were not my parents. I slid into the backseat and turned away from the sidewalk-side window.

Auntie? Mama was genuinely confused, or seemed so.

Hey man, you heard your mother calling you.

That was the first time Daddy didn't call me Casey or Scooter or even *Man* like my mother and her sisters called me. He said *man* like you say to a homeless person—*sorry man, no change*—and he didn't look at me in the rearview mirror, just tilted his head and gripped the periwinkle-blue steering wheel and bit his lip, turning the metal key in the ignition two or three times before he pulled down the gearshift to drive us home.

Thankfully, the Cadillac broke down before long, and we were upgraded once more to one of Papa's favorites—a nickel-gray, early eighties Mercedes-Benz.

The Benz, as we called it, did not smell like I was owed a lead-paint settlement, did not get my clothes dirty, and did not have a slot for eight-tracks. It had only one flaw: whenever the speedometer glided past 45 mph, the Benz stalled. We'd be on I-35 in the middle lane or zooming through a yellow light to turn from Marsalis to Loop 12, and the line would tickle 45 mph just before we pooted to a stop. So there I was again, crouched in the floor hoping nobody I knew saw me and Mama waiting for help.

The Benz was not what I had hoped a Benz would be, though it remained faster than feet and cleaner than public transportation. And its greatest fault was not *what* it was but *where* it was and wasn't. Even this did not matter until my tenth birthday, an event that mattered only because I had attended BB's tenth birthday party the year before, where it seemed she got more money and more respect than she had theretofore received. So since I was eager to make it to a higher station in the world, I was also eager to be ten. But, thanks to the Benz's absence on that day, I received, instead of honor, a question.

Hell if I know!

That's what I yearned to shout at Aunt Carla, my daddy's baby sister, when she barged into the house on Marsalis on my tenth birthday and yelled *Hey y'all!* to no one in particular and *Where's your daddy?* to me in theory but, as loud as she was, to everybody. She was the family member I imagine you also have, the one who knows exactly the right thing to say to make public what you had only recently become privately shamed of, like getting pregnant out of wedlock or your daddy missing the biggest event in your life.

In fairness, I didn't send him an invitation or anything, just assumed that he would be there on time or at some point. But he often told me *Scooter, when you assume you make an ASS out of U and ME*, and as the celebration kicked off he was just as right as always, though he was also, for the first time, not where I wanted him to be, which Aunt Carla did not fail to point out again. Sherri, the next-oldest Gerald girl and BB's mother, carried no fucks in her purse and so she rolled her eyes and said *Carla shut up you know Crow'll be here in a minute.* This, too, was said loud enough for me to hear, either because all my family speaks in an outside voice or Aunt Sherri wanted to pass along comfort without speaking to me directly. Whatever the case, it worked, and so I left the front door area and went to find BB, who Aunt Sherri had just whipped, and discovered her in Tashia's room in damn good shape, all things considered, tears wiped and everything, playing with two dolls. Aside from suffering well, BB was also a great sharer and a trustworthy person, so she handed over one of the dolls and agreed not to tell my daddy, though I did not yet know this was an unnecessary precaution.

The front door opened. Maybe I ran to see or maybe I held the doll still to listen or maybe I don't remember what I did but I know it was not Daddy at the door because I heard Aunt Chandra, Luke's mother, who didn't always speak so loud but did often yell and clap with glee, sometimes without reason.

Oh my God, Casey Wasey, you're tennnnnnnn!!!!!

Aunt Chandra was a mortician so spent most of her days making dead people look better (and survivors feel better) than they otherwise would. Such skills transferred well to my tenth birthday party, at least for a while, especially since Luke was with her and had brought a gift for me: a pack of toy cars, maybe ten or fifteen of them, just like Hot Wheels, almost. Since a day did come when Luke shared his room and all his food with me, I want to say that he was, like BB, a wonderful sharer, but I wonder whether he shared out of the goodness of his heart or, like so many awful rich people I've met (not that he was rich), out of surplus, a greedy sharing that, in each gift, is a reminder of how much the giver has left. He was only eight at the time, so I will give him the benefit of the doubt, but I don't know for sure. All I know is that people kept dying and thus money kept flowing into

Luke's household, enough for him to have his own set of toy cars, a fluffy comforter on his bed, a word processor that we enjoyed until somebody looted their house, and the first nice basketball goal in the neighborhood. And some mix of Luke's belongings and the fact that he was an abnormally cool dude for an eight-year-old led to another surplus: the great heap of friends that Luke had; so many friends that there were days when funeral home chairs had to be unfolded in Luke's room to contain so many little boys, and the back door to Luke's room had to be opened for ventilation. This surplus, too, Luke shared, and so his friends became my friends, chief among them BK—Big Kid or British Knight, still unsure—who was even willing to protect me with his reputation by the time we started high school, since legend was that he had knocked a boy's eye out of the socket in the Black-Mexican War of 2001. (He grew up to be an ad man, you might like to know.) That was all still a few years off, though. For now, I appreciated Luke's gift but did not need his room, and BK was not my friend nor at my tenth birthday party—and neither was Crow, as Aunt Carla reminded us once again when Aunt Chandra cheered *Ooh come on y'all it's time for cake!*

I don't remember saying a word or cutting that cake, though I do sometimes still feel that little sensation—*he's on his way*—which I suppose is the sensation of hope. At some point cake was cut and eaten and everybody went home and I sat on the couch next to the front door and waited for him even after Mama and Tashia went to bed but I got tired after a while so went to bed, too. He did come back that night or the next day, but soon enough he was gone once again, which would not have been a problem if I had not lied.

The lie in question involved Luke. He and I were on the phone, just holding the phone one boring afternoon as we often did for hours. He was playing a video game, playing with so much focus that I bet his tongue was hanging like it always did when Luke felt he was being excellent at something. I was sitting on my bed, listening to Luke extract great joy from that video game, so much joy that I could imagine enjoying a video game myself. My imagination got carried away, I guess, and I began to hallucinate.

Oh, thank you, Daddy! I shouted. *I been wanting one of these!*

What you talking 'bout, Casey?

My daddy just walked in with a Playstation, Luke. Man that's crazy.

Luke had this little giggle in those days that would inspire even the holiest person to slap him in the goddamn face. He released the giggle.

Fool, Uncle Crow is next door. Y'all's car been parked out there all day.

Young Luke was a lot of things at that time but he was not a liar. And aside from strong eyes he had good enough sense to know that the only people who visited the house next door were dope fiends, unless they were relatives of Dean, the chief dope fiend of that residence and a real decent guy despite or even because of his hobbies.

Dean must have been our parents' age, but he had more kindness and creativity than your average grown person. Was more resourceful, too—I remember a stretch of days when he carried a cardboard box through the neighborhood, selling toiletries for one dollar apiece. I'm sure he acquired those toothpastes and deodorants by honest means, because he was decent, as I said, and never stole a thing from anybody that I know of (and I would have heard about it). Dean was also always there when you needed him, like the evening he taught me and Luke how to install Aunt Chandra's front door—*Okay gentlemen y'all watch me now I'ma do what I gotta do soon as I figure out what I gotta do!* Twenty years later that door still stands and Dean's approach still works.

I tell you about Dean because I haven't seen him in a while and feel better when I think about him, especially that time he showed up with his head shaved and basketballs tattooed on his scalp. Didn't even know Dean liked basketball. But I also mention Dean because I want the record to show that I don't give much of a shit that my father began, sometime before my tenth birthday, hanging with dope fiends. Nor am I up in arms that he acquired and consumed a controlled substance himself, heroin mostly, according to him and to any number of news outlets. I never witnessed it myself and I am trying to tell you things for which I have solid evidence, or at least more interesting things than the claim or fact that a man tried heroin once and, soon after, became addicted. My best bet is that heroin must be pretty incredible, must lead to enough ecstasy to make a man's veins and future seem a small price to pay. Besides, I was, through my twenties, addicted to Skittles, enough of which will have you broke and strung out and dead, too—and while that may seem like comparing apples to oranges, so to speak, addiction is addiction and it just so happens that we've built ourselves a nice society that places all the folks addicted to fame and money and complaining a little lower than the angels and, down below waterbugs and Hugo Chavez, places men and women who get high every now and then or all the time. Not that I'm endorsing any of it. I'm just not going to be the one to jump all over the addicts we don't like. At least not for being *addicts*. Daddy could have enjoyed all the heroin in the world for all I cared—I just wanted him to show up for my tenth birthday party and to inform me of his visit to Dean's so I wouldn't be caught up in a lie. And I wanted him to be more careful so I would not have to snuff out that fire on his shirt when I found him outside asleep in the Benz that night, and I wanted him to go back to Ace Pawn Shop and retrieve my old Sega Genesis and my Giga Pets and other items of mine, or at least give me a cut of the proceeds, and I wanted him to pick me up from school on time like he used to. That's all.

Instead, the three o'clock bell rang one fall afternoon in 1997 and I stood out on the front steps with all the other kids. I watched them stampede to the car line, to the arms of grandparents, to the sidewalk for a short stroll to Caravan Trail or Solitude Drive. Watched them all and waited on the steps. Some authority asked me twice or three times *Honey, where's your ride?* which is what I wanted to know myself, but knowing not, I lied and said *On their way* and kept on waiting until the steps were empty except for me and the parking lot was also almost empty. I went to the edge of the hill to look down at Granny's house. The driveway there was empty, too. I did not have a key and did not want to go there, anyway. I decided to walk.

The house on Marsalis was three miles away, an hour away on adult feet, much longer for a ten-year-old with a book bag. But I knew exactly how to get there—down Red Bird Lane to the cemetery gate, right on Marsalis, keep on walking to our front door—and since no place you know how to get to as a child seems too far, I began the journey with a real sense of adventure and a fair amount of energy to boot. Both were gone by time I reached the cemetery. The sun was gone, too, not nighttime yet but cloudy and cold.

I made the right on Marsalis. Less than halfway there. I kept my eyes down, one foot, other foot, and when I next looked up I saw an old woman standing in a schoolyard, packing up her things but still wearing her tangerine crossing guard vest. She smiled on me.

Where you going this late, honey? Headed home, I hope.

Yes, ma'am.

All right, hurry on, then.

I couldn't walk any faster. But that woman made me feel, if only for a few blocks, that she cared that I keep walking, that I reach my destination, and that gave the journey a little Purpose, aside from the original purpose, getting home, which seemed unlikely once I reached the corner of Marsalis and Loop 12.

There are many cities around the world that encourage and even honor the pedestrian. Dallas was not one of them, at least at Loop 12. Three lanes in each direction, a tiny strip of median, cars whizzing by eager to murder old ladies and little children trying to get home. Not even a walk signal that I recall. I stood back and let the light change once or twice. Walked down to the curb. Grabbed my book bag straps. When the light turned green I ran, eyes on the far corner, book bag flinging up and down my little back. Somehow I reached the other side. Still another mile to go. Walking slower now, feeling colder now because it was getting late and I was sweating, but I kept on going, past the creek that trickled under Marsalis, nearly to a shopping center where I could have bought some water if I'd had some money.

A car pulled up beside me.

Casey!

My sister's voice. The Benz. I had imagined rescue a few times on this journey, but not how mad I'd be if it happened. Mad or not, I was tired, so got in, slid my book bag off.

Where have you been, boy?

Tashia sounded like she had been searching for a long time. I reached between the front seats and grabbed her arm, started to explain everything. But then I began to cry and decided to just do that for a little while.

You knew I was gonna pick you up, Scooter. Daddy used the same tone he always used when I did something he thought ridiculous, like when I claimed there was gold in the rocks outside our apartment in Columbus— gold and other precious stones in all the rocks of the earth, actually. He laughed and sighed and said, with just enough mockery, *Scooter, there in't any gold in those rocks.* Then he walked through the front door and closed it behind him. Of course he had been right that time, but times had changed and he had changed and *I* had changed even though he did not notice, and so to him I was still the crazy one. Maybe so.

It is fitting, then, that at this very time, I came under the supervision from eight a.m. to three p.m. each weekday, of the only woman ever to escape the North Texas insane asylum, according to her.

Little children! Gwendolyn Davis, my fifth-grade teacher, speaking. Shrieking, you could say. *Do you all know what is in Terrell, Texas?* Nobody answered. *The insane asylum! That is where I am from. I . . . am the one . . . who got away!*

You didn't doubt it, watching Ms. Davis stand at that giant wood-and-iron desk strewn with manila folders and uncapped pens and other chaos, her lashes fluttering behind the small glasses pinched on her nose, red fingernails flashing, always long and her own, freshly painted, tips never dull—perfect for tapping her desktop, your sternum, her temple when she wanted you to think. She especially wanted us to think about the consequences of not turning in her assignments.

Oh!

Another shriek. This time after classwork was passed, student by student, thirty sheets in all, to Ms. Davis. She held the full stack as though it were contaminated, scowled the way she always did when she believed there was a sheet missing. Never even counted to be sure.

You all must think that I am Willie Foo Foo, just jumped off the turnip truck last night. I know you do. Must! She had a sinister snicker that made you snicker, too, till you remembered what the snicker was for. *But if you do, baby loves, then you have made one of the biggest mistakes of your natural-born lives. That's all right.* She'd smile, such a wonderful little smile, often a smudge of lipstick on one tooth—for effect, I bet—and Betsy Sue, her paddle, now clutched between those red fingernails. *That is alllll right. You can turn in my assignment today, or you can turn it in next year. Because I, Gwendolyn Davis, will be here. And you, whoeeeever you are, will be right here with me. Same bat time, same bat station, same bat assignment.*

Betsy Sue was not for effect. The paddle was made for times such as these when some poor student mistook Ms. Davis for Willie Foo Foo, whoever that was, or did anything else she had already explicitly told us not to do or expected us to know we shouldn't do unless we were also Willie Foo Foo, in which case we should have stayed home instead of coming to her class. And yet for all the fear she put into the hearts of many of her students, I never was afraid. I mean it when I say I'd changed.

While the adults went off and lost their goddamn minds, I'd taken on the task of fixing myself. Gone was the courage of my conviction that rocks were full of gold. Gone the threats to die for freedom. The kind of carelessness that helped me drive my mother's car into the Drug Emporium, gone, and the guts to pass a note in class or, if pushed, to smash a classmate's face with a Little Golden Book. I had once been the kind of boy who protested when my parents refused to let me wear my overalls backward, in the days of Kris Kross. *I just won't wear 'em, then!* I cried. And did not wear them. That was the old me, though.

The new me did not speak in protest if at all. Was glad that Thornton required uniforms. Damn near impossible to get a uniform wrong, and getting things wrong made the new me sick, a queasy feeling that first appeared during my jihad against the times tables—mistake after mistake, torn flashcards, aborted worksheets, tears. No Tums, no ginger ale, just work, *keep working boy,* and soon enough I could proclaim that twelve times twelve is a hundred forty four and folks would think I'd known this since I was born.

I didn't care about perfection for perfection's sake. Was still a messy boy in my head or in whatever private space I had or made. But I had learned that the authorities loved nothing more than obedience, submission . . . or at least if I submitted they would not bother me too much. Even Granny cooled her jets once I kept my mouth shut and vacuumed the carpet like she requested: twice in each direction, no crooked lines, no footprint tracks. Came to my defense once after that, if you can believe it, when my sister kept trying to convince me that drawing dresses was for girls. *Let that boy alone! Let him draw a dress if he want to!* And yet the best solution, I found, was to stop drawing dresses and attention, and that worked just fine. It was simple, really: identify who was in charge, find out what they want, give it to them immediately.

We ain't seen nothing like it. Ms. Davis's sidekick, Demorris Vance, recalled first meeting me. *Davis and I said when we first got you . . . Where did this boy come from? I mean, boy, you would just sit there and watch us, them big ole eyes . . . Wherever we walked there them eyes were, watchin' us. Wouldn't say nothin', just watch. Didn't wanna miss nothing.*

And you did not miss a thing, Casey Gerald, Ms. Davis caboosed. *Not one single solitary thing.*

I did miss one thing: some day in fall '97 I missed Ms. Davis's exact instructions for a homework assignment. I knew she'd ordered us to write a speech. Topic: *I'm the Mayor Now and This Is My New Plan.* But I couldn't remember whether she'd said we had to recite these speeches from memory, so I assumed the worst. It was bad enough that I'd never written a speech before—not even sure I'd ever *heard* one except for that same snippet of "I Have a Dream" we've been pacified with for a half century, and those thirty-second spots we learned for Easter Sunday. But I also had not given any thought to what the mayor should be doing. So by the time I got home I was desperate enough to ask for help and found it thanks to my sister, who was still magnetic and so retained a retinue of clever, attractive high school friends, some of whom were at our house in my time of need and who, contrary to what was said about them in the papers, had damn good ideas for the mayor's new plan.

There was nothing special about what happened that evening. I transcribed some teenagers' ideas and, when that was finished, read what I'd written again and again until I could say it without reading it. Then the day of reciting arrived. I watched, horrified on their behalf, as idontknowhowmany kids walked to the front and held big sheets of paper and proved that they had no problem staying in fifth grade forever. Another delinquent, another read speech, so many read speeches that I grew ashamed, figured *I* had the problem. But I didn't have time for too much shame because I was next. I walked to the front, empty-handed. Stared at the clock on the back wall (I hated looking people in the face and had heard that audiences couldn't tell whether you're looking at them or at the wall behind them).

Began to say the words that, by this point, I could see in my head, enough to make it all the way to *thank you*. Stood there and looked at Ms. Davis. Considered saying *sorry*. Then she shrieked—

Oh! You are IT, Casey Gerald!

I didn't know what I was so just walked back to my desk, head down, hoping it would all end soon. But she was still staring at me, red fingernails on her hips, smiling.

My my . . . I cannot wait to see you on that stage, baby love.

Turns out I had gotten myself in a big mess. This homework assignment was actually an audition for the annual oratorical contest, in which I had no particular interest but for which Ms. Davis decided, because of my misunderstanding, I had the right skills—and her decisions did not require consent from child nor parent. I was *it*, and until she saw me on the stage for real she wanted to see me in rehearsal, with the talented and gifted teacher, whose qualifications for such a role I can't put my finger on, aside from the fact that she seemed to have a lot of free time.

All I remember is one of those rehearsals (not even the contest, by which time I had other things to worry about, which we'll get to). We gathered in the auditorium. My name was called. I walked onto the stage, to the X that had been taped at center. Stood there and looked at the clock on the back wall. Said my first line and, at some point, said *thank you*. I went back to my seat, next to Ms. Talented-and-Gifted. Looked at her with that *did I do all right?* face that even some famous people make after television interviews.

She put her incredibly wrinkled hand on my arm. *Well, honey, you forgot to say half your speech.* I hadn't even noticed.

That was just how far down the road to perdition I had been up until that time—so carefree that I could stand onstage and not even realize that I was forgetting my speech and ruining my reputation, and not even *mind* until someone notified me. Maybe that's what childhood is supposed to be like, I don't know. All I know is that I have not forgotten a single line of a single speech since that woman's intervention—that from that moment on I spent untold hours picking words that people would like and saying those words again and again and again and again until, at some point, I could lower my eyes from the clock and look folks in the face and give them what they wanted, a little thrill; and with a bit more work I could also move my hands with purpose, *gesticulate*, a finger pointed here, a clasped fist there, a pause, a smile, and *thank you*. To give a speech was to walk a minefield but, boy, to get it right . . . to get it right made the terror feel, sometimes, like real great fun, especially when the people clapped and took your picture and hugged you like they were your kin or at least something more than strangers. And it's only now, all these years later, that I've realized it is possible, if not likely, that deep down I despise the act of standing in front of anybody saying anything. But when I was a child I did not speak much and then, one night, in slavish fear, I got my homework so wrong that it was perfect. And that made all the difference. Or enough.

I think of how it all began and think of another boy in my fifth-grade class, Mauricio, who must have also had some strange things going on in his life at the time. One afternoon, he decided to lie down for a while in the middle of the road. Mauricio's plan was to lie there until a car ran him over, which would have worked if the first prospective car had not been driven by someone who noticed a small boy in the road ahead, on his back. Mauricio didn't flinch as the car approached (that's what I heard) but didn't put up too big a fight when the driver picked him up and carried him to the principal's office or wherever he was taken. He was back in class at his earliest convenience but for some reason, perhaps the same reason that led him to lie in the road, did not return with his homework assignment.

Mauricio! Ms. Davis cried. *Now you listen to me. You can go on out and lie down in the street alllll you want to. But until somebody truly runs you over you had better not walk in my room without your assignment. You are not THAT crazy, baby love.*

But what if he was? Or what if he had more sense than anybody else in that classroom? Maybe Mauricio took a few good looks at the strangeness of his life and, having seen more than enough, decided to just lie down in the street and take his chances there. And young Mauricio, who might have had the right idea all along, was struck with the paddle and doused with medication and, I bet, given another chance to try fifth grade—while I, his mad submissive counterpart, toed the line so well and for so long that somewhere along the way somebody said I had a gift—a *gift!*—when what I had was more of a sickness. And Ms. Davis and Ms. Vance might very well have saved me—never made me go home after school, told me I was *it*, whatever it was, and I am grateful but I ask myself should I—should *we*—have joined Mauricio in the street? Two mad boys and too much strangeness, one reformed, one revolting. Oh, Mauricio, I sure wonder what you're up to these days, haven't seen you in so long, but I do think of you sometimes and wonder.

I understand now why someone had stenciled a slogan in green paint above the entryway to Thornton's upstairs corridor, reserved for fifth and sixth graders.

WHAT YOU ARE TO BE YOU ARE NOW BECOMING

So it was. For me. For Mauricio. And even for my mother and father, by the final night the family spent together at the house on Marsalis, toward the end of 1997.

It wasn't a full night. Sometime after dark but before bed, Tashia allowed me to hang in her room for a while. She had flushed most of that too-cool-for-little-brothers stuff out of her system, a process that coincided with her newfound commitment to the local animal shelter. We heard a scream: Mama. Daddy had pulled a fork on her. Not an industrial fork or anything, just the kind of fork you eat dinner with until you decide to stab your wife. Deciding thusly, Daddy pulls the fork and Mama screams. She runs into Tashia's room and picks up the phone. 911, of course. Either she hangs it up, just a warning, or Daddy runs in and hangs it up on her behalf. Whatever the case, the police do not like people playing on the 911 line and so they rushed immediately to our house and began their investigation. I was not questioned. The police also hate to show up anywhere without producing some results, good or bad, so they advised the woman to leave with her children. We three left in our nightclothes, in a hurry, Mama's face on but runny in places. I assume we left in the Benz, since the cops didn't take us anywhere and nobody picked us up and we didn't walk. We arrived, someway, at Old Ox Road like Indians following the leaning pole in a daze of divine insight. No knocks no doorbells no explanations, that I remember.

The way Granny stood over me as I ran water for a bath made me worry that we could not stay there, even though we had no where else to go. She hovered in the doorway—*Now what is going on?*—but didn't holler when I kept looking into the water, silent. Just shuffled away, going from room to room—*Now what IS going on?*—as if she would find her house empty again if she moved from station to station, asking the same question. She returned to the bathroom door. I was still there. Still didn't know what was going on, what chain of events had turned a smiling husband and wife into a fork-wielding man chasing a screaming woman. Still don't know. Sometimes we don't have the luxury of a slippery slope and find, instead, a cliff. Maybe that's what happened to them that night or maybe, bless their hearts, they had spent a great deal of energy keeping it together— since my tenth birthday, since the seizure, since the beauty convention or the move to Columbus or the first time they met. Who knows? It's amazing, either way, how quickly you can become a thing you'd never thought of being and may not even want to be.

chapter FOUR

Dead, for example.

It still seems odd, how quickly Papa died. One day he was admitted to the hospital, after a new stroke or due to effects of an old one. A few days later, Daddy—who, by the way, moved in with us on Old Ox shortly after we fled him and the house on Marsalis—said *C'mon Scooter*, and though I probably did not hurry I still grabbed my shoes and went.

The hospital seemed far too big for the few patients and visitors inside. We were shown to Papa's room, which seemed too big for him. Too cold. He lay in his big bed, propped up. Asleep. *Say something to Papa, Scooter,* Daddy said.

I didn't want to wake him up, so I just patted Papa's arm, which was also too cold, I thought. I whispered *Hey Papa* and, not knowing what else to say, patted his arm again. Daddy dragged a chair over to Papa's side and said, respectfully, *Hey Daddy*. Papa was covered with a thin blanket and Daddy rubbed the blanket, perhaps to add a little heat. He rested his hand on the blanket, over Papa's shin. Laid his forehead on the back of his hand.

He let out a cry so loud, so untamed, that I thought at first he might be laughing like the good old days, but then I saw that there was wetness streaming down his hand to the thin blanket, and then, though I had never seen nor heard him cry before, I knew that he was weeping. Uncle Moe, his eldest brother, who had been standing in the corner, took me out into the hallway and pulled the door shut behind us. *He'll be all right.* But on the other side of the door I could hear my daddy calling out through all those sobs. *Wake up, Daddy,* he begged. *I'll take you on home,* said Uncle Moe.

Later that evening Daddy called me at Granny's house. *I'm on my way to pick you up,* he mumbled. There was wailing in the background. *Why, Daddy?* I asked. He hung up in my face.

I don't remember speaking to him, even seeing him, again before Papa's service. Or at the service, though I know that he was there. It was hard to see anybody in that great mass of mourners, genuine and not—some both, like me. It is true that I was sad, shed honest tears, but it is also true that whenever Luke began to cry I started crying, too, just to be sure nobody thought that anybody was more sad about this death than I was, or that Papa meant more to anybody else than he meant to me. And sure enough, every time I began to weep somebody looked upon me with concern and somebody else put my head in their bosom and I suppose that you could surely say I was an awful human being at eleven . . . but death makes people, even children, do strange things.

For example: around the time Papa died, Daddy sold the house on Marsalis for twenty-seven thousand dollars, which did not include the value of all my and my sister's belongings that were left behind or moved to storage and then lost when the fee went unpaid. The Benz must have been sold, too, since some post-death morning Daddy stumbled into Granny's house and said he'd been in an accident. Outside, instead of the Benz, was a silver Buick with its windshield bashed in.

In April, Uncle Moe called Granny's house phone and said that Daddy had been shot and was in the intensive care unit. Later he appeared on her porch and said to me and Tashia *C'mon y'all, you need to go see your daddy.* That was news to me, but I complied, of course, and rode out to the hospital and stood at the foot of Daddy's bed. Aside from the staples running down his stomach he looked like he was going to make it and he did, depending on what you mean by *making it*.

I did not see him for some time after that. My sister did, one morning on her way to school. She was riding with Granny down Marsalis, when there, on the corner, she saw her father. They saw each other, in fact. He did not recognize her.

That was August, I believe. In September, Daddy was arrested for stealing cigarettes from a corner store. Twenty-seven thousand dollars had not lasted long. Sure would have been nice of him to share a couple dollars with me or my sister or with Mama, especially around Christmastime. Just like the past two years, I'd ripped a single sheet of paper from my notebook and titled it "Casey's Christmas List," wrote *1* on the left side of the first line, and *Computer* next to the *1*. Submitted it far in advance. Early Christmas morning Mama presented a large wrapped box, big enough for a CPU. I rushed to tear that shiny paper to shreds and find my satisfaction but instead found a two-tiered VHS rack. I didn't have any VHS movies, though, besides the *Ben-Hur* that Auntie O had bought me some years back.

Mama flashed that yet-shining smile. *You like it, Man?* I flashed a smile right back. *Mmhmm, Mama, I sure do. Thank you!* I remain one of the very best liars you will ever meet, thanks to my mother and father, who also taught me never to ask anybody for anything.

For example: I did not ask Clarice to courier me downtown to the Lew Sterrett Justice Center to see my daddy. And yet she surely did, at least once, pick me up and drive the back roads to the jail, pulled into the underground parking lot, past the enclosed outdoor exercise area. Walked with me inside, where I was inspected like I'd committed a crime myself, and then sat, waiting, in those welded-together chairs until it was time to go sit in a single bolted-down chair and look at Daddy through that dingy thick glass and talk to him through that spit-aroma'd phone receiver. I hope you don't get the sense that I had something against people in jail or even my daddy, though I guess I did have a few things against him at that time. It's just that I did not and do not understand why moral support has to come at the expense of children. I would have gladly, maybe, written a letter or something, but I had no interest whatever in going to jail to see anybody and I bet many of the other children—all those I've seen dragged off to prison to take a portrait in front of that palm tree background like they're at Disneyland or somewhere similarly magical—would also like to stay away from jail, just as everybody else I've ever met prefers to stay away from jail. If we are fighting, as we should, to set folks free from jails, then we should also have sense enough to keep innocent children away from jail, too.

But even if I had not been tramped down to the prison, I would not have escaped my father altogether. When a once-great man decides to lose it, or accidentally loses it, somebody is liable to write about it in the papers, even if you're only twelve and have done a decent job keeping your business to yourself.

Casey—Ms. Davis slid up to my locker one March morning—*are you all right?* She looked so concerned that I wondered for a moment whether I *was* all right, not wanting to lie to her.

Yes, ma'am.

She hooked her arm through mine and shuttled me to her desk. Handed me, folded over between her red fingernails, a copy of that day's *Dallas Morning News*. On the front page, above the fold, was Rod Gerald just where I'd last seen him, behind the glass down at Lew Sterrett, with the headline *Lost Options: Once the Pride of Texas, S. Oak Cliff Star Saw Life, Dreams Sacked by Drugs.*

The story also took up the space below the fold and some of the inside of the first section, photos and quotes, you name it.

It's not sad, Clarice told the *News. It'd be sad if he wasn't guilty.*

I thought it was pretty sad either way, but what did I know. I was only twelve and was too young to have an opinion. Not, of course, too young to die or be caught up in the Rapture. And no longer too young to be taken to the Facilities to see my mother.

There were so many of these places around Dallas—Green Oaks, Timberlawn, Cedars, etc. etc.—and each was the same, more or less: an office-like building hidden behind trees, full of whispers (*What's the patient ID?*) and brochures ("Signs Your Child Is Suicidal") and buzzers. Door after door of buzzers. Mama and her associates were kept behind the final buzzered door, though not for yearlong stints, if only because by 1999 the insurance companies didn't put up with anybody asking for too much help. So she was kept there for a week, two weeks, maybe, and Tashia and I were taken there, wherever *there* was, to visit once these stays began, sometime after Papa died.

Each Facility had its own approach to visitation. One, within a larger hospital, reserved a lounge where you could sit with your relative without supervision, as long as you whispered and never needed to go to the bathroom. Another designed separate wings for drug recovery and psychiatric care, each wing with its own communal visitation area and its own little lawn or smoking corner. Thanks to the *News,* I know that Tashia and I visited Daddy at least once pre- or post-jail in the recovery wing. I'm inclined to say we visited Mama in both wings. I'm also inclined *not* to say that. Multiple people alleged that she needed recovery around this time, and she confessed to it at least once, and I've repeated it. But a drugged person sometimes closely resembles a manic person, and both drugs and mental illness can rejigger the brain in such a way that memory becomes unreliable. So since I never saw my mother use any drug and I am not convinced that her people, me included, did enough work to know the root cause (let alone the effects) of her behavior—and since I know of many children who would lie to protect their mother's honor—I will only say for sure that we visited her in the wing where she received psychiatric care, if you want to call it that.

I won't tell you what I saw in there. Either you've been to such a place yourself and know, or you haven't been and should be glad. All I'll say is this: if I ever get the chance to hold someone accountable for what I saw and heard, what was done and not done to and for my mother and all those other patients . . . well, I sure hope I have the guts to take it. But I also hope I'm in the mood to be honest and tell whoever was responsible *thank you.* The Facilities never failed to keep her in one place for a while. But a while ain't forever and so, in those days, the day always came when she was sent back into the world, a free woman, threw off the yoke of catatonia, with plans, big or small, and places to go, and a new promise: *I'll be right back.*

To be fair, I remember her telling me that only once. I was standing or squatting in the front yard. She flung the screen door open, rushed down the two small steps, not panicked, excited maybe, face on and shades on. I believe she had her purse. She cut through the yard, between the hedges and a chinaberry tree. Smiled at me as always and tossed those words— *Baby, I'll be right back—K Mama see you later!* I took her at her word. I also assumed that *right back* meant *in a few hours* or *later today* but nighttime came and then the next day and maybe a few more next days, too, I can't remember. But I do remember glancing up the street every few minutes while I played in the yard and I remember staring out the window in the living room once I went inside and I remember listening for the front door in the night, however many nights went by before she came right back.

As I later learned and proved myself, once you get away with a major lie a whole new world of possibilities opens up, possibilities that don't require lying at all. That might explain why she only said *I'll be right back* that single time. There was another afternoon she simply was not there when I got home from school and, some unknown string of days later, called, cheery *Hey Man I'm over on Moonglow tell somebody to come pick me up.* We did that right away. And an evening when Shon spotted Mama speed-walking behind the little shopping center on Red Bird and invited her to get in the car and come back home. She arrived, still smiling, talking fast, no gifts but herself.

I want to say I remember yet another capture-reunion: a sunny afternoon, me in the backseat of Granny's car, Tashia up front. Up ahead, alongside the highway, I saw a woman with burnt-blonde hair. *Granny there go my mama right there pull over!* She pulled over. Put her hazard lights on. I stuck my head out the window and yelled over all the highway traffic, waving—*Mama c'mon get in the car!* And boy she was so glad to get off her feet she hurried down the grassy hill and hopped on in.

The only problem with that memory is I know that, many times, I mistook random women on the sides of roads for my mother, imagined many schemes for stumbling upon her, trapping her even. So I can't swear that this highway sighting was real. Hope and delusion, often hard to distinguish, also make folks do strange things sometimes.

For example: I turned to sorcery. It wasn't any serious voodoo business, really. Some days of absence had passed and it struck me, as from above, that I could conjure up my mother just by walking perfectly: from the top of Old Ox Road at R. L. Thornton down to Granny's house, placing one foot, one foot only, in each sidewalk square. I could not let two feet land inside the same square. Could not let any part of any foot touch the lines between the squares. Could not skip a square, all the way to the last square at the last blade of grass that separated Granny's lawn from her driveway. I bullshit you verily not: it worked. No missteps, reached the driveway, looked at the porch, saw my mother there, cigarette in hand. *Hey Man! Hey Mama where you been?* She didn't tell me but it didn't matter.

It worked only one time. And yet I still tried it every now and then, even once with my eyes closed. And I still stared out the window when I passed through the living room, still listened for the front door in the night, still waited for the local news to inform me of a woman's body that'd been found in the Trinity River. None of these were reliable ways to fore-tell when or whether she'd be back, but that didn't stop me. And if insanity is doing the same thing and expecting a different result, then I guess you could say I went insane, but I did not feel insane at all in those days, though I did sometimes feel a gnawing pain in my stomach, not like I wanted to vomit but a bit like I have felt, maybe you have felt, when you rush to catch the train and make it just in time based on the schedule and you stand there at the platform's edge, leaning over, peering down into the dark and empty tunnel where the train was meant to be, five, now twenty minutes ago, and arrival times have come and keep on going and you wonder *where's the train* and you worry that you'll lose your job or you know that you will miss your big appointment or you wonder if your mother's dead. And you just don't know.

All I know is that she came back home one day or night, and was off to a Facility some day or night soon after. At some point in that stay, the phone rang at Granny's house.

Casey? Granny called out, gently, from her bedroom. Didn't sound mad or nothing.

I popped my head inside her doorway.

Well now that was your mama's doctor called. Said she checked herself out the hospital today.

She on her way to the house?

Chile, I don't know. I figure she'll be down here after while.

I figured, too. She even called once. Said she'd be home soon. So to my regiment of windows and front doors and news bulletins and strangers on the sides of roads I added phone calls—the phone rings, that little ding of hope goes off, *hello?* Bill collector. *Next time.* She didn't call again.

And now I figure this: If ever your mother asks you to choose between her death and disappearance, have her die. Always. Though not immedi-ately, of course.

Death has a certain elegance to it. A date. A time. A body. A clean hemline, so to speak. Death *is*, more and more by the day it seems, very expensive. Whatever the cost, pay it.

A disappearance, on the contrary, is a messy, sordid enterprise. It is hard even to pin down when, exactly, someone disappears. For the cops, it's after a certain number of days, or proof of foul play, or once they decide your people are worth tracking. For friends and family, it depends on when each person hears the news, whether they trust the messenger, whether they give a damn, and so on. The hardest point to determine is when the Disappeared would say they disappeared, since they never disappear to themselves. All you know for sure is that they're not where they used to be, with you. And since there are so many missing people who wanted nothing more than to vanish, it is unclear whether you, the Left Behind, are suffering a hardship or committing an injustice when you canvas the neighborhood and staple posters to light poles and pray or ask for prayer. What kind of just God, after all, would help you hunt somebody down? And in the event that you stop searching—stop waiting, close the curtains in the living room, switch the station from the news, sleep soundly through the night, see many women on the sides of roads and speed up, don't look back—it is unclear whether you have set the Disappeared free or simply given up.

And all this ambivalence, the muddle that a missing person leaves behind, might explain why I've said for all these years that my mother disappeared when I was twelve, in '99. Even told a president. I was just about to tell you the same thing, but happened to be rummaging through my few personal effects that survived those days, and stumbled across another artifact, near that photograph I told you about—if you want to call a middle school science folder an *artifact*. Nothing special, just an assignment from January 2000, definitions—*epicenter, fault, seismic waves*. Back then schools demanded parental involvement, so near the top of this document Granny had signed her name. Made sense: Mama had disappeared, Granny lent her imprimatur thereafter.

Now, I have never been able to leave well enough alone, so kept looking through those files. Worksheets. Pop quizzes. Outlines. A drawing:

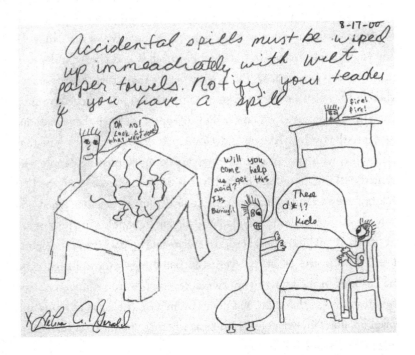

And there it was, at the bottom of that drawing: an ornate signature in blue ink. My mother's. At the top of the page was a date, also in blue ink: 17 August 2000. *Maybe her mind was so gone in '99 that she wrote the wrong year.* I kept looking. There it was again—August 23, a quiz on lab safety. And again—August 31, a bell ringer re: the respiratory system. October 18: a test on circulation. October 26, in the margins, notes on cells and chromosomes. Then, 2 November 2000, Granny's signature returns.

This made no sense.

I wondered, for reasons you will come to understand, whether I had drawn those signatures myself. I hoped like hell I had. Was so desperate for some clarity, for vindication, that I asked my sister, without really asking her, when her mother disappeared. *Were your parents at your hs graduation?* I texted. I knew that Tashia graduated May 2000, that everyone who could have been there should have been, to see that little girl with those shiny plump bronze cheeks walk across the stage. To see what she'd grown up to be: valedictorian, champion of lost animals and little brothers alike, provider of her own home training, defender of wayward parents. She'd even given a quote to the *News* in '99, she was so loyal: *I love him with all my heart. I'm going to be behind him 100 percent as long as he's doing right.*

Ummmm not daddy . . . i can't even remember if Mama was . . .

I was so thrown off by my sister's reply that I let her know why I'd asked. Even with the stakes raised, all she could remember was that I broke the disappearance news to her sometime before Thanksgiving 2000. The signatures were authentic, sure enough.

I consider the fact that my mother was around on 31 December 1999, on my thirteenth birthday, for my sister's graduation, on August 17 and again on October 26—around for a whole year after I, for years, swore she had disappeared. Consider the fact that I, who was meant to remember, cannot remember any of it, that my sister cannot remember any of it. And I ask myself—ask *you*—what if all the terror of the world, not *all* but *some* of the Big Terror, is actually lost forever? Too much to remember, too loud a terror to listen to again. What if to remember nothing *is* to remember something: to remember that you, at some point, had to forget? Did I, in my rummaging, discover a scandal, or a tragedy, or a choice? A choice to remember the end on my own terms—or better yet, to remember my own private beginning? Is that not how our world was ordered? One day, a man laid out a calendar and marked *year 1, anno Domini.* His purpose (like I knew that man) was not to mark the day the Hittites died, or the Parthenon was abandoned, or any other tragedy that befell the BC peoples.

He chose year 1, pulled it out of his ass, so to speak, so that we would re-member, always remember, a certain New Thing. And he didn't even do *that* right, turns out. His choice still stands. Why can't mine? Or yours? Why can't we rename the years, mark some for sorrows, others for fresh starts, for redemption? Perhaps that's what I did. Or perhaps my mind went bad for a while. Or perhaps I simply made it up, lied for all those years.

All I know is that she disappeared and that 1999 still strikes me as a good year for the end of things, so I'll let her stay gone in my head for all those months she was still, in some form, around. And I'll also tell you of one final departure that for sure took place in the year 2000, but since it was a very 1999 kind of thing, we'll leave it with the other disasters of the last millennium.

I'd known, in the abstract, that my sister was going to college after graduation—she'd been accepted to Xavier University in New Orleans, where she planned to learn how to be a neonatologist, whatever that was. This sounded well and right to me. But then she packed two suit-cases. Then people started showing up to Granny's house the night of her send-off.

I don't remember the meal and I hardly remember who attended aside from my mother's sisters and Shon's husband, who would be driving Tashia the nine hours to Louisiana. I remember the party ending, the seven or so people still there. We linked hands in a circle around Tashia. Somebody prayed. Folks took turns hugging her goodbye. They let me go last.

I reached up to wrap my arms around her, but before I could say bye I couldn't say anything. My throat closed up and somebody just kept grab-bing at my chest, or that's what it felt like, and I couldn't make any words come out. I could only scream. Tashia kept patting me—*Casey, don't cry, I'll be back*—and Shon or somebody said *Y'all let's leave 'em alone* and they left and I wanted to stop crying this was so embarrassing, but my back kept crunching up and I could have made her scoliosis even worse that's how hard I squeezed her. You ever want something not to happen in equal proportion to your certainty that it is going to? *Don't leave,* I kept saying under my breath, into her stomach. She pulled away, smiled, walked to the car. I stood at the front door and watched the taillights ease up the hill, out of view. Gone.

PART TWO

And I saw a new heaven and a new earth: for the first heaven and the first earth were passed away

The Apocalypse of John
Revelation 21:1

chapter **FIVE**

Poor John . . . Alone, exiled to the isle of Patmos, must have had some wild shit going on in his life, too, as he wrote down his apocalypse—new heaven, new earth, *the works*. I understand, brother. I do. Compared to that my dreams were pretty tame: all I needed was a new *home*, a need that was not revealed to me by God but by my cousins, who began to joke, around the time my mother disappeared and my sister left for college, that I was *homeless*. And as with many things I laughed at in those days without actually being amused, I worried they were right. I was not without a place to leave my clothes, have a meal, lay my head—a place to *live*, if only in the most basic sense of the word. But I could not tell them where my home was at that time and even now you'll have to let me look beyond the brick and mortar to trace some outline of my home in all the places I have been. The first of which appeared on the first day of the first year of the new millennium, when D'Angelo released the second single from his second album, *Voodoo:* "Untitled (How Does It Feel?)." On the same television that I watched Peter Jennings bring in the year 2000, I watched D'Angelo's video for this song. A lot. So much that after the first few (dozen) times I had it memorized, and watched it crouched before the screen in the dark with the sound off, so that everyone in the house thought I was asleep.

Have you seen it?

The opening frame is empty but full of blackness. You know something is coming. You can sense the camera is moving. As it moves, the magic meaty top of a golden brown ear comes into view. It's D'Angelo's.

From the ear your eyes follow the back of his head, the tight brown flesh between narrow rows of braided hair. You scan the perfect rows around to his left ear, past the jagged sideburns, across the glowing cheekbone and finally come to rest on his eyes. You are so close to his eyes you cannot see the forehead above or the nose below. He cannot see you because he is not looking.

Open your eyes, D'Angelo. The eyes flutter once, twice. He looks at you.

His eyes are calm like he's been watching since the dawn of man and already knew what you were doing when he wasn't looking. You want to die, it's that perfect.

The stare is too much and he knows it. The camera rushes down the bridge of his nose and rests on cool gleaming lips. You are a child but those are not the lips of children, they are man lips god lips spread lazily over a tiny gap in small marble teeth.

Pan out from the lips that you've fallen into, see the goatee that runs to a trace of beard lining the beatific jaw and around to those ears and into the blackness behind him.

The strong neck offering a path to shoulders that shine in the studio light of God and—wow—a real man chest that is flanked by one tattooed wing on his left arm. The chest is bare except for a simple gold link chain that hangs down in the valley carved in the middle of his heart. At the end of the chain is a gold Jesus hanging on the cross.

The feet on the cross point down his sternum to a crooked belly button that has come into view inside the ample muscles between the strong veiny arms that swing at his sides, above the place you can't believe the camera is panning back to show. He is naked.

You can't hear him but you know what he is asking at this moment, in the song.

How does it feel

You don't know.

He takes a glance (nervous?) to his right—the first time he is not watching you or down below or God behind his eyelids. We are not alone and we do not know who's there. But D'Angelo doesn't stop. You feel that if you are caught, he will make it okay.

The shot goes back to his face, up close. His head drops. His eyes close. His hand grabs at his chest, which now fills the entire screen—the most perfect chest you've seen, adorned with the tiny golden replica of the most perfect sacrifice.

He is sweating now. The drops run down to the navel but don't enter it, they just keep running down. The camera does, too. How far? How far down?

Oh wow. You are watching a stomach drenched in sweat and writhing all by itself. It doesn't matter that you can't hear a word D'Angelo is saying. The words don't matter. You haven't breathed in two and a half minutes, as far as you know.

He starts to turn. You think it might be the camera, moving to show a different angle. But he asked you how it feels, not what you think, and you feel like he's turning away. You worry you may never see him again, though he has the back of four men's backs and that wing across his left arm, so you know that you could mount him and fly away. Where are you going, D'Angelo?

With his back turned and his arms partly raised to show his clenched fists, he lifts his head, which now is bathed in the light. You watch him cry out, again and again. Then he's turned back around to face you, but he's not really here. It looks as if he's close to tears. His stomach is pumping like he can't catch his breath. He's staring down—at what?—and lifts his right hand to put it behind his head. He starts to smirk. He's smiling. Something is happening down there. Inside of him. He raises his left hand but doesn't put it behind his head—instead he puts a fist to his temple like his mind is about to ooze out of his ear.

What. Is. Happening?

The camera draws you quickly to his face. He throws his head back and opens his mouth wide enough to let the scream flow, wide enough that you can see the dark pink line running down the back of his throat. An exorcism? You see the blackness inside his nostrils. You see the muscles in his neck. You see his eyes, clamped shut. He is not there. He has swerved out of the frame.

This is what your life is supposed to be. This feeling. He looks at you again now and you know it is a different look than the first one he gave you. Different than any look anyone has ever given you. D'Angelo is not fucking around this is not a game this is not lust this is an earnest plea and a question that only you can answer: *How does it feel?*

That's what he's asking. Crying. *How does it feeeeel?* And his face is full of pain like he needs to truly know how it feels or else his mission cannot be complete. He punches the air and sweat flies across his face and runs down his brow.

He doesn't take his eyes off you again until he opens his mouth and looks far into the darkness above him and the darkness sends down light. When he looks at you again you wonder if he's angry but you know he's not ashamed. You are not ashamed anymore, either.

You have wanted so badly to escape. Once a month, sometimes more, you've prayed the prayer of salvation, hoping to feel the Holy Ghost and to know that even *your* sin can be forgiven. You keep praying because you haven't felt it yet and fear you never will. But now you feel it. You feel it in the way he shakes his head, how his body rocks and his knees buckle, the sincerity in his eyes when he looks at you and mouths what no one else has said to you before: *I want to take you away from here.* You feel naked and beautiful and right.

For thirty seconds more, D'Angelo swerves in and out of the frame, his fists punch the air, his head rocks back and his mouth bursts open. And then it's over. He looks at you and lets his mouth rest. The screen blacks out. But you have seen and felt it all. Found a piece of what you needed. At least I had.

You see, I have been on this earth for thirty years and have not met a single faggot, starting with myself, who survived without finding another place, real or not, to call home. If you know what I mean, I hope you've found it. Will do what I can to help. If you *don't* know, if that word sounds harsh, it should.

There was a boy I met around this time, D, who everybody knew either because they went to school with him, or because he was one of the top track stars in the city, or simply because he was loud and Oak Cliff was small. Even as a teenager, everybody also seemed to know, or insinuate, or violently allege, that D was *sweet*.

On New Years Eve 2010, D was stabbed to death in his apartment in Houston. He was twenty-four. His roommate found the body the next afternoon, and the news reached us all within a week. A few days later, Luke, BK, and I went to a sports bar to watch the NFL playoffs. During one of the commercial breaks I brought up D's death.

Say man, remember D? Did you hear he got killed?

Nah, all I know is he was a faggot, one of them responded.

The commercial break ended, Luke went to get a beer, and I realized that a decade earlier, hardly anyone I knew would have stopped short of a full, perhaps silent, endorsement of this death.

So it meant a great deal back in the year 2000 that every Saturday after

Showtime at the Apollo ended and *Flava TV* came on, I could crouch in the dark for four and a half minutes and know that there was a home out there somewhere: a place that, even when it's gone, I could still feel inside; a place that, as wrong as it might be, was still worth going to. At least a place where D'Angelo stood stark naked and offered to take me away—I was a thirteen-year-old boy, not a saint.

Instead of D'Angelo, it was my father who took me away after Tashia left for New Orleans. He had paid his debt to society, had spent his time in a halfway house with great moral vigor—read the Bible and went to church so much that he was called to preach the gospel like his father, in his father's church that was now being ruled and ruined by his older brother. Even sang the lead for one of the male chorus's most popular songs. The legend was now also a living testimony to the Lord's redemptive power.

I doubt Granny asked him to take me away, because she has never liked my daddy, as far as I can tell, and has surely never put anybody out of her house. So I figure he and some other wise adults felt that a boy's home was with his father.

At Clarice's house now, where Daddy moved upon his release, there was far more space to live. The front room was all mine, and it came with a door that locked, a full-size mattress on actual rails, a black dresser and walk-in closet to put my clothes, and a small brown mouse that sometimes ran across the pillow that I slept on, until BB and I caught it and set it on fire in the backyard, which was almost as large as the practice football field at my middle school. The school itself I could tolerate only because I was in the eighth grade and would soon leave it forever. I'm pretty sure middle school was awful for everyone, and I've come to believe that the general role of school in American life is to introduce young boys and girls to inescapable misery at an early age so they won't complain too much when they reach the workforce.

Long before I heard of Yale or Harvard, W. H. Atwell was the best school I had known, according to the Dallas Independent School District pamphlets, the Texas Education Agency (which had not put it on probation), and the people who taught in the building. Tashia had gone to Atwell when we first moved back to Dallas in 1995, and her then-boyfriend Roderick (no joke) was the prototypical Atwell Archer—with his baby-blue-and-scarlet letterman's jacket, his perfectly creased Girbaud jeans and spotless Nike Air Max, his hair full of waves like Puerto Ricans I'd come to know, his two-story home in a neighborhood where being a black person in a two-story home was nothing to take note of whatsoever, his mother and father who owned this home and lived in it together, and his nauseating sense that he was well on his way to becoming a Strong Black Man.

Much of this sense came from the head football, basketball, and track coach at Atwell: Fred Walton, who trained Roderick years after he had the honor of training Michael Johnson, who went on to be a great Olympian, and years before he had the misfortune of training me.

Coach Walton was at least six-foot-three and that was just the start of him—that belly firm but hanging over the gym shorts he always wore when he wasn't in a suit . . . those hands that seemed made solely to hold a wooden paddle . . . that afro that didn't look large but might have been larger without all the grease and sweat therein. The sweat rested in the hair or on his forehead until it ran when he began to bark orders and reprimands, which was damn near all the time, since he came to work each day determined to make us men.

Every practice ended with conditioning—twelve to sixteen wind sprints down the practice field and back, forty thirteen- and fourteen-year-old boys near death before we reached the halfway mark, standing along the goal line, panting, hawking spit, the big boys throwing up, clasping our hands behind our heads to beckon even the smallest poof of air.

Goddamn it, men! Get your hands from behind your heads. Don't you know that's how the police are gonna make you stand when they arrest you?!

You did not come to my practice to get arrested! Put your hands on your knees if you need some air!

I'm almost positive there's science that says you should put your hands behind your head to open your lungs. That meant nothing to Coach Walton.

He demanded that we wear a suit and tie on the day of every football game or track meet, because men had to know how to be professional. Fine with me—I could borrow Daddy's jackets, put extra cuffs in his pants and tie my belt super tight once a week for most of fall and spring, which was easier than trying to create new outfits from the few clothes I had. When school ended, we forty would file into the gym and sit against the wall to wait. Coach Walton would appear suddenly, mysteriously, from behind his office door, two or three times, catching us mid-grab-ass, which we'd cease immediately, backs to the wall again, while he paced the gym floor, looking down at us.

Listen, men, he'd let out after a long silence. *When a man's yard isn't cut, you know there's trouble in the home. You hear me?*

Yes, sir!

He'd return to his office and close the door until the next revelation, and the next, until finally he'd order us to change into our uniforms.

Coach Walton was full of those kinds of insights, whatever they meant, but he offered specific guidance to me only one time. It was during the single game I played in (I was the third-string running back), when the Atwell Archers were up by some ungodly amount and Coach Walton decided that my time had come.

It was night. The crowd was still thickly sprinkled throughout the stands under the lights at Sprague Stadium, which sat right across the street from Community First on Westmoreland. Coach Walton made a signal with his hands from the sidelines, and the quarterback yelled out *42 Trap* (or something like that) in the huddle. The name sounds like nonsense, but it's pretty straightforward: the first number told us what running back should get the ball; the second number told that back what gap in the offensive line to run through; and the *trap* told the offensive line how to block—trap a particular defender so the running back could slip through the hole.

The only problem was that *I* kept getting trapped. I ran the play once and was clotheslined as soon as the football plopped in my breadbasket. Ran it again and fumbled before my second step. Coach Walton's hands motioned for a timeout, then one hand motioned for me. I loped over to him. His other hand grabbed my face mask. I could hardly see him for that giant hand over the face mask bars, but could feel him towering over me. Could hear his voice bearing down.

Goddamn it, son! Listen to me. You're embarrassing yourself. You're embarrassing your family. Get your ass low, keep your eyes open, and run for your life!

And wouldn't you know it, the very next play—42 Trap for the third time in a row, to show how much faith Coach Walton had in his men and how little imagination he had in his playbook—I scored my first and last touchdown as an Atwell Archer. It wasn't the thought of embarrassing myself that did it, as I was no more or less ashamed than usual. It wasn't the fear of embarrassing my family, none of whom came to any of my games, which I knew because I spent most of my time on the sidelines looking up into the stands to see if anybody was there to watch. I really just needed a little instruction, that's all: get your ass low, keep your eyes open, and run for your life. I ran like that all the way through my life, right up until I couldn't run anymore.

The next day at school was my best, if only because one of the lunch ladies had come to the game and told me as I walked through the lunch line that she was *so* happy I'd finally *put that ball in the end zone.* She gave me an extra slice of pizza for free even though I already didn't have to pay for my lunch thanks to some program the state or somebody had.

Aside from having one fan and a free slice of pizza, this triumph changed much of nothing. I still didn't have any Nikes. I was still one of only two students in advanced English class sitting next to Ms. G's desk putting intonation marks over words I could already pronounce but didn't understand while she paid me no mind. I still watched the door at the eighth-grade athletic banquet to see if Daddy would walk through. And I was still a faggot. The girls reminded me of this on the playground when they heard my voice, which sometimes sounded like my sister's, and pointed out *Mmm it's always the cute ones ain't it?* My coach reminded me when he saw even the slightest limp in my wrist or ankle as I horsed around in practice, and mumbled *ole fruity ass boy* as he shook his head. And in the middle of the biggest track meet of the year, Jeremy and Brandon Scott (no relation), the most beautiful boys and most gifted athletes in my class, reminded me when they yelled down from the stands while I warmed up—*Say, Casey, look! We're gay like you!*—pretending to hug each other while the crowd around them laughed, which would have been worth all my free lunch had it been real.

I do owe Jeremy eternal thanks for ending the worst thing that happened to me in middle school: my relationship with Naomi Watts. Naomi was one of the most popular girls at Atwell, the daughter of the best high school football coach in the city, and looked like the skinny, pin-curled version of a bad attitude that nobody complained about. One day in the spring of eighth grade, Naomi's best friend cornered me in the hallway after school.

Hey, Casey. So um, Naomi wanna go with you.

Oh cool aight ... I'll think about it.

Well I already told her you said yeah, so here's her number. Call her, boy.

I truly could have died right there in that hallway, a satisfied still-single boy. But I had no choice, so I called Naomi that afternoon from Luke's house, on a cordless phone that I kept walking with into empty rooms, half hoping that Luke would hear me talking to a girl, half hoping the phone's battery would go out.

There was something about her voice that made me feel I was going to be sick. I think it was that she sounded like a girl, but after about ten minutes, the conversation was about as pleasant as the worst thing that's happened to you could be. She was a nice girl, I thought, even though I look back now and realize that she was the Oak Cliff version of a rich uptown girl who takes the subway out to Bed-Stuy to slum it up at house parties with boys who will never meet her parents.

For a whole week, I'd get off the bus in the morning and find Naomi, who was always dropped off by somebody, standing there waiting for me to escort her into the building. I had never up till then, and have never since, found so many reasons to scratch myself as I did on the mornings Naomi demanded that we hold hands. If God really destroyed Sodom and Gomorrah, he should have done it for this kind of nonsense, not for staring at some pretty angel boys.

Anyway, the coup de grace came on the eighth-grade class field trip to Medieval Times—quite possibly the dumbest amusement venue in America (even dumber than the Henry Ford outside of Detroit). All afternoon, I had to sit in a dark stadium pit, watching two grown men in cheap costumes pretend to joust on shitting horses in a field of straw that, combined with Naomi hanging all over me as we shared a dry medieval rotisserie chicken, sparked my worst allergy attack of the year 2001. There I was, nearly crying, eating my tasteless chicken and watching the hay fly and Naomi's smile glow, and wondering whether I would have a rash after it all.

In the locker room before track practice the next day, Jeremy asked if I had kissed Naomi yet.

Nah, man.

Nigga, c'mon you gotta get that. She wants you to.

Uhh have you seen her lips? Man, they crusty.

That was the best excuse I could come up with on the spot, and it seemed good or funny enough for Jeremy to drop the interrogation. But the next morning Naomi was not waiting at the bus depot. She was standing outside the door of my first period class. Arms folded.

What did you say to Jeremy about me?

Huh? I didn't say nothing 'bout you.

She rolled her eyes and left. By the time I sat at my desk, her consigliere had appeared.

So, uh. Naomi said she don't wanna go with you no more. We still cool, though, right?

Oh yeah. We cool.

Rarely have I felt the deep relief I felt the day my weeklong love affair with Naomi Watts ended. Home was clearly not in the hands of girls and surely not at school, but that was nothing new. Aside from the sanctuary I found with Ms. Davis and Ms. Vance, I'd never liked school much anyhow—the rush of bodies, the stench of hallways full of fascist monitors, the heavy books, the invisible voice pouring on me from the intercom. As early as kindergarten, during the year Tashia and I were sent to Dallas, I began most mornings with a wailing fit, thrashing about, ripping at Granny's shag carpet, hoping to get out of the ordeal. Granny brought those tantrums to an end the day she grabbed my wrist and walked me, still crying, up the street and right to Ms. McLemore's classroom, where, worst of all, in the middle of each afternoon, we were told to take out mats and spread them across the floor. It was nap time.

If I hadn't been so disoriented by the cartoon animals smiling down from the walls in the dim crowded room, I might have made a run for it. Instead I sat there on my mat and scanned the scene, all those thumb-sucking, snot-dribbling fools littering the floor around me. Didn't they understand how little sense this made? Why would I leave my house, which I did not want to do, come to this school, where I did not want to be, and then be forced to do something there that I without question did better at my house? I have spent an inordinate amount of time in the

American education cabal, but very few school rituals baffle me more than this one.

I decided to boycott nap time. Didn't call it that. Didn't say anything, really, just sat there and tried to keep my eyes on Ms. McLemore, the smiling animals, and the sleepers simultaneously. But my nonconformity was not acceptable.

First came the threat of violence: twelve strikes in my palm with Ms. McLemore's ruler. I still refused to sleep, which gives me some hope that someday, should the time come, I might have deep down what it takes to give my life for a worthy cause.

Next came bribes: Ms. McLemore announced that everyone who slept could have a piece of candy when nap time ended. Lord knows how I loved candy, and this clever move got me at least to lie down. But still I would not sleep. I just halfway closed my eyes and let a little drool trickle to seem more believable. This didn't work and I got tired of pretending for once in my life, so I gave up on the candy and sat back up on my mat. To this day, a burning suspicion rises within me anytime I am offered—*lured with*—performance-based compensation. There's always something hiding behind the gumdrop and the annual bonus, and I will not fall for it.

Finally, perhaps because I really had not bothered anybody during my protest, Ms. McLemore called me to her desk and asked what I wanted to do instead of sleep. I might have shrugged or simply stared at her, but I didn't know.

She reached in her big metal drawer and pulled out an unwrapped pack of blank index cards along with a black plastic filing box.

If you're not going to sleep, Casey, I want you to take these and write every word you see on the wall. One word on each card. This will be your little word bank, okay?

Yes, ma'am.

For the rest of kindergarten, while my classmates lay under the spell of tyranny, I sat cross-legged, eyes bulging in the no-light of nap time as I strained to make out the words on the wall. And if I could find Ms. Mc-Lemore again, that stocky, sweater-vested woman with the incredible gray-blonde Dallas hair and the ruler hand that struck like a jackhammer, I would thank her for not forcing me to sleep and for teaching me that home is what you think about when you don't want to be where you are—like Clarice's house, not least because she did not want me there herself.

Let me be very clear: Clarice Gerald is one of the highest-performing Christians I have ever known—Pope-esque, actually, especially in public: from the fact that she would never touch a car door, would always wait for you to open it and shut it behind her once she was seated; to the vestments that filled three large closets which we were not supposed to enter; to the time it took to run errands with her because of all the people who stopped to kiss her as we moved through the bank and the Salvation Army and the grocery store—*Oh, Mother Gerald, it's so good to see you!*

Clarice never missed a birthday, never was at a loss for words when it was time to pray, and, as she told the family at Christmas a few years ago, she never was a whore. *Y'all know what that is: W-H-O-R-E.*

I'm nobody's shrink, but I know from personal experience that sometimes tireless service for others is a perfect way to keep them very far from you, so I wonder whether this is why, even as I knew Clarice would give me her last dime, I overheard her telling one of her many visitors *I don't know why he can't go stay with Ms. West.* Which was a fair complaint, when I think about it.

She and her baby son made a terrific pair amongst the people and at their residence. By early 2001, Daddy was juggling three girlfriends, and one night while he was occupied with one, BB and I heard a knock at Clarice's front door. Thinking it was Aunt Carla, we opened the door and were pushed out of the way by another, who had come—informed by whom, I wonder!—to levy justice.

The tawdry details are not worth my ink or your time, but I will say that when the melee died down, it was me and BB who received Clarice's talking-to: *Y'all know better! Don't let nobody in my house this time of night, I don't care who it is or what somebody's doing.* She shuffled off back to bed, the sweet melody of her morning hymn—*What are you gonna do when the world is on fire?*—just a few hours off.

There was no talking-to for Crow, of course. He was on his way to Winner once again, going from strength to strength in his love life, at work (he was now a code enforcement officer for Dallas County), and in the pulpit, where his preaching schedule had increased to about once every other month.

The last sermon of his that I remember was preached during a night service. A word had been laid on his heart, to encourage the congregation to put their tragedies into perspective and trust that God has a plan, no matter how bad things might be:

If my daughter tells me she's pregnant out of wedlock, I gotta count it all joy and give it to God! If my son becomes a homosexual, I can't do nothing about it, I gotta turn it over to the Lord! Come on, saints!

I don't remember what he said after this, but I can still feel the eyes of all the saints on the back of my faggot head and on my whore sister's belly, even though we had not yet done what Daddy said we would do.

His sermon's end made way for the invitation to discipleship and for the choir—which, it might be important to note, had lost, in the early nineties, its minister of music and choir director and half of the tenor section to AIDS, each member eulogized by the pastor, who never called out their sins directly but shimmied his hand as he reminded *somebody in here* that they would not enter the kingdom of God. The remaining mighty voices rose to sing one of my favorite songs: "His Yoke Is Easy," led by the choir's prize alto, who began, earnest, a bit labored, with only an organ behind her:

Since I met Jesus
There's a burning
Oh such a burning deep down within

He holds me with his unseen power
And He keeps me from all sin
And He changes me from day to day
As I walk along this old narrow way
Since I met Jesus, since He changed this old soul of mine
It makes me wanna run on
Shout hallelujah
Right to the end

The organ picked up a little speed, the drummer set a new tempo, somebody grabbed a tambourine, and the choir was ready to go:

His yoke is easy, His yoke is easyyyyy
Burdens are light, burdens are light
Walk where He leads me, walk where He leads me
Always be right! Always be right!
Cherish the race, cherish the race
Running with haste, running with haste
And by His graaaaace
I know I'll make it
I'll make it home some day!

And even though Jesus had not come the way folks said He would, even though they claimed I could not have Him anyway, I found—thanks to this song's description of what Jesus was truly like—that He was in fact still alive, and was living in the Internet.

For at the dawn of the new millennium, there was no greater unseen power than the orgiastic churning of a landline modem going at far less than 56 kilobits per second all the way across the information superhighway until it reached the home page of America Online, where you heard that you had mail.

In the often-freezing back room of Clarice's house, where Papa had slept and studied, his desk, stacked with cowboy hats and VHS copies of his sermons, still sat against one wall. Opposite was another wall, a shrine to Daddy, including a picture of him, Papa, and Woody Hayes arm in arm at the Orange Bowl. These walls of honor formed a corridor, at the end of which I set up an old folding table, placed my computer on top, and arranged a high-backed chair to face my father's and his father's legacy, only because it faced the door.

I don't know what it was like to be fourteen out on the frontier of the American West, but it's hard for me to believe that it was much different, aside from the Comanches and dysentery, than being fourteen on the Internet in the early 2000s. Nobody in my family seemed to know how to use what Granny simply called "The Computer," which made me useful if not important, as I was the one who wrote down directions from MapQuest (we didn't have a printer) when it was time to go somewhere new; the one who looked up homework questions and health diagnoses on AltaVista, since our encyclopedia set was from the seventies; and the one who downloaded music from Napster and Kazaa, making decades worth of radio-dubbed cassette tapes obsolete with the click of my mouse.

Once everybody went to sleep, I'd tiptoe through the darkened house, stringing a long telephone cord from the living room about thirty feet back to the modem on the grimy green folding table, and sit in the chair with a blanket wrapped around my shoulders, the glow of the computer screen shining in my face. Sitting there alone, it seemed that anything was possible. I didn't even need money, thanks to the AOL free trial disks that came in the mail and to my school, where I slipped them in my book bag. I should have thanked Steve Case, the man who founded AOL, when I met him a few years ago, but I was drunk and tired.

With the modem connected and blocking any calls, I'd sign into the master account, which was mine. A faceless, armless, yellow man on the screen signaled how close I was to being online, and when I finally reached the home page he said *Welcome*.

Why, thank you, Mr. Internet.

At this time, there were about twenty-five million users on AOL, but it was unclear how many of these were real or different people. And it didn't matter. One little telephone cord had connected me to a whole new world, where my name wasn't Casey anymore. And I was only fourteen, or a boy, or in Texas when I felt like it, because the most-asked question on the Internet—A/S/L? (age/sex/location)—was not a request for the truth, just for a choice. And with that choice of who you were, which might change from day to day or hour to hour or chat room to chat room, you also received access to the countless lives, real and not, organized by category—Food, Leisure, Sports, Gay & Lesbian (clearly named by the AOL marketing people)—and gathered in chat rooms— StatenIslandM4M, HotBabesFtLauderdale, RoughSkinAnime—created by random cyborg pioneers in screen-lit rooms across the American night.

At the outset of this chat room revolution, and even still at its near-apex in 2001, the new frontier disturbed a great many adults and experts. In a 1986 *Washington Post* article, a reporter warned: *It's certainly the illusion of intimacy—the instant gratification of human contact without responsibility or consequences or actual involvement . . . but the danger is that going online instead of going into the real world ultimately turns conversation into a spectator sport.* But what the authorities call danger is often nothing more than a better option. I mean, what was in the real world, anyway? Names we hadn't chosen, families we couldn't leave, language that had to be spelled out instead of the much more sensible *LOL* and *BRB*—whole lives confined by the school you attended or house you lived in or country to which you pledged allegiance every morning.

I had no interest in the real world, and I imagine that one-third of those twenty-five million AOL users were reputed to be homosexuals because they were not too fond of the real world, either—not bothered by the idea that "conversation," which wasn't possible in the real world anyway, had been turned into a spectator sport, or that "human contact," which had only come in the form of ass-kickings, could be made without consequence.

So I sat in the glow of Jesus on the Internet, His easy yoke and very light burdens, and chatted for hours, first in the near-endless chat rooms, then over AOL Instant Messenger, until I ventured out into the new cyber landscapes that popped up before social networks were something to make a movie about: CollegeClub, Yahoo Chat, BlackPlanet, and so on. I even broke my first heart on the Internet, when some man from somewhere I don't remember asked when we were going to meet. *I want to see who you are in real life.*

Um, never. And I never talked to him again, because aside from probably being a murderer, he had outed himself as an old person who missed the whole point of the Internet: Who I was in real life was not important. The only thing that mattered was who I wanted to be at any given moment.

This might sound like the bizarre fantasyland of childhood. But years later, in my late twenties, I met a boy in Norway—quite possibly the most beautiful boy in all of Scandinavia, with a lithe vegetarian body, a golden feline face that made him look like the one domesticated cat that the Museum of Natural History will preserve to show off to future civilizations, and a floating air about him that let you know you'd likely never see him again— not because he was loose, but because he could not stand attachments.

Late in the night, I asked him to tell me about his family.

Ah, my family. Well, I was adopted actually. He sounded just like Tiny Tim, I promise.

Oh. Do you know who your real parents are?

Nope. I'm a proper orphan. Just dropped off—bloop—on a little doorstep in Colombia. Five months old. Yep. A man and woman from Norway came to get me when I was two, and they've been my parents since then.

But don't you kind of want to know who your people are?

Nope. Nope. Nope.

He said *nope* with so much bliss that you thought it must have been one of the first words he'd learned in English.

Well, I said, *why don't we just make it up?*

Make it up? He considered this for a moment, blinked the long lashes that framed his eyelids, rested his mane of hair on my chest, and mouthed with a skeptical smile: *Okay.*

I closed my eyes to focus, then it all came to me: his mother was a mermaid and his father was a revolutionary. They left their beautiful baby on the orphanage doorstep just before they tried to escape execution. They abandoned him to save his life, and lost their heads a few days later.

Ah, he giggled. *That's it. I'm a mermaid.* And then he closed his eyes and slept for what seemed like half a day.

Anyway, I tell you this so that you know we never lose the need for make-believe, for carousels and fake IDs, imaginary friends and mermaid mothers who dropped us off to hide us from the nasty truth of this dark world down here. In that way, the Internet was just about the best home I'd ever known, where the unexpected things that happened felt like magic, not like death.

Back in the real world, life was still the same. Until one night when Daddy knocked on the back room's door and hollered *C'mon Scooter.*

I slipped on my shoes and walked out to the white Lincoln Town Car recently purchased by the third girlfriend—a woman that everybody else in Daddy's family seemed to like, if only because she had money and lived in Houston. I hated this woman and made it clear by never saying hello or looking her in the face, and by telling all my cousins, who laughed at her jokes, that they were dead to me. The same policy applied to the other women still on the scene.

And wouldn't you know it, this most exciting love triangle—

quadrangle, I suppose—is why my father had invited me on a ride that night.

Scooter, man, I got three women and I gotta decide, you know? I got one who's got money, got one that's beautiful, and got one that can cook like a son of a gun. What you think, man?

Mama had been gone for two years or so. Daddy had not said a word about it to me, that I can remember, not a *How you doing* or a *Sure hate that*. And now he wanted my input on which of these three harlots he should choose to replace or supersede or blot out my dead or disappeared mother.

Thankfully I had carried out additional reforms on myself—could now speak in a low easy voice, with very simple pleasant words, whenever I wanted to slide a butcher knife across somebody's throat. I responded, nicely:

I don't want to talk about that.

The noise of tires on pavement filled the car. I looked over at Daddy. He seemed calm, surprisingly calm, both hands gripping the steering wheel.

Man, FUCK YOU! His hands flew to the roof of the car and slammed back down, making the Lincoln swerve. *Don't nobody care what you wanna talk about!*

He went silent again, clenching his jaw, chest laboring under an open button-down shirt. He ground his hands into the wheel, over and over. He did not look at me—or if he did I didn't know, because I turned to look out the window, into the night. Silent too.

I want to say that I was smiling, but I'm pretty sure that's just the *now* me trying to make the *then* me seem tougher than I was. I want to say that I felt peace—the peace that comes when someone finally admits the thing you've long suspected. But between peace and emptiness, the line is thin.

Maybe that's what it was. The beginning of an emptying. That's the image I see now, the one that feels true. A little boy with a heavy sack on his shoulder. He's trying to get somewhere but doesn't know where exactly, or how. This sack is so heavy he's starting to limp and he can't go any further. He stops on the side of the trail and sits down on a rock. The cool night wind feels gentle on his aching neck. He unties the heavy sack and looks at all the things he's been carrying. He smiles. *No wonder this walk has been so hard.* He decides to leave some of the things here on the trail—the heaviest things, the jagged things, the things whose use he doesn't know. These are the things that he takes out first. He sees a stick nearby and uses it to dig a hole next to the rock. In the hole, he buries the things in his sack that hurt too much to carry. He doesn't know he will need them later. Doesn't know that they will wash up in the next rains. For now, all that matters is that his limp is gone and his sack is light and he's on his way—*I'm free.*

And I really did feel free. Free not to listen to my daddy, or to anybody else for that matter, especially all the people who begged me, as fall 2001 approached, not to go to South Oak Cliff High School—which some called *School of Crime* or *Sex on Campus*—because they felt it was not safe, that I would not learn, that I could not reach my full potential there. I enrolled anyway.

I walked through the massive golden doors of that building, past the snarling taxidermic bear that stood inside the foyer, twenty-five years after my father became one of the school's biggest stars, and a few months after I supposedly emptied him from the knapsack of my heart. But the first thing I did was sign up to play his position, quarterback, and ask for his old number, 8. I even spent a few afternoons with him trying to throw the football better, and stood in an awkward meeting with him and my coach where he made the case for why his son should not be on the bench. This does not make sense to me now. And if I look closely enough at fourteen-year-old me I can see a boy to whom the world made little sense and who made even less sense to himself—and, because of this, a boy who watched everything as though his life depended on it, because it did.

And I learned, as I watched, that if you only see the surface of things, you might as well be blind.

On the surface, there were adults in charge at South Oak Cliff just as everywhere else in the world. I studied them as I always had, to see what they wanted so that I could give it to them immediately. But from the first day, Ms. Ford, my freshman English teacher, had no interest in anything I had to offer—not my supplicant smile, not the speed and accuracy with which I turned in my assignments, not the way I stared at her for the rest of class with eyes that promised *I'll do whatever you ask.*

Ms. Ford was eager to talk only to a certain horde of boys in long white T-shirts with red *Tall Tee* stickers, boys in brand-new Jordans, with the booty haircut popular at the time (low fade all around except for a butt cheek of hair on the back of their heads), boys—black, Chicano, all friends—with golds and no books whatsoever. I couldn't understand why she was so into them and why, for that matter, these grown-looking boys were in a freshman English class.

I came to understand through unofficial reports (gossip, likely the truth) that Ms. Ford had a little exchange program with these gentlemen: they sold her marijuana, she gave them decent grades. I was and remain a supporter of the barter system, but had no access to drugs (Dean would not have sold them to me) and so was all set to fail that English class. But South Oak Cliff had many rams in its bushes, including my distant cousin Joan, who taught a typing class and coached the majorettes, and to whom I went to beg for help. It could have taken up to a week or forever to be moved, but she saw her cousin's panicked face and did not ask any questions. Just stood up from her seat and said *Oh, naw. C'mon, boy, we gotta get you out of there.* Sure enough, she did.

Her intercession took me to a new English class, where the teacher smiled and gave me free CDs and let me work from the eleventh-grade textbook instead of staring out the window. Took me to advanced biology, where Mr. Alijahdey still taught, decades after teaching my mother and years after getting rid of his "slave name," Mr. Morrison. Took me to Algebra II, where I would have been doomed, since I'd finished but not learned the prerequisite Algebra I and Geometry at Atwell, but the teacher remembered Tashia and offered extra help. And took me to Ms. Jacques's world history class, where I sat for an entire school year, did every assignment, even earned an A—yet aside from telling you King Tut was from Egypt, all I can share of my learning are the opening lines of a poem we had to recite: "Myself" by Edgar A. Guest.

> I have to live with myself and so
> I want to be fit for myself to know
> I want to be able as days go by,
> Always to look myself straight in the eye;
> I don't want to stand in the setting sun
> And hate myself for the things I have done.

I shared this poem with pride one night in a tomb I'll tell you about in a little while, and another person there—an actual poet who spent a great deal of time amongst original Shakespeare folios at Yale's Elizabethan Club—kindly informed me that Edgar A. Guest was one of the biggest jokes in all of literature. That didn't change the fact that, at fourteen and for many years after, this poem was far more useful instruction than a primer on the ancient Sumerians would have been.

Anyway, once she transformed my schedule, Joan shepherded me to the coaches, the registrar, the most respected teachers that I would have in the coming years, and even the principal—who swaggered through the halls like Joe Clark, shouting, slamming a baseball bat on trash cans— and told them all that I was a good kid and a smart student and, most of all, *her cousin*, so they should look out for me. In one week, Joan did what women—kin and stranger—have done for me since I was born: saw me wandering through the world and grabbed me by the wrist to say *C'mon here, boy.*

But for all the good she did with the faculty and staff, there was little she could do to keep me safe otherwise. For beneath the veneer of rules and regulations enforced by men and women, South Oak Cliff was a world ruled by the violence of boys. That's what made the place so fun.

In the freshman locker room, darkness might fall, suddenly, and you would hear a beat on a bench near the door, and a yell from a shadowy figure standing in the doorway—*Yeah freshmen!*—and another three or four shadows chanting—*Draws! Draws! Draws!* You knew, although you wished it were not so, that they had come to grab one of you, at random or with premeditation, and pin you down while another boy or two ripped your pants and underwear off, and another turned on the lights for all to see what you had or did not have.

In the hallway after lunch, the lights might flicker and the shuffle of feet and slamming of lockers might be replaced by screams or utter silence aside from the sound of a boy's head being bashed against the wall. In this same hallway one morning, I smelled Tank Jones walk by before I saw him, blood running down his dingy white shirt. Tank was the only true bully I knew of, with the bad odor and extra weight and low self-esteem that bullies always have. This particular morning Tank had attacked another boy across the street and, when the boy did not cower, had pulled out a pistol to assure the boy that he'd have a bullet in his ass if he did not do what Tank demanded. This boy must have had incredibly swift hands, because he grabbed Tank's pistol and, as Tank tried to run away, shot him in the back. All that blood was spurting from the hole in Tank's hide blubber, where the bullet was still lodged when he rushed by me to the nurse's office. God *is* just, sometimes.

These were simple skirmishes. Some days there might be war.

In the first few weeks of school, on a hot August afternoon when the

Texas sun sat right on your chest and blew fire in your nostrils, I walked outside and, through the nearly blinding light, saw a caravan of boys racing down Marsalis into the school's gravel parking lot. Some were packed into an old-school Cutlass, others into a Chevy Caprice with spinning hubcaps, television screens behind the headrests, at least one subwoofer making the whole car tremble, Dirty South Rydaz playing inside and out. One boy was perched outside the passenger window as the Caprice turned in, hands signaling something for somebody. These were the boys from Highland Hills. They had come to end a conflict with their enemies from Beckley-Saner, another Oak Cliff neighborhood where boys had nothing but the pride of a few blocks they had inherited—blocks that, absent any other cause to believe in, were worth dying for, I suppose. They would find out this day.

Walking out to meet the boys from Highland Hills—shirts off; fists their only weapons, unlike their enemies, who carried choppers in the trunk—were the boys from Beckley-Saner. They were led by SirJon "Juice" Harris, a sophomore and track star who was only an acquaintance at the time, since we shared a few classes, but would become, by the end of the spring season, something like a big brother.

I can't tell you what exactly went down once the two sides met. (BK made sure we took the back way to his house.) But I can tell you that nobody died and that Juice became untouchable because of the blood he shed that day to defend his turf. And for some reason, he lent this grace to me for the rest of our time together at South Oak Cliff. On other days of war, Juice told me where to go to stay safe. When he snuck a girl into our hotel room at the state track meet, Juice let me slip out without a sneer. And when a few senior boys tried to call me *faggot*, Juice laughed but said—*Say, man, y'all leave that nigga alone.*

Maybe he protected me because I helped him with his homework a few times, or because he liked the way I struck people with words a bit like he struck them with his hands, or because I was his biggest fan during track season—yelling his name from the stands because he was an incredible runner, an even better show-off (he had his personal best 800-meter dash time cut into his hair), and never had any family there to cheer him on. But none of this would be enough to explain his care for me then, or why years later, when I graduated from Harvard, it was Juice, not my father, who called and said through tears that he was proud of me. *Man, I saw you on that video and said gahlee, look at my little nigga Case J!*

The only way I start to understand it is by looking past the surface of the violence, into the packs of brawling gangsters, to see my friend and brother Juice, who was just like me in ways that we both recognized but could not articulate. We both knew he was smarter than he let on. We knew that he never complained about the nights he and his older brother slept in the park, nowhere else to go. And we knew—or I know *now*—that beneath the mask of viciousness, Juice was just a little boy. We were all just little boys, you know. Somebody must have forgotten that. Forgotten *us*. So we found each other.

And even here, even here, in this forgotten world, there was joy. The joy that comes from freedom, a teenage thirst for life outside of rules, beyond reach, without the illusion of security at a time when many boys and girls across the land were learning that illusion was all security could be—when they saw those planes bring down the towers, when they watched the futile shock and awe, when they heard the lies passed off as evidence. I was lucky. I learned early.

That year, I felt the joy of making life on my own terms in whatever way I could—stayed at so many houses that I can't tell you where I slept most nights, bathed only when I could no longer bear my stench, drank from water hoses instead of faucets, lived on a diet of Zebra Cakes and Fanta and hot wings. Spent aimless hours, days, with my friends, who were often as free as I. We started to grow up or at least get older, we shared what little we had of food and money, we made football fields in the street and devastating jokes in the barbershop. And out of the naked crust of lost boys, we made something like a family.

And as the school year ended and the summer opened, all this joy hung in the balance, because for the first time in my life, somebody kept a promise: My sister came back for me.

chapter **SIX**

What an ungrateful boy.

I bet that's what they said when my sister returned from New Orleans—leaving her degree and her dreams behind—and, upon seeing what a wild street urchin I had become, took me in to give me some love and instruction and a home. I was supposed to be grateful, but I wasn't.

So many people I knew had either left college or never gone that I saw nothing wrong with Tashia ditching that nasty swamp, long before the levees broke. Her life, her freedom, her future—just leave me out of it. I'd always been able to pretend that something that was clearly happening was not happening at all, but beneath this skill was a raw hot panic when I got even the slightest suspicion that plans involving me were being made. I sensed that now. Jobs were acquired. Questions were asked—*Where are you going? What time is the game this week? How much homework do you have?*—the kinds of questions that suffocated me.

And Tashia did not only want to ask questions. She wanted to grin and cackle and retell all the stories from our former life.

Remember when that boy hit you in the head with that two-by-four and I came to the bathroom and your head had that hole in it and you said oooh Tashia I really did it this time?

Yeah I remember, what's it to you, what are you getting at?

Oh, she was getting at plenty. Dallas County—through HUD and Franklin Roosevelt, who gave me so much before I was even born—had little vouchers you could use to rent a place to live if you didn't have the money to pay for it yourself. And sure enough, this nineteen-year-old Judas was in cahoots with her father to secure one of those vouchers, and began browsing two-bedroom apartments in the Section 8 listings. *Don't tell me nothing about it, Tashia. I'm happy for you, you've really gotten on your feet in no time, you're living Lyndon Johnson's American Dream, with your job at the IRS making $35,000. I don't know nobody making that kind of money, girl. Before long you'll be rich you'll be pulling in $100,000 a year. Got your gold Mitsubishi and now your own roomy apartment. Cute. I'm gonna spend most of my time with Luke over Aunt Chandra's house. She got the Internet and a big-screen television with cable and she buy bags of mozzarella sticks that I can eat whenever I want. And when I get sick of Luke's house I'll go across the street to hang with BK and Porodie and Antimox and we'll play Monopoly for hours or Madden all night. But I'll definitely come stay with you sometime. We can hang out when I'm free.*

I said all that in my head except for the very last part.

Casey, I got a two-bedroom for you. You are not sleeping on the floor anymore, boy. You're gonna live with me.

You know, every time I see a stray dog on the side of the road I want to yell or whisper in its ear—*Say man you better run for it before some crazy bastard comes and picks you up and gives you a bath and takes away your sperm and makes you sleep in a tiny dog house till you die.* I mean, really, who the hell do these people think they are, just walking in our lives trying to save us?

I was trapped. Tashia and I didn't even have a conversation. We just collected all my few things from their various holding places and moved into our apartment, which had recently opened thanks to some deal the city had made with a developer whereby apartments were built for people who probably shouldn't have been living on their own. And after I holed up in silence for a few hours or days, waiting to be lobotomized or hosed down with cold water, I looked around from my own room on the second floor of this little apartment, and realized I might just be in an episode of my absolute favorite book from first grade: *The Boxcar Children*.

Aside from the circumstance that these were children who lived in a boxcar, I remember only the scene where, for the first time in many days, there is butter for dinner. *"Oh butter!" cried Jessie, her eyes shining.* Benny, the youngest at six, is old enough to spread his own butter, but since they're orphans all they have is a spoon—which is a problem because at some point in his life Benny has been taught that he needs a knife to spread things like butter. Without one, the poor boy can't spread a damn thing. Then his brother, Henry, at fourteen the eldest and the man of the non-house, comes to the rescue:

"Now this spoon is a magic spoon," says Henry. "Turn it around and use the handle, and it is a knife!"

Holy shit.

I never forgot this moment because it taught me that sometimes it doesn't matter what you have. All that matters is what you're trying to do—there's always some way to do it. *The Boxcar Children* also helped me hold space in my mind for something other than the villains of the Bible and the racists of *Black Like Me* and the fruit balloon from *James and the Giant Peach*. These were the only books I had read by the time I was fifteen (aside from *Left Behind*), and they pretty accurately described most of the people in my life. But Henry, Jessie, Violet, and Benny pushed me to consider the possibility that things might just be okay. And I'm not sure that ever in the history of America, a nineteen-year-old girl and a fifteen-year-old boy had more fun making things okay than Tashia and I did.

We moved in together in the fall of 2002, my sophomore year of high school, and the first thing I remember is Christmas. We had never had a real Christmas tree before, but we were making a home now, and on television people with homes had real Christmas trees. So without asking anybody for money or permission, we drove to the Christmas tree lot and bought a Christmas tree. It was that easy. Around March we finally took down that beautiful tree, which by then was turning brown and shedding pine needles that bloodied our feet. And we decided together that we would never have another real Christmas tree in our home. Not because we couldn't—we just didn't want to. It felt good to have choices.

We also decided we would end the rationing of precious commodities like sugar. All our lives we'd been told how much sugar we could use—*you don't need that much sugar in that rice, boy!*—but now we bought big bags of Domino sugar and I would pour and pour that fine white sugar until I decided the Kool-Aid was sweet enough. And all my sister said was *Ooh boy that's sweet!* Never *You used up all my sugar.* It was our sugar now and we could get more.

And the air-conditioning! It was always so goddamn hot outside, and sometimes Granny would keep the thermostat at almost eighty, or at least it felt that way. Or she would leave the air off in the car and roll down the windows and act like she didn't see me drowning in a pool of my own sweat, talking about *gas is high* when it was only ninety-nine cents a gallon back then. No more no more. Tashia and I ran our air conditioner so much and so cold that the pipes froze and spewed ice all over the carpet and the maintenance man had to come fix it twice. But we laughed so hard each time and turned the air back up and agreed that we would never be hot unless we wanted to.

Not everything went this well. Tashia, attempting to make hot-water cornbread, called Granny to get the recipe, but I guess since we did whatever we wanted now, she took a pretty loose approach to following Granny's instructions. She decided that if you heated a large skillet of oil, added water, and dropped in balls of cornbread mix, then *poof* you'd have hot-water cornbread. All you actually had was a stove on fire.

We had an endless supply of water, though, which lent itself to us to douse the flames and to take showers that lasted forever—long steamy showers that pruned our skin and opened our pores and even set off the smoke alarm, which hadn't happened when we set the stove on fire. Sometimes I'd sit in the bathtub and let the water rain down on my satisfied body until I felt like I was taking a nap in the womb. The water never went cold and we only turned it off when we wanted to, not when somebody came and yelled at us for running up the water bill. It was our bill and we'd run it up and happily suffer the consequences.

All this was ours—our fine white sugar, our freezing air-conditioning, our steamy water, our kitchen fire. And our laws. For who shall provide the law at the bottom of the world? What means shall justify which ends? When shall the score be settled, in this life or in the life to come? *Now*, I say. *Now* is the time and we must write the law ourselves, not draw it from on high. At least that's what I figured when I took my mother's money.

It had been three years or so since Mama disappeared and left her things like she was coming right back. One night, going through this pile, I found checks—blank fresh checks connected to a bank account that I figured still contained money, since I reckoned she was dead by then and the dead don't spend much. For years Mama had received US dollars, thanks again to FDR, who knew before my mother was born that she might be so ill that she could not work and, without money, would not be able to provide for me. So into her bank account came about seven hundred dollars a month on my behalf. And although she was gone, these checks continued to appear, like an apparition, like a connection to her in that other world, like the jackpot that I needed to hit. If I didn't *need* to hit it, I wanted to hit it. And if you take your dead mother's checkbook and turn it around, it's an inheritance. *My* inheritance.

After hours of practice, I got the signature right enough, and took the first of many checks to the bank. And after the paranoid suspense at the teller window, my sister and I finally had fresh monies to spend— enough to help pay rent and buy new clothes for school, and enough for

Tashia to throw me a surprise sixteenth birthday party at Granny's house, an event that I had explicitly requested not to happen because one of the only things I hated more than a birthday was a surprise. But Tashia was a sneaky bastard and conspired with the family without tipping me off to anything, so by the time I realized what was happening I had already been betrayed. I walked in to the shrieks of *Surprise!* and Bobby Blue Bland still requesting somebody's love light, all these years later. And after my silent fury ran its course, everything seemed rather nice, especially when I saw that Tashia had ordered a buttercream cake from Sam's Club. The cake even had my name spelled correctly, unlike the last cake somebody bought me when I turned thirteen, which read *Happy Birthday Crunchy!* That's what it looked like to me. But I stood there before the five or six people who attended, and smiled that sincere fake smile I had perfected while they sang the birthday dirge, then told everybody *Thank y'all really thank y'all so much* when all I wanted to ask was why they couldn't even spell one of the simplest names in the family.

Tashia did not make those small mistakes that tip you off to a person's lack of care, so I gave her and the gathered a considerably more sincere fake smile and longer hugs and added *Aww!* to the *Thank y'all really thank y'all so much*. I accepted a plate of enchiladas or fried catfish or chicken tetrazzini (those are the most likely options) and sat laughing and eating with the family for a little while before sneaking off to the bathroom. I turned on the faucet and leaned over the sink to look in the mirror that took up most of the pink wall. I let a batch of tears go down with the water. *Where are you, Mama?*

Anyway, maybe I felt that she left the checks to commemorate my sixteenth year, or that taking them was my revenge, or maybe I simply felt like a clever criminal with nice school clothes for a change. All I know is that after three or four months I felt no guilt, no guilt at all. And if I had fallen into moral disrepair, there was yet much further down to fall. Not long after I turned sixteen, I finally met a boy.

chapter SEVEN

Stop.

That is the only word that escaped. I whispered it in his ear. Mouthed it when he looked at me. Closed my eyes and said it to myself.

Stop, Red. I have to go.

His breath was a hot blanket on my lips. *Nah, where you gotta go?*

I did not know so did not answer. I stepped back and he stood there. Watched me toddle right into the sink. He came closer.

Stop, Red. Please.

He laughed. *Nobody ever touched you, huh?*

I smirked but did not answer this one, either. Just stared at him. There was not a single blemish on his face, odd for a boy—as odd as his lips, the likes of which I have seen only once more, in a movie, on a pale French boy on a frigid day. That boy's lips were bruised; Red's were simply large and dark and beautiful, as were his deep-set eyes. His nose had an almost imperceptible crook, and his body looked as if it could not break, so I didn't try. I wrapped my arms around his neck and said *stop* but he must have known that this made no sense, that I was just a foolish boy, because he paid my words no mind. Too late. Much too late.

I could have stopped at his first message months earlier—*Don't let these bitches say nothing 'bout your pictures*—but I felt the paralyzing joy of having been figured out. I had invited "the ladies" to tell me what they thought about the pictures on my BlackPlanet page, but this strangely pretty boy or man, posed in his digital portrait with a basketball in one hand, gym shorts running down to his shins, and no shirt whatever, had been brave enough to call my bluff in the most interesting way. So I responded.

I could have stopped when he asked for my number—the number to the cordless phone that I snuck into my room each night, picking up before it rang a full time, and the number to the tiny mobile Shon bought me, where his name was listed only as *R* just in case somebody found my phone and wondered who was calling me *baby* all the time like I was grown. Late in the night, I'd cradle the phone between my ear and the pillow to listen to him talk until I fell asleep. When I woke, his texts read *I listened to you breathe in your sleep.* That seemed maniacally romantic. On game days, in the lull between the time you mummify your ankles with tape and finally walk out for the coin toss, the empty gap that's typically filled with the same song you listen to each week and the same cheerleader you meet behind the gym before boarding the bus, I tucked the mobile phone between my hip pad and my jockstrap and waited for him to wish me luck. He filled my lulls just fine.

I could have stopped him when he said, a few months after that first message, that he was coming to see me in June. He did not have a car to drive all the way from Shreveport, where he lived with his mother and father, who pastored a Pentecostal church, so he would catch a ride with a friend who was headed to Dallas for the Juneteenth celebrations and didn't want to drive alone. I actually did try to stop him then, but he said that he was my boyfriend and that this was what boyfriends were supposed to do. That was news to me—instruction, too—so I just said *Oh, well all right.*

And as the days of May crept by, I thought he might forget or that I could stop him at the last minute, even if he was already on his way to town. Maybe I'd explain *My sister won't let me take her car,* or remember *Oh dang I gotta go to the family cookout,* or warn *We'll get in trouble if we're caught,* no matter whether it was true. But I knew that he liked trouble—that he took great pride in the fight that broke his nose, that he was as ready to curse at his father's parishioners as to electrify them with his singing voice which was, like Prince's, much higher than his speaking one. There's no stopping a man like that.

The appointed day came and a text appeared on my phone: *I'm here.* The apartment was empty and the car was outside—not his friend's car, as I would never have given him my address, but my sister's Mitsubishi. I climbed in, ignited the engine, steered three exits down the highway—holding the seat belt away from my freshly ironed shirt—to the parking lot of the only and last Walmart non-Supercenter. Saw his friend's metallic gold Ford Mustang in a near-empty section of the lot . . . saw him, in the passenger seat. I parked across from them, stayed in the car, did a decent job playing it cool until he stepped out and walked over and opened my sister's car door without knocking and sat down.

I could have run away and left him in that car or insulted him or suggested we go to the movies or cried and cried or smelled bad instead of bathing twice—I could have done *something* other than what I wanted to do with such a marrow yearning that it took the shape of a command, but I did nothing to stop myself. And in that nothing there appeared a space for a something, a space for him to stand here, before me, in this small dim hotel room, held up by the sink, my lungs stuck like a man so full he can't get up from the table. I could hear the thumping in my ear and the low hum of the hotel air conditioner. Could almost hear the glow of the one lamp that was still on, its light confirming that he was lifting my shirt, paid for with my dead mother's money. I asked him not to wrinkle it, not leave any marks on my neck, now exposed. He said nothing. There was nothing left to say.

Nowhere else to run, either, and only him to watch, which I did so long and with such intensity that he finally switched off the lamp and told me to lie down. I could not see a thing now and did not want to, so rested one side of my face on the floral quilt and closed my eyes and held my body still and kept quiet. I was so still and so quiet that he made me promise that I'd never done this before, so quiet that his soft kiss on my forehead may have been heard down in the lobby, so quiet that the silence sounded like awe and the pain felt like freedom. It was Juneteenth, after all.

One hundred and thirty-three years had passed since Major General Gordon Granger stepped out on a balcony in Galveston and announced to the crowd below:

The people of Texas are informed . . . that all slaves are free. This involves an absolute equality of personal rights and rights of property between former masters and slaves, and the connection heretofore existing between them becomes that between employer and hired labor.

If it was comical to tell these white Texans and their black property—which was still being bought and sold months after this balcony decree—that they were now *absolutely equal*, then it was perverse to tell them this news so late: almost three years after President Lincoln wrote the Emancipation Proclamation in September 1862, two and a half years after he issued it on 1 January 1863, and two months after his army finally had killed enough Confederates to make Robert E. Lee surrender at Appomattox on 9 April 1865, which was less than a week before Lincoln himself was killed on April 15. When Gordon Granger showed up on June 19, the war was over, its champion was dead, millions of formerly enslaved people across the South were getting on with their lives, and 250,000 black Texans were just finding out that they had been party to the worst overtime fraud in the history of the world.

And there was yet more time to wait, for the news of emancipation took a while to snake up from Galveston and through the Neches River Valley and on down the little roads that led to the remote hamlets that had been too far even for Abraham Lincoln's long arm of death to reach. The news finally found them, as did the violence, for *the war may not have brought a great deal of bloodshed to Texas, but the peace certainly did*. I have read of the lynchings and the vigilantes, believe almost every word, but I sure wish I could sit and talk with Clarice's grandfather, one of the 250,000 who received the news on that day—though he must have been quite young or else Clarice must have been telling a story about this man having been born a slave. I don't believe she was, though, because I've been to Pelham, where she was born, where she took me and my cousins to pick cotton, and where, in 1866, a group of former slaves founded Forks of the Creek, Texas. She spoke of her people's days there like Old Blues speak of the 29–29 loss to Harvard in 1968, like some pre-Stonewall gays speak of the nights they were ambushed out of the clubs—nostalgia, memory, belonging, compelling lies.

Gahlee, Granny, how did they even survive?

Clarice never failed to refuse my sympathies.

Chile, don't be believing what folks say about how bad slavery was. Everybody had a job, and a place to stay, and something to eat. Now if somebody came and paid your rent, you wouldn't be sitting up talking about you wanna leave, would you? Master don't mean owner. Master mean provider.

There's little question that some of this is the rambling of a woman who has spent many years turning ideas and questions over in her head, so that some things that don't make sense to anybody else seem perfectly reasonable to her. Some of it must be the residue of all the efforts of the United Daughters of the Confederacy and the Sons of Confederate Veterans and the local newspapers and regional Klansmen and Woodrow Wilson to convince her that the natural place for a black person in this country was one of submission. But aside from her husband I have never seen nor heard my grandmother submit to anybody, so some part of her second look at slavery had to be worth at least trying to consider—a near-impossible task until I got home from that hotel, looked into the mirror after checking for blood, and wondered what I was supposed to do, now that there was no going back.

I understood Clarice, then. I could slip at least my pinky toe in the raggedy sandal of her grandfather, who woke up on June 20 or some morning not long after with a serious problem on his hands: he had to choose for himself the means by which he would live in the world, having been tossed out of the only one he'd ever known. The story of that terror, of that confusion, of that blind grasp for the solidity of liberation is what informed my grandmother's view of history—a glance not toward the virtue of bondage, but rather toward the incredible price that must be paid to be free. And now I saw it, too.

When my mother disappeared and my father grew too hard to carry, there was one verse from the Psalms that I wrote over and over in my spiral notebook during class, and repeated while I warmed up for the mile relay during track meets, and remembered when I could feel tears trying to sneak out of my eyes: *When my father and my mother forsake me, then the Lord will take me up.* And in the moments when I felt like the last boy in the farthest reaches of the Milky Way, the void too large, the air too thin, I would close my eyes and sing—

> *Walk with me, Lord*
> *Walk with me*
> *Walk with me, Lord*
> *Walk with me*
> *While I'm on this tedious journey*
> *I want Jesus to walk with me*

And the second verse, my favorite—

> *Hold my hand, Lord*
> *Hold my hand*
> *Hold my hand, Lord*

Hold my hand
While I'm on this tedious journey
I want Jesus to hold my hand

I can't explain it in scientific terms, but I felt something there, walking with me, holding my hand. Maybe it was just my imagination, I don't know. But when you seem to have lost everything else that matters, the imagination is not a bad thing to have left. I'm sure some of these rituals were just that—ways of being that I learned from folks around me, whom I had watched from the day I was born and who, even before then, had worked to increase the odds that I would come into a personal under-standing of the Christian God. If this had not been so, I might very well have been an atheist, or a Shintoist, or a Hare Krishna; might be waging holy war somewhere today. But I wasn't and I'm not. I can no more escape the particular cosmology of my inheritance than I can turn my brown eyes deep blue.

Yet my rabid search for the person of Jesus, for the path to Him and, through Him, to the next life, was also shaped in those years by a desper-ate need for something not to fail me. *Give me a place to stand,* Archimedes says, *and I will move the earth.* Well the preacher always shouted *On Christ the solid rock I stand, all other ground is sinking sand,* and this made sense to me. The Psalms had sent those tears back down and the hymn had held my hand on many days, but now that I had crossed the threshold from a boy with sinful thoughts to a boy *living* in sin, the world which held at least some promise of comfort was thrown into a battle between wicked free-dom and repressed safety—between love and ruin. At least that's how I saw the choice at that time. Red knew as much, or so he said. And though I did not care to realize then, he was either awfully brave or crazy as hell, for choosing to love me, anyhow.

To be sure, I was a terrible lover for many reasons which cannot be blamed on God—a sneaky whore, prone to paranoid rages over missed calls and new friends, demanding on the most arbitrary points: Wish me happy birthday at the time I was born, not just on the day. Never call me out of my name. And so on. But aside from these abuses, which I mostly outgrew, Red had to endure being the symbol of my eternal damnation. For every time I chose him—not in the act of sex, which might simply be a temporary victory of the flesh, but in the more dangerous choice to see him as a legitimate human being whose heart meant something to mine, as much as that is possible at seventeen—I chose death.

Many nights we'd hang up the phone and I would turn the small television in my room to TBN, the Trinity Broadcasting Network, to watch the services of E. V. Hill, who reminded me of my Papa, or John Hagee, who reminded me of the Old Testament God. Pastor Hagee's Cornerstone Church was based in San Antonio, and this large man with his milk-white jowls and thick Elvis hairdo seemed obsessed with two things more than all else: prophesying the end of days and saving America from spiritual corruption—most of which the "homosexual movement" had caused. One of his classic sermons was called Homosexuality: Alternative or Abomination. He opened with a reading from Romans 1:27.

And likewise also the men, leaving the natural use of the woman, burned in their lust one toward another; men with men working that which is unseemly, and receiving in themselves that recompense of their error which was meet.

Hagee repeated for emphasis: *Receiving in themselves that recompense of their error which was meet. Certainly that would include AIDS.*

He followed with the greatest hits—a stroll through Leviticus and on to Genesis for the long story of the men of Sodom, who sounded to him a lot like the homosexuals in the streets demanding to be recognized as a persecuted minority, when they truly were perverts who made a choice to live in conflict with the laws of God, just as America was doing this very day, for which President Clinton and anyone who supported him would be held accountable at the Judgment. Even then, I was never afraid that my sister would kick me out of her house—when we finally had an explicit conversation years later, she said *I was waiting for you to tell me. You're my baby, I don't care how wrong you are.* And even though this confirmed that she believed I was wrong, it still meant a great deal in practical terms that she could accept my sinfulness enough to care and provide for me. Jesus, according to John Hagee and most every other pastor I'd heard, would not be so understanding. *Abomination*, he said, *means the ultimate, worst kind of sin*—punishable by death and separation from Christ. I could not afford to lose Jesus, or did not want to at that time, even if I could.

Over the nearly two years that we were more or less together, Red and I separated—that word makes it sound so serious!—at least three times. I told him that I simply could not do *this* anymore (either because it was true or because it was the easiest way to end things). He was always understanding, even said he'd pray for me. But his prayers were not enough, so I decided one night to dial the toll-free number that always scrolled across the bottom of the screen as I watched TBN. The host had been saying all night that God's warriors were waiting by the phone to pray for anybody who needed it. I figured he was talking about me.

The voice of what sounded like a young man came through from the other side. He was either nice enough or I felt guilty enough to tell him my name and age, and to admit that I had been sleeping with a man and needed to be delivered.

Now you and this man, Casey, were you always safe?

No, not always.

God, that's dangerous, Casey, you know?

Mmhmm. I know.

But I'm so glad you called. I want to pray with you, okay? Close your eyes and repeat after me.

I can't remember what exactly he said, but the prayer was a mix of the standard prayer of salvation, along with specific amendments for my health and my deliverance. It was all rather soothing, actually. When he finished, I felt much lighter and a bit sleepy. Even shed a few tears for good measure. Before we got off the line, the young man told me that my walk was just beginning but that he would be there for me—*I want you to call me every evening so we can pray and check in, okay?*

I told him I would call the next day, but I never spoke to him again, or anybody else at the Trinity Broadcasting Network. My walk was interrupted almost as soon as it started, by a new Musiq Soulchild song that asked in the chorus: *If you can't have the one you love, then where are you going in your life?* I thought this was a great question and didn't know the answer, so I asked Red, who knew so much and whom I had not spoken to in weeks. All I know of his response is that it was good enough to convince me that he should visit, which he did one weekend when my sister was out of town. He even brought me his favorite dog tag, which had *U Aint Gotta Lie to Kick It* punched into thin gray aluminum. All this felt a lot better than listening to John Hagee, though I kept doing that as well.

For a stretch of junior year—it must have been spring because I didn't take on extra projects during football season—I decided that I would not only cut Red out of my life; I would quit sin altogether. I went to sleep to John Hagee, woke up to Joyce Meyer, stopped cursing, and refused to laugh at dirty jokes, which was even more difficult than not being a homosexual because all my friends were in the same first period US history class, where we had staged a mutiny against the teacher, who finally surrendered when we decided to break into spontaneous rounds of the wave instead of learning the Constitution. It was so hard to resist, but I had to. Could have kept resisting all of it had I not become so sad and tired, had I not started having trouble paying attention in class or to what anybody was saying. Most days I'd just sit at my desk in the back row, the glaze of redemption over my eyes, and watch the clock until 3:45 p.m. came around. A week or so into my sin fast, I went to Luke's after school and logged into Yahoo Chat to see if Red was online so that I could tell him how miserable I was. This was the dumbest thing I could possibly do in the midst of renouncing sin, because he made me feel better, which made me feel much worse, and the next thing I knew he was on his way back to Dallas. By seventeen, I could tolerably manage a double life. This triple life was too exhausting. His next visit needed to be his last.

Instead of a heart-to-heart over dinner—we never went to a restaurant, but he did buy me Taco Bell once—or coffee, which I didn't drink, we rented a room at our go-to spot: a Motel 6 on the desolate edge of Grand Prairie, a suburb so unremarkable I have a hard time describing it other than saying that it was close to the freeway. I didn't have the thirty dollars it cost to pay for this secluded clean bungalow in which to un-elope, so I appreciated him letting me save my lunch money along with my soul. I appreciated many of the other things he did on our Motel 6 visits—years later I drove through the western stretch of Kansas on my way to Colorado and, unable to drive any further into the night, pulled into a Motel 6 instead of the cheaper Super 8 next door, in remembrance of Red—but this visit was unlike the others because I'd made it clear before he came that this would be goodbye.

With only the television on and the stale white sheets around us, I could still see him lying there on me. His skin always seemed to glow in the dark and his face was so close to mine that I didn't have to strain my eyes too hard to stare. If I could have turned him into a speck of cornea and carried him around transparently, forever, I would have done it—he knew that as confused as I was about so many things, I was unwaveringly obsessed with him, which gave him good grounds to tell me so often: *Boy your ass is crazy.* I took real pride in that. To provide a final piece of evidence, I lay there on my back, tucked my nose into the nape of his neck, and cried. *I'm gonna miss you.* He said nothing, just kept wiping my eyes with his rough thumbs until his hands were wet and my face was dry.

———————

I see us there, in my mind, and think that Red should have done to me what the chief Vithobai did to the Christian missionary Pinmay in E. M. Forster's story "The Life to Come." Ever read that?

The story—tragedy, really—begins when a British missionary, Pinmay, is sent into an unnamed forest to convert the pagan natives, starting with the most stubborn among them: the chief, Vithobai, who hasn't given the time of day to any of the seasoned missionaries, not even the brutal Roman Catholics, who've come and gone before Pinmay shows up.

Their first encounter goes as everyone expects, except Pinmay, who hasn't even bothered to learn the language or customs of the people he intends to save. Vithobai has a servant inform Pinmay that he's barking up the wrong tree, so to speak, and Pinmay is forced to spend the night alone in the forest, since he can't reach his missionary camp safely until the morning. He finds a tree trunk to rest beside. He has a little lamp, the clothes on his back, a Bible, and nothing else save his disappointment. In the middle of the night, a figure appears. A man, naked except for a garland of flowers. It's Vithobai.

I wish to hear more about this god whose name is Love, he says.

The missionary can hardly contain himself. *Come to Christ!* cries Pinmay.

Is that your name? Vithobai asks.

Pinmay straightens that out and invites Vithobai to join him by the tree trunk, to hear about his god. He reads the words from a letter the Apostle Paul wrote to the church at Corinth—*If I speak in the tongues of men or of angels, but do not have love, I am only a resounding gong or a clanging cymbal . . . etc. etc.*—words which move Vithobai so deeply that he rests his head in Pinmay's bosom and blows out the lamp. Darkness covers whatever follows.

The next morning, not long after Pinmay returns, ashamed, to his missionary camp, word comes from the forest that Vithobai and his entire tribe have decided to give their lives to Christ. Pinmay must have been one extraordinary lay. Whatever the case, Vithobai is changed—his new name is Barnabas—and Pinmay is changed, too: now mean and dismissive toward his first, most important convert. The table is set for disaster.

Come to Christ, Barnabas implores Pinmay the next time he sees the missionary.

Not yet, Pinmay replies.

He refuses to see Barnabas for five years, years during which, as you might suspect, the natives become riddled with disease, Barnabas loses his land, and Pinmay decides to marry a woman. Barnabas is on the outs big-time, but still attends Pinmay's wedding with a fine gift and one final plea: *Come to Christ.* God has commanded them to love, Barnabas reminds the missionary, whose *not yet* becomes *never*. Pinmay fines his former lover for backsliding. At this point in Forster's story it seems that Barnabas has either a seizure or a nervous breakdown, not totally sure which. He recovers, physically at least, and retreats high into the mountains with the woman he's forced to marry. Next thing we know (though some years have passed), broken-hearted Barnabas is near death, thanks to a consumption outbreak that was started by one of the workers who'd come to civilize the village. Pinmay hears the news and, out of duty if not care, goes with Mrs. Pinmay to visit the chief one last time.

He finds Barnabas lying on an asphalt roof, naked. That is not the way a good Christian should die, Pinmay explains. Barnabas needs a shawl or something. He also needs to know, according to Pinmay, that what they did in the forest those many years ago was *sin*, not *love*, and Barnabas must repent before it is too late. *Repent* Pinmay begs—and also begs Vithobai, as he's again become, to kiss his forehead, as a sign that the forgiveness is real.

Vithobai, nearly dead but not a fool, asks Pinmay to lie down on his now-skeletal chest so the kiss may be planted. Pinmay lowers his head, rests it on Vithobai, continues his entreaty:

We have erred in this life, Pinmay says, *but it will not be so in the life to come.*

Hearing this, Vithobai gets a little pep in his dying step—he had forgotten that his new religion comes with a major perk: once this life is over, he'll receive a brand-new one. He asks Pinmay whether they will meet in the life to come, and whether there will be love in it. Pinmay assures him that they will and there will be.

Life, life, eternal life. Wait for me in it! the chief shouts.

And as he shouts these words, Vithobai drives a dagger through Pinmay's heart. Poor man is dead before he even knows what hit him. Of course, since almost every homosexual story written in the twentieth century had to include a death or a suicide, after murdering the missionary Vithobai jumps off the roof and kills himself. I'll excuse Forster for that— he couldn't even publish this incredible story in his lifetime.

Anyway, I say all that to say that Red should've stabbed me, but he didn't. And he didn't jump off the Motel 6 balcony to his grisly death. He just held me and wiped my tears and drove me home. And I'm so glad he left me alive because I was having such a hard time securing salvation in the life to come that I couldn't afford to jeopardize my chances in this one.

chapter **EIGHT**

Go to any Texas high school. Sit in a classroom. Stand in a hallway. You'll see it: the glow above the head of the football player—his letterman jacket full of patches, his locker empty of books, the swagger that must be taught to most fashion models but that comes naturally to him, a seventeen-year-old boy on the varsity. He doesn't know that this may be the pinnacle of his life. That his friends will never be as popular, that sex will never come as easily, that his name might never again appear in the paper for anything good. No matter. Even in the most meaningless worlds there are places of privilege. He is it. The Alma Mater says it all.

> *Hail Alma Mater!*
> *Hail Gold and White!*
> *We're right behind you*
> *As you go into the fight*
> *Loyal and faithful,*
> *Ever we'll be.*
> *South Oak Cliff, we love you;*
> *Win a vic-to-ry*

Victories don't fall from the sky. Somebody's got to suit up. Somebody's got to lift and run and vomit and strain and weep. Somebody's got to stand there in a jersey with salty sweat running down his cheeks and accept your loyalty and your faith. That's what the boy down on the field is for. I wanted to be him. I wasn't alone.

So many of us who became that boy have been broken because of it. They will put our body in the ground a little earlier than the rest of you. Our brains might be sitting in a lab somewhere. But man, even if it was just a little twinkle of light that we held on to like a dying firefly for the rest of our lives, the game gave a lot for all it took.

Some of it goes right back to what Oscar Wilde said: *Everything in life is about sex except sex. Sex is about power.* Well Texas high school football is perhaps the only thing in the world that was about both. You may not have been a star, but you were a member. And the only thing worse than being an insignificant member of something is to not be a member of anything. Jefferson should have put that right in the Declaration, so true is it of life in this country. As long as I was part of the team, I had a crew. I had memories to gin up and stories to steal. I had reliable Friday night plans and a secured seat during lunch and the right to leave class early for pep rallies. These gifts alone were worth a shorter life.

Then there were the uniforms. All you have to do is watch the drag queen Dorian Corey sit in front of her mirror for almost the entirety of *Paris Is Burning* and you will understand how much care my teammates and I devoted to tearing perfect strips of bright white or jet-black tape to spat our cleats, pulling long thick socks above our calves, adjusting neoprene sleeves until the seams formed a straight line from our elbows to the opening of a sticky pair of gloves we begged for, fastening our glittering pants like corsets, squeezing too-tight pads over narrow shoulders, and finally placing a shiny domed crown on our heads—a helmet, with black paw print stickers on the sides and, for the chosen few, a clear or tinted or

mirrored visor that kept stadium lights out of our eyes and fear in our opponents' hearts. *Look good. Feel good. Play good.*

But first, the wait. The agonizing wait in the bowels of a rancid locker
room. We sat there all dressed up, listening to the voices in our heads and
the thick silence around us except for the patter of cleats on the concrete
floor, sounding out the same journey over and over. To the mirror. To the
toilet. There may be no worse wait than the one you know will end. This
is one of them. We watched the clock wind down. Chewed our mouth-
piece. Told a nervous joke. Then, by the awful grace of God, came game
time.

For most of high school, my wait just led to more waiting. I spent
sophomore year on the junior varsity squad, where we wore hand-me-
down varsity outfits and played on muddy fields before crowds of seventy-
five on a good day. There were only five or six games to our season,
instead of the standard ten, and since my time at quarterback as a freshman had been such a disaster, the coaches decided to put me at defensive
end. I was small for the position, but I was fast and wild. A bit like a rabid
lemur.

One night we were being embarrassed by a team I've long since forgotten, and our offensive coordinator, Coach Wesley, was fed up. He hated
losing and resented wasting his time with chickenshit underclassmen instead of the college-bound wide receivers he coached on the varsity, or the
state champion–caliber sprinters he trained on the track team, where he
paid special attention to me since I was among the fastest boys in my year,
thanks to my father's genes and Coach Walton's instruction.

With the offense stalled, Coach Wesley devised a new plan.

Casey!

I was idling on the other end of the sideline, probably staring off toward the highway. I hurried down to the offensive huddle to see what he
wanted.

Put ya helmet on, man. Aight listen, fellas. Casey, you get in at quarterback. Shotgun. Now when the center snap the ball, I want everybody to run right. Casey, you run left. Understand?

Yes, sir.

Sure enough, the center shot the ball back to me, the other ten boys on the offense ran to their right, and I took off to my left—around the left tackle, right by a linebacker too slow and a safety too confused to catch me, and into the end zone for a touchdown.

Shiiiit same thang! Y'all run this way. Casey that way. You aight?

By this point we had run Team Right/Casey Left or Team Left/Casey Right about seven times in a row and I was sucking wind. But even if I wasn't indefatigable, I was obedient.

Yeah. I'm good, Coach.

And it kept working. At least for that one game.

The following week, or maybe a few weeks later, we met the Lincoln Tigers in Pleasant Grove—the most feral neighborhood in Dallas and a perfect neutral site for the boys from slightly less feral South Dallas to come kick my ass. All night, the main attraction of the South Oak Cliff junior varsity was our Casey Run the Other Way package. But the Lincoln boys were a lot less dumb than they looked and a lot more vicious, so when my teammates ran the other way, they left behind a sea of death in purple jerseys.

The boys from Lincoln didn't just tackle me. They hit me after the referee blew his whistle to end the play. They held me up to let their teammates spear me in the side. They pushed my helmet in the grass at the bottom of a pile and yelled into my ear *Stay down ole bitch-ass nigga!* They saw me trying to run out of bounds and sped up to throw me headfirst into the rocks that framed the playing field. But I kept getting up—kept running the ball, kept my mouth shut, kept taking the blows. Sometimes I just closed my eyes and savored the rush of being pummeled, the crack of another helmet on mine. I grinned, called a few time-outs to patch my wounds, went back for more.

My arms were so bloodied by the end of the game that I went to school the next day with dirty bandages in place of shirt sleeves. My friend Junebug, who was already a varsity running back and who sounded like a chopped-and-screwed Sly Stone record, saw me in the locker room and slurred *Damn, kinfolk them niggas turned you into a mummy!* Everybody on the varsity had either seen or heard what the Lincoln Tigers did to me the night before, so they also knew what I had not done: quit. Thanks to one play and one night of punishment, I had what I'd long wanted—a little respect and a spot on the varsity. This was the first time I learned how far you can make it in America if you have enough disregard for your personal welfare. Maybe that's why football is the national pastime.

Listen up, fellas. Lemme tell you why the game of football is so incredible. Where else can you beat the shit out of another man and get away with it? No goddamn where.

That was Coach Jasper, a man so squat and black and round that he looked like a doo doo bug who had grown up to be a *Homo sapiens*. I can still see him now, waddling up and down the practice field with those gray cotton shorts riding up his heart-shaped ass, and those little hands desperately clinging to each other in front of his stomach. Every now and then he'd waddle over to a huddle, tilt his too-small head back, put his tongue under his jutting front teeth, and share his thoughts on the game of football, or life, or our futures.

In the middle of a lackluster practice junior year—one of those practices that gets off to such a lazy sloppy start that all you can do is wait to run gassers and go home—Coach Jasper blew his whistle to stop our drill. He leaned that little head back.

You know what? You niggas is sorry. Look at ya! Missin' tackles. Forgettin'
assignments. Loafin' around here like it's a goddamn picnic. Sorry! And you
know what? Most of you niggas gone be like this for the rest of your lives. You
gone talk sorry. You gone work sorry. You gone . . . fuck sorry! I can't even stand
to look at this shit no mo'.

And he waddled right off the field.

Coach Jasper's prophesy remains one of the funniest things I've ever
heard, but it also said a lot about the purpose of high school football in the
eyes of the adults who led us. The program did not exist to develop boys
into men or even better players. It was a stage—a place to reveal, based on
the slightest evidence, whether a teenage boy already had what it took to
perform. One play could make you a star. One mistake could end it all.
Your bad day, your meltdown, your injury was just a symptom of the fact
that you were a *sorry-ass nigga* and would always be one. A cancer. A pussy.
A has-been. We were not a team but a collection of final products that, if
we stayed healthy and in the coaches' good graces, could be displayed to
the men who came looking for us like johns after virgin prostitutes: the
college recruiters.

Say, man, lemme tell you somethin'. Any recruiter that come up here I'ma
tell 'em to look at Casey Gerald. I tell you niggas all the time: be good to the
program and the program will be good to you.

Coach Jasper again, this time in the hallway outside the varsity locker
room. He pulled me aside in the spring of junior year, which he and the
other coaches said mattered more than any other because it was the year
we earned our scholarships. *You got to show up on film this year, fellas,* they
stressed. Ten short weeks in the fall would set the course for the rest of our
lives. We had one shot.

That was all I needed. My junior season had been a banner year for the
Golden Bears, since we had more top-shelf talent than any school in the

district: a wide receiver headed to Kansas, a defensive end headed to Missouri, and a freak of nature headed wherever he wanted. Larry Hughes was the best guard on a basketball team that would win the next two state championships; ran a 20-point 200-meter dash, a 47-second quarter-mile, and could hurdle when he wasn't too bored by it. He was the best receiver, the best running back, the best safety, the best quarterback, and the best kicker on the football team; one of the most sought-after recruits in the country; and the most gifted athlete I have ever played with or against.

The only thing Larry could not do better than everybody else was read, which he could hardly do at all. I wouldn't have known this if I hadn't taken economics a year early and sat across from him his senior year in a crowded classroom where Coach Taylor typically instructed us to watch a movie or pretend to copy stock prices from the business section of the *Dallas Morning News* or just sit and talk for fifty minutes, as long as we weren't too loud.

If you dumbass niggas don't lower your goddamn voices we gone pull out the book and work!

At least once, Coach Taylor made good on his threat and so out came the economics textbook. It was time for "popcorn reading." One student was called on to read aloud, then that student chose the next reader, and so on until the passage was complete or the whole class had participated. Juice shot his hand up first and flashed his gold-clad incisors. *Lemme start, Coach!*

Juice began to read and the more sentences he put behind him the more his lips spread into a grin, a damn-fool grin. He finished his passage.

C'mon, Larry, you next! Juice shouted, cackling.

I don't know that I've seen many sadder scenes than Larry Hughes trying to read—or the rest of us watching him read. *C'mon, Larry,* the snickers, Juice cracking up. Coach Taylor finally showed a mercy—*Aight, man, call on somebody.*

Despite it all, Larry never stormed out of the room, never shed a shamed tear. Perhaps he knew as well as anybody that of the hundreds of college recruiters who showed up to watch him practice or on film or from the stands of SOC games where they sometimes took up half a section of bleachers, not a single one would ask our coaches or his father or the boy himself whether he could read. And they'd never meet one of his teachers, who would not have told them the truth anyway.

And by this boy's stripes, I was helped.

It was a late fall practice the week before we faced one of our main rivals, the Kimball Knights, and our head coach, B. J. Price, wanted to keep Larry fresh because he'd just recovered from a shoulder injury and there were four other positions he had to fill. Since I was almost as fast as he was, especially when I was scared, Coach Price substituted me for Larry on a play that had a complex name I no longer remember. I was to go in at quarterback. Shotgun. The center would snap the ball to me. I would then fake a handoff to the running back standing to my left or right, and then run the other way. Sounded familiar.

On my first try, I fumbled the snap. Want to say the ball was wet but the truth is that I was nervous. Could hardly say *hut*.

Well I'll be John Brown, son! Take the goddamn snap and hold on to the ball or else I'll get your numbnuts-lookin' ass outta there!

Coach Price was, like the rest of his staff, a brother of Omega Psi Phi fraternity, which meant that most of the things that came out of his mouth were barks, sexual testimonials, comedy bits, or withering insults like this one, delivered in his piercing high-pitched voice.

Stop the tape, Coach. He'd whine during a film session. *I'll be John Brown. What in the shit is this? Fifteen niggas missed the tackle! Some of you niggas missed him twice! I'm telling you guys. You think I'm fuckin' around. Them niggas from Roosevelt gone come over here and put they foot so far up your monkey ass you gone be walkin' around bent over like a question mark!*

Once, Coach Price brought the legendary Bobby Knight to speak to us. Nobody gave much of a damn. But Coach Price was so inspired by the General's example that, the next practice, he brought out a yardstick and threatened to strike Terry Newsom, who instead of taking his lick grabbed the yardstick and drew it back above his head. *Nigga if you ever raise yo' hand to me again, I'll kill yo' bitch ass. You ain't my fucking daddy.*

Coach Price never raised his hand to Terry Newsom again. He kicked him off the team and forced him to transfer to another school before the year was out.

I didn't have Terry Newsom's testicles, and Coach Price had always been better to me than I likely deserved, so when he berated me for fumbling the snap I just said *yes sir* and returned to the shotgun to call for the ball again. The center shot it back and I took off—around the left tackle, past a linebacker too slow to catch me and, now that I had survived the Lincoln Massacre, *through* a senior safety who intended to teach me a lesson, then on into the end zone.

Shiiit all right, son. Okay! Coach Price yelped. He decided this new scheme would be our opening attack against Kimball.

Since there was no film of my junior varsity days, no mention of my name in Kimball's scouting report, and no cheers from the crowd of fifteen thousand when I stepped on the turf of Sprague Stadium, where Coach Walton had taught fourteen-year-old me to run for his life, this simple play still worked. I was so afraid of the Kimball varsity defense that I ran even faster than I had in practice, even faster than Larry Hughes, who walked over on the sidelines after the first drive and slapped me on the ass—*damn, keep running like that, boy.*

We lost a close game to Kimball that night, but under those radiant lights and the wall of sound coming from the Golden Bear band blasting Stevie Wonder's "Jammin'," and the crowd chanting *Who ya rootin' for? S-O-C!*, and the old-timers coming up to tell me that I ran like my old man used to run, and Coach Price letting me switch my jersey to number 1, that performance was the high point in a career composed mostly of low points or none. And thanks again to Larry Hughes's bounty, my four or five brilliant plays did not go unnoticed—recruiters started courting me, too.

There was nothing more precious to receive than the letters these men sent, starting with a sprinkle your sophomore year, a deluge by the time you were a junior. Some boys kept the letters in their book bags. Some kept boxes full of them like messages from a lover at war. Some boys who had their own room at home might fill up a whole wall with letters instead of posters of Michael Jordan or Emmitt Smith. The better you were, the more letters you got. The more personal those letters would be. Larry Hughes wouldn't even open a letter from a school like the University of North Texas. Should a letter come from a powerhouse like Michigan, he might file-13 anything other than a handwritten note from the head coach himself.

> *Dear Larry,*
>
> *I'm here in Ann Arbor thinking of you. You did a great job last week and I can't wait to see you here in a Wolverine uniform. Please give your dad my best.*
>
> *—Coach*

By junior year spring, these letters led to in-person visits from recruiters, who showed up to watch the boy's best game film and to ask his high school coach one question: *Is he a good kid?* A question that meant far more than it let on, intended as it was to solicit answers to two impolite if not illegal questions: *Can we get him into school?* and *Is he hungry enough to stay?* No recruiter wanted to waste time on a boy who would not be accepted by the college admissions committee (the better the athlete, the lower the bar). And no recruiter wanted to court a boy who would not submit to his demands—who did not feel such deep gratitude for his opportunity that he'd do almost anything, be almost anybody, not to lose it. This was the threat behind Coach Jasper's *Be good to the program and the program will be good to you.* And not long after he signaled that I'd held up my end of the bargain, the SOC coaching staff tried to hold up theirs.

A few weeks before the end of junior year, Coach Taylor ran out to find me in the parking lot, where I was bumming a ride home, excitement all over the big flat brown face that made him look like an adorable teddy bear despite all the cursing. He'd just finished showing my Kimball film to a recruiter, who had been convinced to visit a school on the other side of the Trinity by another coach who made many such visits yet never convinced anybody that I know of to attend his podunk college in Kansas and who told the recruiter of a boy he'd seen on tape who might have decent enough grades to be worth a look. *Boy, I'm glad I came. We don't have anything that fast in the whole program,* the recruiter told Coach Taylor, who rushed to tell me all about it.

Man, ain't nobody from Yale ever showed up here!

Where is Yale, Coach?

It's up in Connecticut. East Coast. That's a real good opportunity, Casey. I'm tellin' ya. Think about it.

Aight, Coach. I will.

What I really thought was *Ain't nobody from SOC ever gone to no school in Connecticut—where is that, anyway?* Here was my own coach, saying in so many words that I was such a pathetic football player that he'd send me halfway around the world to play peewee football for a team nobody knew anything about. Not that I was angry at him, but I sure was insulted and embarrassed. Guess you could also say ignorant and proud—in other words, I was a seventeen-year-old heading into my last year of high school, which should instead be called the first year of real life: when, after a long blind walk pushed along by the winds of fate, a boy rubs the dreamy crust of youth from his eyes and looks upon the world as a man. A man with choices if not options, with no clue and little doubt, in heat to *be* somebody, even an awful somebody, which I was. I'd paid my dues on the outskirts of the world—had worn the too-little pants and the run-down shoes, had pretended not to hear the *No you take him*s and the *He's not my responsibility*s, had been a nobody for so long and to so many that I could still taste other people's leftovers, could still see the empty seats in the stands, could still feel a violent smirk come across my face when I sensed somebody sniffing around my life to figure out whether I was worth their time. Maybe I had not been worth it for seventeen years, but now I would be. Now I was on track to be valedictorian like my sister, and I ditched any class that demanded too much work so that I could put more distance between me and the second-ranked student. Now I was captain of the football team and *I* did the inviting to lunch and the bossing of underclassmen. Now I was the senior class president, thanks to the pressure BK et al. put on other students to vote. Now I was the voice of tyranny flowing out over the PA system for the afternoon announcements, the face in the Sports-Day section for the fall season preview, and the name on the South Oak Cliff marquee:

Dallas Mayor for a Day
Casey Gerald

The City of Dallas had launched the Mayor for a Day program to give one senior from each public high school a day of exposure to the world of power beyond their backwater, and to give the city leaders some comfort that, despite the stench of failure in the school system, there existed at least a fine mist of success. One fall morning I put on my only suit and was dropped off at city hall—one of three buildings in Dallas designed by I. M. Pei, a testament to what one longtime civic leader told me: *Dallas always believes it is one great building away from being a world-class city*—and spent the day shadowing Mayor Laura Miller. This included taking one picture with her, standing to be recognized in the city council meeting, and sitting in the backseat of her chauffeured car while she handled city business on the phone. This whole exercise still seems like almost as big a waste of time for a teenager as it was for the leader of one of the largest cities in the country.

But if everything happens for a reason, then perhaps I spent that day with Laura Miller because Somebody knew what I only recently learned: Six months before I was born, my father spent a day with Laura Miller, too. He was not a senior in high school but a lumber hauler at Home Depot. She was not the mayor but a journalist, profiling him for a special issue of the *Dallas Morning News*'s magazine: *When Bad Things Happen to Good Athletes*.

The article opens with those familiar lines: *As a high school quarterback growing up in South Dallas, Rod Gerald possessed two of the fastest legs and two of the steadiest hands in America* etc. etc. . . . And there he is, in a nearly full-page photo, standing under hazy fluorescent light between aisles of wood in his orange Home Depot smock, showing that same mustachioed smile he wore in our family portrait, telling this woman all the things I'd need to know but would not hear directly.

If you're good enough, the college can handle anything. If you don't have the money to go to college, the college can handle it. If you don't have the shoes or the clothes, they can handle it. If you tell them you're embarrassed to go to college because you don't have the car, the clothes, the money—they'll make sure you have it. Until you mess up.

Rod Gerald had messed up and now, with his seed that would become me growing in my mother's belly, he was earning seven dollars an hour at the Home Depot in Red Bird Mall.

In 1986, Laura Miller saw this as a parable—the most prized product from a school that had reportedly sent more players to the National Football League than any other high school in the nation, now chewed up and spat out.

Gerald's is a familiar lament among stellar, blue-chip former high school football stars. He is but one of thousands of 17- and 18-year-olds across the country wooed each year by college recruiters and proud high school coaches into believing that pigskin is their savior—a free ticket to a college education, a stepping stone to the pros.

In the time that had passed since my father's day with Laura Miller, some things had changed. South Oak Cliff had sent only one player to the National Football League in the preceding eighteen years and would send only two more in the years to come, including Larry Hughes. (We had sent one player to the pro basketball Hall of Fame, Dennis Rodman, but everybody said his sister was the real star at SOC, so nobody made much of a fuss about him.) The Home Depot was no longer near Red Bird Mall. Neither was RadioShack or JCPenney or the McDonald's down the street, which was closed temporarily because one night, when Luke and I stopped to pick up a hamburger after leaving the mall, we saw a boy lying in a pool of blood behind the cash register. Somebody had come and shot him in the head about a half hour before we showed up.

But aside from these changes, and the fact that I'd gone from living in my mother's womb to living without her altogether, everything was mostly the same nearly two decades later. The fast legs were still running, the steady hands were still catching, the recruiters were still lying, and Brenda Battle—now Brenda Cox, another slight change—was still delivering the same tired lecture in her classroom that she'd given to Laura Miller in that 1986 article:

A kid is a kid, and I think society looks at that kid as a commodity. Let's face it, sports is big bucks. I think what happens is your universities and your recruiters do not look at the kid as a possible future executive. They look at that kid specifically for what he came there for—and that is to get winning points for that particular team. And you take a 17-year-old kid who is praised for his running ability, his tackling ability, his shooting ability, and that's all that he can see.

A decade-plus later, in 1997, I stepped into Ms. Cox's class for the first time—saw the face that was so racially ambiguous that she was often privy to the private things white people said about nonwhites and

Mexicans said about non-Mexicans and blacks said about blacks and non-blacks alike; heard the voice which carried her father's twang from South Dallas by way of Waco and her mother's harshness from Louisiana, where she picked up the skin and hair of her French-speaking grandparents and two degrees from Southern University in Baton Rouge, making her one of the few teachers with a masters in her subject when she joined the South Oak Cliff faculty in 1974 (and one of the few with an afro, which the principal tried unsuccessfully to make her cut or perm).

I'd walked the three blocks to SOC from the house on Marsalis with my mother to be a witness for some presentation that Tashia was to deliver after school. I don't remember anything Tashia said and very little else about that day besides my fear that the building might swallow ten-year-old me up, clutching Mama's hand so tightly I could have cut off her circulation if I hadn't been so weak, walking so close up under her that I kept tripping over the back of her shoes.

Boy, you were hiding behind Debra like a shadow! Ms. Cox always taunts. *You were so leetle and your eyes were so big like you were tryin' to catch everything. I thought you were gonna pee yourself, you were so scared.* She pauses— *I just said to myself . . . Somebody needs to protect this little boy.*

Seven years later I was back in her room and Ms. Cox had, by then, decided that *she* would do some protecting—but I was no longer a little boy, no longer hiding behind my mother, no longer looking around trying to catch anything, and no longer mute. I was talking a lot. Lying a lot, actually, and I have the record to prove it, thanks to the fact that the *Dallas Morning News* seems to have conspired to record my life just so I could tell you all about it someday.

In November 2004, the paper ran a big article on the front page of the sports section—"SOC Defensive Back Forges Own Identity"—that included three testimonials that reflect the lies my family told ourselves about ourselves and one another.

There was my sister, reprising her role as Moral Force of Hope. She now spoke of her baby brother instead of Daddy. *I'm just grateful he hasn't let his circumstances define who he is. He's risen to the challenge. He's grown into his own man.*

Now what shall we call a boy whose college application is a thousand-word pastiche of trauma pornography? Whose letters of recommendation echo all his stations of the cross? Who looks down into the camera with pitiful eyes for a portrait that will be the banner of an article about his father and his mother and his poverty and the troubles of his world? A boy so far from growing into a man that even the things he believes most deeply he believes only in response to someone else? I say we ought to call him a boy *defined* by his circumstances.

Perhaps we all are—just seven billion Eves made from the rib of our Adam-circumstance—but why do we lie about it? Why don't we want to believe it? Is it that it shames us to admit how limited our power is, how much we can submit—*have submitted*—to the things we did not choose? I reckon it's some of that. Real shame. The trouble isn't that we are defined by our circumstances. It's that we are so defined by *running* from them that we don't understand what they mean, what they did and are still doing to shape the way we see and move through the world. And we call the running *rising to the challenge.* Not so. Not so.

Then there was Clarice, offering her highest praise when the journalist noted how remarkable it was that I was not an angry boy despite all events.

You can't ever tell if he's upset or not. He doesn't show emotions. He just moves on.

Perhaps she could have *asked* if I was upset, or how I felt at all. Perhaps she or anyone could have knocked on the bathroom door after twenty minutes of hearing the faucet run. Perhaps instead of being proud that a kid could endure so much, she should have been troubled that there was little sign of any harm. Where had it all gone? Did it just evaporate? How did this boy—all these boys—become so brave?

Have you ever watched the losing team at the end of a high school football game, especially the seniors after the very last game of their very last season? If not, you've missed the clearest sign of how many tears are trapped inside so many boys. All that sobbing, all that hugging, all that snot going all over the place, all those boys muttering *I love you* to one another—you would think their best friend has died in their arms, so struck with grief are they. This spectacle is just a shroud. Don't buy it. Football simply ain't that sad. But nobody's ever judged a boy for weeping over a ballgame, so the moment comes and he squeezes his rag while he can. Then *moves on.*

It's a masterful sleight of hand and a real virtue, until it isn't. I can only liken it to something I later witnessed and will soon tell you about—when the whole world almost came tumbling down behind a similarly noble idea: if you take a small piece of bad debt and wrap it up with other little pieces of bad debt and maybe a slice or two of good debt, the debt ain't so bad anymore. It might even be an asset! Until one piece of debt falls. Then another. Then the stock market and the pensions and a few prime ministers. Now how about the human heart? When you bundle its little nicks and cuts, can you turn a broken boy into a stoic? No, you'll turn him into a ticking time bomb, and, probably, a fool. Which I was.

The most foolish thing in this charade of an article, which I loved so much and carried around like I was a breathing scrapbook, came right after the lede:

Casey Gerald knows some folks are still fascinated with his father. It's fine by him if he's referred to as Rod Gerald's son . . . But being the son of a troubled former SOC superstar accounts for but a sliver of who Casey Gerald is. He has carved out his own identity.

The journalist didn't make this up. I helped him with my doozy of a quote: "*I don't really focus on trying to be like him,*" Casey said of his father. "*I focus on being myself. Hopefully I'm better.*"

That's me, lying through my teeth so convincingly that I believed it at the time. My saving grace was not that I was *good* but that I was inadequate—I avoided having my life ruined by the high-stakes gamble of big-time college football because I was not better than my father. Not even close. As the article went on to point out: *Casey, while talented, is not as gifted an athlete as his father was.* So like thousands of other seventeen- and eighteen-year-old boys across the country, my stream of letters and recruiter visits dried up to a few real and disappointing options to play football. There was a glimmer of hope that I'd go to Texas Christian University, as SOC's last great player had done, until Coach Price confided that TCU's head coach was wary of recruiting boys from the inner city. Then TCU's head coach came to my house with the truth: he could not spend one of his athletic scholarships on me, but would let me walk onto the team as a regular student if I wanted. I wasn't about to go live in Fort Worth to carry some other bastard's shoulder pads, so TCU was out.

My best shot, Coach Walker stressed—aside from the US Air Force Academy which, when I visited, seemed less appealing than going to prison—was to head east to Yale, where I didn't have to worry about earning a football scholarship because they didn't offer them anyway.

Son, just take your visit up there and see how you like it. Ain't no harm in that.

chapter NINE

No harm my ass, I thought on that long ride south from the Hartford airport to New Haven—the snow stacked up to sternums in the fields, battering the windshield, nearly blocking the view of all the factories that lined our route.

Don't worry, guys, said the tall pale man with sunken eyes, the coach who'd visited SOC to see my tape. *The weather doesn't get much worse than this.*

I rolled that comforting lie around in my head and stared out at the storm and at the smoking boxy factories and all the no-people in the streets of the little New England towns. Before long, the black van mounted a slope and came down on the other side to ease off I-91 and onto Grove Street, lowering us into a valley lined with buildings cast in the mold of old-world castles, a mold meant to lend an air of grandeur but which made me think, only and immediately, of Harry Potter.

Through the valley we crept at parade pace past the Grove Street Cemetery and Eli Whitney's body, past Payne Whitney Gym (named after one of Eli Whitney's descendants), and on to Vanderbilt Hall (Vanderbilts being Whitneys' kin by marriage). Mr. Vanderbilt's hall was just a pit stop to drop off my luggage and meet the boy who would host me for the weekend—with his clipped midwestern accent; the photograph of a black man, white woman, and him, a family portrait, on his mantel; and his best friend (another mixed-race boy from the football team) in the common area. Since I went on to host many recruits in my time at Yale, I can tell you that the coaches pulled out all the stops to make sure I was paired with the closest things they had to my own kind.

We continued to the athletic department headquarters, which was attached to Payne Whitney Gym and looked as divine. Literally. If the tour guide wasn't lying, then the Payne Whitney Gym was supposed to be a cathedral, per the terms of Mrs. Payne Whitney's gift to the college. But the college didn't need another church at the time. It needed a gym. So somebody hatched the idea to build a gym that *looked* like a giant church, and pray that the Whitneys didn't protest when they discovered the truth, since it would also be the largest indoor gym in the world, which might please them all the same. It did, apparently.

From the athletic department headquarters, we—now thirty or so boys—went on to see the Gutenberg Bible at the rare books library, and the statue of Nathan Hale at Connecticut Hall, and the tomb of the secret society Skull and Bones. None of these meant much to me but they were nice enough. Then we filed back onto the tour bus to take a drive down Whalley Avenue—ignoring the homeless people along the way—and out to West Haven to see the Yale Bowl, the first and almost the only sign that some semblance of respectable football existed at this school.

Here was a stadium, said the short grim Italian tour guide/coach named Larry Ciotti, that could pack more than sixty thousand people on the wooden benches that loomed end to end above a playing field sod with the grass of history—a field where the game was invented, where the first pass was thrown and two of the first three Heisman Trophy winners had run and twenty-seven national champions had been crowned (never mind that all but one of those championships came before the First World War). Here was a stadium that had inspired the Rose Bowl and housed the New

York Giants when Yankee Stadium could not do the job—a stadium that would still be standing, likely without lights or turf, for many years to come because it meant so much to the country that the Yale Corporation would not allow any changes to be made.

You young men will have the privilege—Coach Ciotti paused to look away from us and out into the distance so that we, too, would look into the distance and see the privilege for ourselves—*to play on that field. To wear the Yale Blue. It's a privilege. An honor. You know, a Yale coach once walked into the locker room before his team took this field. And he told them*—Coach Ciotti sniffled and grimaced and turned to us—*"Gentlemen, you are now going to play football against Harvard. Never again in your whole life will you do anything so important."* He turned and strode back to the bus in silence.

If Coach Ciotti had not been a Connecticut high school football legend, as we were constantly told, he could have been one hell of a used car salesman. And I would have bought his old jalopy on the spot, just like I bought into his big Privilege speech. I would never be good enough to walk on the field of the Horseshoe and play Michigan as my father had done, not good enough to get a taste of the Red River Rivalry between Texas and Oklahoma or even line up for Stanford against Cal. But if there was any truth to the things Larry Ciotti said—which I couldn't be sure of because he was a Catholic and I'd never met a Catholic who was *open* about it—then, without even trying, I had stumbled onto something even grander, older, and more important than all the things I thought I wanted. And if my visit had just been this first day, then Yale would have only been buildings and history to me, and that would have been fine. But the second day came. With it came people. Parents.

When I was young, I'd walk into Granny's kitchen in the middle of the night. I'd stand on my tiptoes and reach for the light switch and brace myself for what was to come: a frenzied march of roaches, little ones about the size of a half fingernail, jetting across the floor and flitting over the stove and into the sink, headed somewhere with the remains of yesterday's dinner and a first taste of tomorrow's sandwich. There was nothing very threatening about them, and as long as I stayed on my tiptoes I could avoid smashing our little friends with my bare feet, and they'd go on about their business.

But every now and then, in the stillness of the dark, I'd lie on the couch or my mattress and hear a violent thud in the corner of the room. A winged scurry, like baby scratches on a cardboard box. I'd jump out of bed in a blind panic, reach for the shoe whose place I'd noted before lying down, and gird my loins before turning on the light and lunging at a prehistoric flying cockroach that might have only been the size of my big toe but seemed to be as big, at least in terms of danger posed, as an atom bomb. Recalling these battles still causes the heart to speed and the breath to catch and the hand to reach for something hard and the will to reach for violence. I had at eighteen, and still often have now, a similar reaction to parents.

And here they were, a few dozen well-dressed smiling talking cockroaches, crowded around me with their sons, who were supposed to be my future teammates. But how was I supposed to trust and bleed and sweat and vomit and weep with boys who hugged and laughed with roaches? At least real roaches kept their mouths shut or spoke softly enough for only other roaches to hear. Not parents. Bastards talked like it was going out of style. And if other parents were around, if they were talking to these other parents about their children, if they were talking about the children they were proud of, you couldn't shut them up. Then they got to asking questions. I'm not old enough to have witnessed the Inquisition, but I'm willing to bet it was more interesting, if not less painful, than living through a herd of parents who catch the question spirit.

All throughout the second day there were questions—questions about Nathan Hale, about financial aid, about room rates at the Omni Hotel; questions about the last question asked because everybody didn't hear the question; questions for the coaching staff, and the admissions committee, and for other parents and for sons and, at dinner, for me.

You're from Dallas?

Yes, ma'am.

And what school do you go to there?

It's called South Oak Cliff.

South Oak Cliff?

Yes, ma'am.

Hmm. You know, I think my husband went to South Oak Cliff. (Turning to her son) *Didn't your dad go to South Oak Cliff, Alex?* (Son looks to mother. Mouth full. Nods.) *Yes, yes, I think that's right. What a coincidence, huh?*

Yes, ma'am. That's crazy.

Well goodness. I'll have to call him to be sure. He won't believe this.

The meekly persistent woman who looked like she could be kin to my kin and who spoke in what I understood to be perfect English had come with her son Alex, who not only sounded perfect but also looked perfect— not in the sense of being beautiful, but in the perfect symmetry of his features and the look on his face that made you believe he didn't sin. Alex had a twin who apparently was also perfect because, toward the end of dinner, their mother turned to me after asking these and many other questions, and said, almost under her breath:

The boys want to go to Cornell . . . She paused to let the horror of that sink in, not knowing I had never heard of Cornell . . . *but their father and I have told them that if we are going to spend our money on their education, they have three options: Harvard, Yale, or Princeton. They are free to choose as long as it's one of those.*

Her statement struck me not as the insufferable bragging parents normally do at dinners like this one, but almost as a note passed across the visitation table from the priest to a political prisoner on the eve of his hunger strike: *Negotiate.* She was firm but did not press the issue. She was, after all, a woman from Albany, Georgia, whose parents had been sharecroppers but whose twin boys had three options—*Harvard, Yale, or Princeton*—and so I suppose she had long ago learned how to say a lot without risking saying too much.

After dinner she rushed toward me, her phone held out like a piece of fresh hot cornbread.

I was right! My husband, Jimmy, wants to talk to you.

I accepted the phone and prepared to endure a few minutes of parenting. The voice on the other end took me by surprise.

Say, man! You're Rod Gerald's boy?

Yes, sir.

Man, listen, I played with your dad at SOC! Seventy-four. He was seventy-five, right?

I think so, mmhmm.

Ack ack ack aw man yeah! That was one cold negro. What a small small world. Listen man I hate I'm not there to meet you, but you just listen to what my wife is saying, okay? And if you need anything, you just let her know. Let us know. All right man?

Yes, sir. Real good to talk to you.

The woman with the perfect English and perfect sons had married this man, Jimmy Bishop, who had grown up right down the road from my family and had played at South Oak Cliff with my daddy. From SOC he'd gone down to the University of Texas and, despite being woefully unprepared for college, he'd looked back at Oak Cliff and decided that by hook or crook he'd stay in Austin until the job was done. He majored in communications and got so good at communicating that when he came back home he was running the TV station. Before long, he left for Baltimore to run the station there, and moved to a nice part of Maryland where he and his wife raised these perfect twin boys who only had three options—*Harvard Yale Princeton*—but who had a daddy who'd grown up with *my* daddy and who still sounded, at least when he was happy or relaxed, like me. And his wife, Gloria, must have heard a little bit of him in me when she listened, because she says she took one look at me and knew that I was from Oak Cliff, that I had no idea what to do with my silverware and even less of a clue what to do with my life, so she decided to keep asking questions and pass along some advice: *take this ticket, boy.*

And when I think about this little coincidence, I realize Jimmy Bishop was the first person I'd ever met who had left Oak Cliff and stayed gone for a good reason, and Gloria Bishop was the first parent I'd met whose questions didn't make me sick, and Alex and Avery Bishop were the first perfect black boys I'd met that didn't make me want to punch them in the face. And all these firsts ope'd a space for me to consider, even if I could not know for sure, that here at the other end of the world there might be yet a little room for me.

I didn't have time to bask in these newfound possibilities, though. By the end of dinner and the close of the second day, the weather and parents and questions had worn me down. I went back to my host's room coughing and snotting a little and looking around for cold medicine, in part to feel better and in part to force myself to sleep. But there was no respite to be had—my host had orders to show me a good time, which meant taking me to a club and arranging for dances or more with a girl who had a reputation for helping secure prospective recruits. The club was Toad's Place, New Haven's version of the Fillmore, except smaller and dirtier, like the dungeon the madman keeps that poor girl in toward the end of *The Silence of the Lambs.* The girl shall remain nameless because she was just a college girl and she went on to have a great dance career and marry an investment banker and buy a renovated brownstone in Harlem.

It'll come as no surprise that I found all types of phlegm in my throat during the two songs I danced to at Toad's. The girl was enough of a saint to suggest that my hosts take me home so that I could get some rest. They relented. I suppose that after three years at Yale they had at least learned that it was better to keep a recruit alive than to get him laid.

We trudged through the snow back to Vanderbilt Hall and settled into the heated chambers of my host's dorm. I was feeling much better by then, of course. I took off my coat, which might as well have been off the whole time, as flimsy as it was against the nine-degree New Haven weather. Sat on the futon to rub my flat feet, sore from walking and my half-size-too-small sneakers. My hosts got comfortable, too. It struck me that now was the right time to ask the only question that had crossed my mind during the visit.

Do y'all not say "nigga" here?

I looked at the two boys much like I imagine little girls look at their mothers the first time they find blood in their underwear. A short quiet nervous laugh came from one of them. They looked to each other. Then at me.

Um, nah.

Oh.

I can't say for sure that I was embarrassed or disappointed or confused, though I figure I was some part of all three. And I can't tell you what I did next other than sleep, which I only know because I woke up the next day—and I only know *that* because I ain't dead. But something miraculous had to have happened in the waning hours of that night or on my third and final day in New Haven, something to outweigh the error of the first two days, when I was forced to walk in a snowstorm and listen to parents and dance with a girl and sleep in a room with black boys who didn't say *nigga*—something to make me ignore how strange and cold and hostile it had been at the eastern end of the world.

But maybe not.

You see, every journey is really two journeys: a *going-to* and a *going-away*. And it's not until the journey is over that you can see what's what, because you can't get away from nothing if you're looking at it all the time, and you can't go toward something you see too clearly because if you saw exactly what it was you'd have enough sense not to chase it. So you stand there at the shoreline of decision—maybe you are more desperate to get away than to go anywhere, or more eager to find someplace new than to leave the place you know, but you need both impulses or else you're in trouble. If all you've got is a going-away, you might end up lost, since the only thing on your mind is running. And if all you've got is a going-to, you might end up sad because what you find is rarely as good as you thought it would be, unless it's different from what you imagined, so it helps to remember how awful the thing was that you left. It's a simple equation, really, and the stranger the journey the better the math works. Just plug in what you were trying to get to and multiply it by what you were trying to get away from, and you'll understand a hell of a lot more precisely why you did what you did. At least this works for me.

At the time, my going-to had very little to do with the propaganda that I received in New Haven, or in packages that came through the mail— large blue folders with a quote on front that read *Yale is at once a tradition, a company of scholars, a society of friends*—or in the conference room near the principal's office at SOC, where the tall pale man with sunken eyes brought Yale's head coach and a youngish man named Tony Reno, who would be my position coach and whose voice reminded me of a character from the Matt Damon/Ben Affleck Southie projects movies. The three men sat there, shaken by having had to walk through metal detectors to enter a school, solemn in the face of their judge, my sister, and her jury: Ms. Cox, Coach Price, and the school registrar.

It had been quite some time since three white men had sat in a room at South Oak Cliff High School. Though I'm sure that contributed to the skepticism, I also know that my people would have been wary of these men even if they had been the progeny of Martin King himself, simply because the men were outsiders. They could tolerate (if not embrace) a liar, a thief, an idiot—as long as he was one of ours. But woe to the man who hears *You must not be from around here.* Maybe the whole world is broken up into two kinds of people: those who are outsiders and those who distrust them. I can't tell you how much good it has done me to have been born into the latter camp, but one by-product is that my *going-to* was as simple as licking my forefinger and holding it up to see which way the wind of my people blew.

When the meeting at SOC ended, the eyes of my people watched from the hallway as the three Yale men walked a few paces to the front door, then watched from second-floor windows as the men walked thirty yards or so across the yard to the parking lot, then watched the car drive down Marsalis Avenue until it was out of sight. Then they watched each other. Then they watched me. Some of them may have never seen me before, but the men slapped my shoulder and grinned and asked—*Son, you the one that's talkin' about going to Yale?*—and the women hugged my neck and put a little lipstick on my cheek and, after church, a twenty-dollar bill in my hand, and sighed—*Baby we are so proud of you!* Most of the men and women were strangers to me by name, but they were *my people* and I felt their breeze and the breeze blew East and the breeze said *Go thou.*

And once my decision was made, once it was certain that the three men from Yale had not lied about me being accepted, I realized that these people had a lot more than a breeze in them. The first week of February marked the most important event in the lives of high school athletes across America: National Signing Day, when eighteen-year-old boys and girls buy brand-new suits and dresses, and wear crisp ball caps with mascots embroidered on the front, and bring their mothers and fathers and little siblings and next-door neighbors with them to serve as entourage and cheering squad as the sons and daughters sign letters of intent to register with the National Collegiate Athletic Association. No matter that all these friends and loved ones have likely never showed up to school even once over the last four years. No matter that the letters are only one-way pledges from the athlete to the college, not the other way around—which will only come to light when these now-shining boys and girls are sent back home as sad young-old people after missing a few study halls or tearing an ACL or sneaking off with one too many girls. National Signing Day is a quintessentially American affair, when our love for youthful innocence and gaudy pageantry crowds out any trace of the dark past and even bleaker future. Perhaps that's why, for the first part of National Signing Day, which took place in the crowded South Oak Cliff library, my father showed up with Clarice. They each delivered a brief speech—about tradition, and family, and pride. I couldn't make this stuff up.

From the ceremony at SOC, Tashia and I—along with the other half-dozen boys in my class who were signing with colleges that day—caravanned out to the field house at the ever-faithful Sprague Stadium for a grand event to honor boys and girls from every high school in Dallas, who were putting their city on the national stage yet again as a go-to destination for any college coach who wanted to win.

The bleachers overflowed with cowbells and posters, with people whose shouts gathered, swelled, and rang down at last, just as their baby's name was called by the announcer.

From SKY-LINE HIGH SCHOOL

Headed to the UNIVERSITY OF OK-LA-HO-MAAA

CHAAARLES HUNTERRR

The bleachers rocked, or at least the section of bleachers where this boy's family stood, and he was escorted by a loved one down a long strip of red carpet in the center of the basketball court, walking slowly enough to drink up the adulation and to give the cameraman time to walk backward in front of him, recording his procession for the evening news.

Perhaps by design, I was one of the last boys called. After the silence that followed the announcer booming my high school, and the gasp that followed his boom of my soon-to-be college, there was a wail that ripped through the field house once he boomed my name. This was the gust of my people—strong enough to make Kimball Knights and Lincoln Tigers cheer for a South Oak Cliff Golden Bear; strong enough for the feet to stomp in the bleachers with more passion for a boy going to play for a team nobody knew existed than all the boys going off to be Longhorns or Sooners or, someday, even Dallas Cowboys; strong enough for the Sprague groundskeeper to call me over to his cart once the ceremony was over. He started to speak, then caught his bottom lip with his top teeth. He rested his worn hands on my shoulders. Tears rolled down his tired cheeks. *Go all the way, son. Go all the way.* I was not sure how to get to all the way, but I felt in the hands of the men and heard in the voices of the women and saw in the eyes of the little children that if I went all the way, then *they* would go, too. And it seemed that they had been waiting so long to go.

So mixed in with, and likely holding together, the standard reasons of going to the best college I could find and joining the best football team that would take me and living just a little over an hour from what they called the best city in the world, my *going-to* was simply tracing those men's hands and those women's voices and those little children's eyes, even if they pointed to a place at the eastern end of the world that I was too dim to have great passion for.

But the *going-away*—that was the greater part of my journey. Because not long after Signing Day, but far too long after dropping off the face of my earth, and ignoring all those times I pled with God, and leaving checks in place of a body, my mother came back.

chapter TEN

It didn't go through, Case.

Huh?

Mama's check. Last one you put in the bank didn't go through.

Hmph.

So I call the bank, right? And the man said her account is closed.

Like ain't nothing in there?

Like it's closed, Case. You know, closed.

Oh.

Mmhmm.

To understand this exchange, you should know that my sister and I began singing what I'd loosely call duets around the time I was six and she was eleven. Tashia and I would sit in the backseat of Daddy's black Ford Probe, or walk side by side through the wide wild field that stretched out before our Columbus apartment and separated her middle school from my elementary, or she would stay in the shower for a day and I would stand outside the bathroom door, kicking it until she let me in to use the toilet. Then, with no cue, the window-staring or grass-swiping or tantrum-throwing would pause and one of us, usually her, would start to sing.

As long as I've known her, Tashia's been a soprano—from the diaphragm, a hint of nasal passage. As long as she's known me, neither of us has known quite what I was: a slobbering no-singing baby; a seven-year-old faltering soprano; a teenage contralto digging for the tenor within. None of this mattered when we sang, though. If I was the lead, I'd open in whatever key felt good to me. If she led, I would join in whatever key felt good to me. I'd glance at her . . . she'd grin. And before the first verse was over, she would have found whatever notes she needed to make my notes right. Not once did she tell me I was doing it wrong, not once did we sound bad (to me), and not once did I consider how much trouble she went through to find the right notes for both of us. But she always did. Always.

Maybe little brothers exist solely to give their sisters extra burdens—so many burdens that the burdens start to form their identity. Maybe that's what all boys do to all girls, then to women, then to the world. Or maybe that's just what I did to my sister. All I know is that I never thanked her for naming me, never apologized for ruining her spine, never thought it my job to find my own right notes, and never heard her complain about any of it. And my blissful tone-deaf singing was the crawl of a sprint to more bliss, more ignorance, more faith (if inaction is a by-product of faith) that my sister would figure it all out—not just those notes but also and especially this new problem, this riddle, this bounced check, this gift which kept us going for two years and which ended on the third day of a fall month because that's the day the money was supposed to come but didn't.

And for the first time I could remember, I wanted my sister to fail.

Some of it was the part of me that in another life would have been a right-wing reactionary instead of a queer, the part that nodded when William F. Buckley said his job was to stand athwart history yelling *STOP*. It's hard enough to get used to a crappy life. But once you do, you see that even crap can be cozy and the coziness becomes important to you. And even the slightest change—in the name of *progress* or *healing* or *uplift*—feels like a threat to your existence, so you ignore it as long as you can. Sometimes you ignore it even after you supposedly can't. This is one thing liberals continually miscalculate: the human desire to leave things just the way they are.

Some of it was rooted in the fact that you can wait so long for something that waiting becomes the thing itself. You take your wait and cut it into little stars and the wait makes the face of heaven so fine that you fall in love with night and pay no worship to the garish sun. I think that's what Shakespeare would say, and I'll agree because of who he is and because I genuinely agree. But I'd go a little further on the point, because I know that if your wait ends, if Romeo lives, if my mother is alive instead of dead or disappeared, then you no longer have something to look forward to in despair, and Juliet's lines are flat, and the lyrics to "Sometimes I Feel Like a Motherless Child" don't feel as raw and deep and compelling. The story has to change, you see, and that's not only a great deal of work to undertake, but also a real risk, as the new story might not be as marvelous as the old sad one.

But the greatest risk was hope.

For nearly five years, I had prayed for this one thing to happen—well, I also prayed to be delivered from sin until a few of my sins got too good to give up—and each prayer required a little more desperation and earnestness, new words since the old ones had not worked, larger mustard seeds since the mountains had not moved. And over time, each prayer brought with it more resentment and formed a callus on the heart to match the knees. And daily prayer turned into weekly prayer then annual prayer at someone else's request, then no prayer at all because even dogs and babies know when to stop asking for the same thing. And this journey ended not at hopelessness—only liars and some mass murderers have *no* hope—but at an *anti-hope*. This anti-hope seems to be in vogue, mind you, especially amongst those who consider themselves too brilliant or too secular to believe in silly things like unicorns and hope and God. They say that anti-hope is the natural order of things, that the most obvious stance for the man and woman of reason is the stance of Cool Customer, leaning against the wall of the world while the moral arc of the universe bends down to crush them, as it must. And they must convince themselves and others that this anti-hope is not only natural, not only superior, but inevitable. Because otherwise they must admit that anti-hope is a choice—a choice birthed by fear, by a cautious assessment of risk, a selective reading of the past projected onto the future, a failure of the imagination and a crippling of the will. They have to make Hope the province of fools so that Anti-Hope is not revealed to be the province of cowards.

I say this from experience. I was once too weak for hope.

I would have gone right on without it, would have found comfort, if not pleasure, in whatever anti-hope I had, had my sister not always followed through on what she said she would—had she not traced our living mother to Saint Louis.

Well, I talked to a lady at some halfway house up there. She was real nice. Said Mama's been living there for a little over a year.

Why she live there?

I'ono, Case. Don't even know. Lady said Mama got arrested a while back, though.

What for?

Good question. Lady said she couldn't tell me.

Hmph.

I guess we should go up there and get her.

To Saint Louis??

Don't you think so? Me, you, and Granny can ride up there after Thanksgiving.

I mean. I guess.

I had reached the age by which every boy and girl has mastered the skill of convincing the people in their lives that there is nothing that excites them—not money, not a surprise birthday party, not raising their mother from the dead. But behind my jaded eyes ran fresh electric wonder: I would get to make new mixtapes for the ride, and print out all the directions twice in case I lost a copy. I would get to see Oklahoma for the first time, and maybe a slice of Kansas, and the Saint Louis arch, which had always been my favorite monument aside from the Statue of Liberty, if only because a rapper I liked put the arch in his music videos. And on top of all this magic, we'd pull up to a stately halfway house—the one I'd visited my daddy in was nicer than the house on Old Ox—and do all the reunion stuff that's cheesy but that looks so nice when people do it on television. Maybe I'd cry a little bit, just a little, but then I'd tell some good mean jokes like *Dang, Mama, what you done killed somebody they got you in witness protection or something?* Or I'd act like I didn't know her and reach out to shake her strange hand like the man at the bank when poor people apply for a loan—*Hi, I'm Casey . . . and you are?* And she'd smack her lips and say *Boy, I'm your mama, shutup!* And we'd giggle outside the car next to the Mississippi River, which I'd also been waiting a long time to see, ever since I learned that the river ran far away from Mississippi just like everybody else that knew what was good for them.

Six hundred miles to Saint Louis. A good nine-hour drive. Got to make that in a day 'cause ain't nobody got money to be spending on a hotel. Fine with me. Leave early, drive fast, take some snacks, let's go.

We left early one morning after Thanksgiving but before Christmas. And as the winter sun snuck west over our heads thinking it was really getting away with something—*I ain't going to Saint Louis with y'all!*—we rode into dusk, then night, then the wailing winds along the river, then the part of Saint Louis I'd bet my last dollar included an MLK Boulevard, then into the driveway of a lanky underfed house that tried to hide its shortcomings with a wide porch and a red awning.

Gone and knock, Tash, Granny said.

The image I have in my head is of the empty driver's seat, the car still running, Tashia's body shrouded by her thickest coat in the mean wind, now mixed with snow, softly lit by a single streetlight at the nearby corner. A light not strong enough to guide her path all the way to the front door of the house, where she stood and knocked and waited.

Now Debra know she need to come on, Granny muttered.

Tashia lingered at the door and knocked again. Looked out at us—at Granny, since when she looked I turned away. She used one hand to try to insulate her neck with her coat collar, and the other hand to knock again. *Hello?!*

I sandwiched my head between the front seats to get a better view.

Chile. Granny, again.

I eased back and stared out the window again, looking toward the empty sad far end of the street. Tashia kept standing at the door. Kept knocking. Granny kept watching her. I had seen enough. Stepped out of the car and let that cat-o'-nine-tails Saint Louis wind rip the decency off my face.

Tashia! Come on. It's time to go, shit.

I had never cursed in front of Granny. I don't think I had ever slammed a door, car or other. But right there and then I knew I could not only curse and slam doors but also knock down an old woman if she said a sideways word to me. Maybe she sensed that, or maybe she was too startled to say anything, or maybe she was cursing and slamming doors in her head as she rubbed her hands over and over in her lap.

Tashia was still at the door.

Natashia. Come on.

She peeled herself from the porch and retraced her path through the wind and snow. By the time she plopped down in the backseat I was already pulling out of the driveway and already certain—though I didn't say it aloud; nobody said anything—that I was going to drive through the night, stopping only for gas that Granny or Tashia would have to wake up and purchase, all those six hundred miles back to Dallas.

But I couldn't make the drive. Got so tired, just about twenty miles outside Saint Louis, that I couldn't keep my eyes open. Hate, sometimes, can be so heavy it even weighs your eyelids down.

Baby why don't you gone and pull off the road, Granny said, almost a whisper. *We can sleep a lil while. Get on up and finish it tomorrow.*

There was a Super 8 an exit or two ahead, on the other side of the overpass. No time to wait for Motel 6.

C'mon, Tash. Your brother'll stay in the car and we'll tell 'em we got two people.

I sat under the yellow glow of the Super 8 sign, wanting to go to sleep right there in the parking lot and wanting everybody else to die, starting with my mother.

Granny left Tashia in the heated motel hallway and came back to the car. *Get the bags, hon. Make sure it's locked, now.* She led me through the motel's back door. Held the door open while I dragged our bags into the small room. *Natash, me and you can climb up in this bed. Give your brother that other'n.*

One of them turned the lights out, yet as tired as I was I couldn't fall asleep. Grew a bit delirious (that's my story) and so texted Red, who hadn't heard from me in months aside from the message I'd sent a week or so earlier, telling him that we'd found my mother and were going to pick her up in Saint Louis.

She wasn't even there, Red. I fucking hate her.

He responded like he'd been waiting all day—*Don't say that. She's still your mom. Get some sleep.* I wonder if he knew how soothing that message was. A few moments after reading it, I finally fell asleep, fully clothed, splayed across the narrow stiff prickly mattress.

Granny woke me the next morning, lobby breakfast in hand, and said to no one in particular—*I'll do some drivin' today.*

And she did. All those six hundred miles, except the few I'd driven the night before, sometimes going ninety miles an hour, strangling the steering wheel with both hands unless she needed one to slide her glasses back up her nose. Granny brought us out of Saint Louis, past that slice of

Kansas, down through barren Oklahoma, and back into the same old crumbling driveway on Old Ox. She never asked a question on that ride, never said a mean word, never let out a tear or sigh or moan, just kept calling me and Tashia *hon* and *baby* all the way, and made us dinner when we walked in her house, and let us eat without saying anything to her or each other, not even *thank you*.

I've been watching Granny for a long time. Have known so many women like her—well, not *so* many, but enough. And as I've watched I've grown suspect of all that strength they show. Granny still has the scar from when she fell out of a tree as a little girl and split her upper lip; still has the picture of her baby Janet lying in that tiny coffin with the lace around her wrists; still has her dead husband's coats and some of his bills. And for all those years I was trying to move on, she still had her disappeared daughter's papers and children—children who had gone off on their own and had done about the best they could, but who were still children, even if she was the only one who knew it. So she carried them, too.

But one of these days, Granny and her kind might crack. They might pick up the last straw that must be right in front of their faces. And when they do, when all the Grannies have had enough, what is the world gonna do? Who's gonna carry the cross and the children and wipe the tears of the old women? Will you be ready? Will I?

I don't know why Granny and Tashia kept trying to find my mother— maybe that's what love looks like, or an appetite for abuse—and I know even less about how they succeeded in smoking her out of hiding. It seems to me that the social services woman was the linchpin, and that she became a diplomatic go-between because of some genuine desire to provide social services, some buckling under Tashia's persistence, and some respect for Granny's age. I'd also bet she was lured by that tone in

Granny's voice that conveys her desire for something and her refusal to beg. This is speculation.

What I do know is that a month or two after I walked down that red carpet on Signing Day to the cheers of all those strangers, I walked across Granny's faded mauve living room carpet to grab the phone from my sister and hear my mother's voice again.

Hey, Man!

Hey, Mama.

I could make up some dialogue to reenact the conversation, but the truth is that I wasn't listening to her, and everything I said was of the *I gotta go* variety. Either she said she would see me soon, or Tashia told me we'd see her soon, or I just gathered from the general shape of things that I'd see her soon, but in any event I did see her soon—after spring break but before graduation.

Granny, Tashia, and I drove out to Dallas-Fort Worth Airport and huddled together under the arrivals board waiting for an update on the most recent flight from Saint Louis. As we waited, I thought about how nice it would be for the plane to crash, and how nice it would also be if the plane hurried up and brought my mama. Then she appeared.

Big crinkly Sunkist hair. Wide gleaming Crest smile, one side tooth missing but not prominently. Face made up in the same way it had been in the last millennium, but with more foundation on the bridge of her nose to cover up a new scar. Ten stitches, if I counted right. All she had was the hair, the smile, the makeup, the nose scar, the clothes on her back, and a transparent plastic attaché bag, in which I believe I saw cigarettes (now Kool 100), a lighter, lipstick, and condoms.

Y'all! Ah! Ohh!

Same sounds she used to make, just louder, more jagged, and less in response to anything anybody had said or done. She reached out to hug me and held me for a terribly long time, maybe three seconds or so. After the hug, I looked at her and felt a tingling desire to slap—no, to *disfigure* her.

And after I disfigured her, I wanted her to grovel. To walk back from the airport, not ride in the car. To go without sleep and food and sit on a mat outside the house and chant *I'm sorry* from sunup to sundown. To let her throat parch with thirst and sorrow. To forget how to laugh and, instead, to cry and cry until crying lost all meaning and the tears dried up and her eyes were filled only with images of all the wrong she'd done. And then, only then, would she be allowed into the house, where she would stand in the corner not looking at anybody in the face but staring at the blank wall, seeing nothing but her mistakes. And she would forget how to speak, would lose all grasp of language except the words *I'm sorry*, which would not be words but would be who she was. Yes. She would become Apology and stay that way until I decided she could be a person again. Then, after a trial period, perhaps she could have a real name. And if she played her cards right she might get some respect. And then, sometime before she died, she might become my mother again, but only on the condition that she earn the title every day for the rest of her life.

Of course, none of this happened. Mama showed up at the airport, rode with us back home, moved into our house, sat at the table with me and Tashia for dinner, asked for a ride to the pharmacy to pick up her medication, said *Good morning* when she woke up, and bought new clothes for my graduation. After the ceremony, she demanded to be in all the pictures and spoke to everybody like she'd just seen them last week, and recounted stories about how she'd made me lunch and Tashia a birthday cake and told us both she loved us.

Almost as if we were producing a blaxploitation Fellini movie, everybody played right along and even offered their own special storyline to this grand delusion, including my father, who despite not coming to my graduation, despite likely having had a hand—though I'm not making an accusation!—in his wife's disappearance, offered not only to bring me a couple dollars as I headed off to college, but to rent a U-Haul trailer and drive me the 1,600 miles from Dallas to New Haven. Not just me, but Granny, Mama, Tashia, and Tashia's newborn baby. (I like that baby, now a girl, a great deal and will leave her out of this.) And for that entire, surprisingly pleasant journey, we pretended that we were not a group of people who had destroyed one another, but a family. Maybe there's no difference between the two.

But all along, from the driveway on Old Ox where aunts and cousins stood to wave us off, to the gates of Vanderbilt Hall where the tall pale man with sunken eyes stood to welcome me, I thought—or I think now that it would have been fitting to think then—of the song my forebears sang so long ago and so well that Roberta Flack decided to sing it, too:

> *I told Jesus, it'll be alright if you change my name*
> *I told Jesus, it'll be alright if you changed, changed my name*
> *I told Jesus be alright be alright be alright*
> *I told Jesus be alright if you change my name*
>
> *Then he told me, he said your father won't know you child, if I change*
> *your name*
> *Yes he told me, said your mother won't know you child, child if I change*
> *your name*
> *But I told Jesus, I said it would be alright, be alright, be alright*
> *If my father turns away now, and my mother turns away now*
> *Yes my brother, my baby sister, turn away, turn away*
> *I told Jesus be alright, if you change my name.*

An Interlude for My Friend

I had a dream about my friend Elijah, who took his life last year. A few or many years ago by the time you read this.

He was sitting in a booth at a diner. There was a small table in front of him, and a small chair on the other side of the table. The dream began with me standing, my hands on the back of the chair, facing Elijah. It was so good to see him.

Before I went to sleep, there was a question that wouldn't leave me alone: How should I tell what happened after I arrived at Yale? Elijah showed up in my dream to answer, which was a surprise since I had not seen him much before he died and not at all since. He had arrived at Yale a year after me, after his own journey from Saint Louis, also a mighty going-away. So maybe he showed up because he understood why I felt so sad. Why I wanted to apologize to all the kids who saw those posters of me plastered over every school in Dallas. *Look Who's Going to Yale! He Did It. You Can Too.* Or maybe he was bored on the other side and wanted to talk. I don't know.

I was about to sit down, but I blinked or something and the diner got so crowded that I couldn't pull the chair back. So I just stood there and leaned over the table so I could hear Elijah over the noise.

Man, you know. Elijah grinned and leaned back in his booth. *We did a lot of things that we wouldn't advise anybody we loved to do.*

I was just about to ask *What things, Elijah?* But I woke up. He kicked me out of the dream. Out of the diner, where he still might be sitting with that grin on his face. *Come on, Casey. You already know.* I did know. I do.

See, if you catch it from the right angle, a boy picking himself up by his bootstraps looks just like a suicide.

chapter ELEVEN

Do you want to be a loser? Do YOU *want to be a loser?? I mean. Do you want to not achieve your dreams? It's your call. Totally your call. Nobody else can control that other than you. The answer is no! Of course not!*

Look at the man on the stage. Lit from above. Pipe organ behind him. Names of fallen soldiers carved into the marble walls around him. A thousand boys and girls in the wooden seats before him. Four years from now, they will be back in the seats, ready to graduate. Tonight they're freshmen. This is their first week. Here from many corners of the world, carrying the dreams of those they left behind. Here to learn to lead, to rule, to prosper, to win.

Never eat alone.

That's what the man says. Yale has brought him to offer wisdom and a free book to its new sons and daughters. This is his message. Every meal is an opportunity to build a new relationship. To grow your network, which becomes your net worth. Say *hello.* Smile. Send a note. Get out of your room. Share your interests. Your passions. Your projects. Offer help. No, don't *offer* help—*help.* Contribute. Suggest. Put your money in the bank of people. Invest it. Watch it grow. Write a check on it someday. You are here to win. Win the people first. The rest will follow.

You don't yet know you will win fewer people than perhaps any fresh-man in the history of Yale College. So you listen to the man. You never eat alone.

There is Zoe Larson. Smiley blonde, sitting in the cavernous Com-mons dining hall with Chris Adams, a tiny basketball player from Jersey. Join them.

Yo, son! You and Zoe should meet. You're both from Dallas.

Cool. Where in Dallas are you from?

I'm from Richardson. What about you?

Ah, yeah I've heard of Richardson. I'm from Dallas, Dallas. Oak Cliff.

Oh, wow.

You're not sure whether eating in silence is the same as eating alone, but it feels like it. You bus your tray and leave. Your phone rings. It's Chris. Always answer phone calls.

Yo, son! You won't believe what she said when you left.

What she say?

My dude. She goes, "Oh my God. He's from the ghetto. It's a miracle he made it out alive. He must be in a gang." Son, I died laughing.

You laugh. Hang up. Never talk to Zoe again. But never eat alone.

Another day, another football practice ends. The practice fields are two miles from the main campus. Don't hop on the bus and sit by yourself. Catch a ride with somebody. An upperclassman, preferably. Oh, there's Jack Delaney. Good guy, Jack. Bet he looks just like his daddy, a boy from Yonkers who grew up to be a Houston oil executive.

Want a ride back to Commons, Casey?

Accepting gifts is a key to making friends.

Oh sure. Thanks a lot, Jack.

You ride through the outskirts of New Haven.

Dang, I never thought it'd be so messed up around Yale.

What do you mean?

Look at all these houses. All these poor people. That's crazy.

Ha. You know, it's all just a by-product of capitalism.

Huh?

That's the way it works, Casey. Everybody's not going to make it. Have to accept that.

Arrive at Commons. Eat with Jack. Ask Jack questions, like why he's racist.

I'm not racist. That's ridiculous. I have great friends who are black. And it's not racist to say that those people need to work hard just like I did.

Tell Jack that he didn't work hard, he just lived off his daddy's money. Yell at Jack. Stare at Jack while he yells at you. Feel the rest of the table stare at you. Bus your tray and leave.

You didn't have money for a computer, so a man who knows your daddy gave you one. Thank God for that man. And thank God for Mark Zuckerberg, who gave you Facebook before everybody else, since it's 2005 and you go to Yale. Make a Facebook group. Name: "Jack Really is a Bigot, Huh?" Invite everyone you know. Not many. Even fewer join. Never eat with the people who don't join. Running out of people now. Find *your* people.

Black Student Alliance at Yale. BSAY. Sounds like the right group. Afro-American Cultural Center. Sounds like the right place. Go there. Be on time for the meeting. Sit in the circle. Just like that one Narcotics Anonymous meeting you saw. Look around. Where's the lotion? There's the pizza. Get some pizza. Eat your pizza and listen to the senior in charge of the meeting.

So tonight we want to really unpack a big topic: What does blackness mean. Right?

You've been black a long time. Your family has been black. Most of the people you've known have been black. You know the words to "Lift Every Voice and Sing." Did you really need to go all the way to Yale to learn what it means to be black?

Try to understand. Thank God you signed up for the class Freedom and Identity in Black Cultures. Pay attention, even though the teacher sounds high.

This is an invocation of a people's subjugation and resistance under the hegemony of race and privilege. Right?

You don't know what this means. You wonder whether she does. You wonder why she and everybody else says *Right?* after every sentence. The teacher assigns a book, *Notes of a Native Son*. You didn't have money for books, so the school gave you some. Buy the book. There's a black man on the cover. Cool. James Baldwin. You've never heard of him. Let's check this out.

I was born in Harlem thirty-one years ago. I began plotting novels at about the time I learned to read. The story of my childhood is the usual bleak fantasy, and we can dismiss it with the restrained observation that I certainly would not consider living it again.

Got it. Poor black dude in a bad neighborhood with a sad family. Not much to see here. You listen in class with wonder. To your classmates, this book is a revelation. To you, it is old news. Didn't even get past the first page.

The next class session is still about Baldwin, but it's better. It's movie day. Instead of a big metal cart, Yale has a projector. You can watch the movie right on a screen on the wall. Don't even have to pull the screen down yourself. The teacher saunters in late, throwing lots of syllables around. She puts on the movie and leaves again. *The Price of the Ticket.* A man appears on the screen.

There are days—this is one of them—when you wonder . . . what your role is in this country and what your future is in it.

You have never wondered either of these things, but you wonder how this can be the same man from the book you didn't read. Book James Baldwin said he was from Harlem. You've been to Harlem once. Got picked up right on 125th Street, and since you didn't know how to get back to New

Haven from Harlem, you went to that man's house even though you didn't want to. And even though you snuck out in the middle of the night, you were there long enough to know that there ain't a single person in Harlem who sounds like the man in this movie who everybody says is the same James Baldwin from the book, from Harlem. And there ain't a single person on this campus that sounds like either Book James Baldwin or Movie James Baldwin. And, for that matter, there ain't a single person on this campus that sounds like *you*.

Maybe that's why nobody understands what you're saying.

You ask for directions to Science Hill. They laugh and say *Signs Heal??* *What's that?* You yell out a play at practice and the upperclassmen have to take off their helmets and call a timeout, they are so overcome with laughter. *Gerald! What the fuck are you saying, man? We gotta get a translator out here, Coach.* You laugh, too. Guess your voice does make you sound dumb. Fix it. Try to sound like them. Just try. Keep trying, it's only been a week. Your jaw hurts? Damn. Okay. Take a break.

Maybe you can't change how you talk yet, but do you have to dress like that?

Why are all your clothes so big? Double extra large? You're a medium, wet. And why do all the clothes match each other? Aww, and you have matching earmuffs, too? It's October! Why do you even have on earmuffs? That's cute. Are you a Yankees fan? No? Well why do you wear those Yankees caps? Do you need boxes for all those shoes? Air Jordans, huh. Doesn't matter, they're just shoes, man.

You would get new clothes if you didn't like these so much. You would get new clothes if you had money. You would buy a coat if you had money. You would buy a plane ticket home if you had money. No you wouldn't. You can't go back home like that. Remember what those teachers at SOC said before you left?

There's no way that boy's gonna graduate from Yale. He's a crack baby. He'll be home before the end of the first semester.

I know, I know. You technically were *not* a crack baby. You were very fat and very healthy, from what I hear. And you *will* be home before the end of the first semester, but just for a holiday. Just to tell your people how great life is at Yale. Just to laugh when they say you sound white now. Just to laugh when Granny says your 98 in Italian class is just two points from 100, but you'll get there next time. Just to laugh when your aunties say they want a Yale sweater when you come back home. You would bring them one if you had money. You would bring them one if you didn't need all the Yale sweaters yourself.

You wear the Yale sweater everywhere you go. You wear a Yale shirt under it. You wear Yale sweats if you don't need real pants on. You wear Yale shorts when it's warm outside. You wear a Yale lanyard around your neck at all times. You put your keys on a Yale keychain that hangs from the lanyard. You put your Yale ID next to your keys. You show your Yale ID to the police instead of your driver's license. You show your Yale ID to the dining hall worker who knows you don't live in Branford College, where the sustainable macaroni and cheese is served. You show your Yale ID to the Yale student who doesn't believe you go to Yale. You wear a blue fitted cap with a big Yale *Y* on it to let everybody know you go to Yale.

You stand on the corner of Tower Parkway and Dixwell Avenue, wearing your Yale cap and Yale sweater. The New Haven Police Department paddy wagon pulls up to the red light in front of you. There are people in the paddy wagon. Prisoners. Watching you. Laughing. One yells at you:

Nigga, you ain't going to Yale! Yo' ass going to jail, nigga!

It's the first time somebody has said *nigga* to you since you arrived. Might be the first time somebody told the truth, too. You appreciate it, in a way. Maybe this *is* jail. You should act like it.

You go to football practice and start a fight with two big boys from some hick town in Massachusetts. The Downing twins, Willy and Tommy. They're prize recruits. Look like they're on steroids. Fuck 'em. Fight 'em.

You try to fight Willy. Tommy joins in. They double-team you. Bitches. The fight's a draw but you won some respect. If not respect, then something close. Fear. *That kid is crazy*, they say.

You go to the only class you do well in, English. The teacher, Professor Ehrgood, is strange. Every time he's about to speak, he stares at the ceiling and rubs his fingers together and taps his lips like he's tasting rich wine or the flesh of a child. He likes you. Well, he may not like you, since you laughed out loud in class when another student said the word *philosophize*. He thought you were being disrespectful. You thought the other student was being funny. You didn't know *philosophize* was a word. You make up for this mistake with your own words.

You really can write, Casey. Overwrite sometimes, but we'll work on that.

You write about the person you've been writing about since Ms. Davis's class: Martin Luther King, Jr. You're also supposed to write about Malcolm X and Socrates and what they all have to do with one another. But Malcolm X is a Muslim and Socrates is a white man and you've never written about either of those, so you stick with what you know. You write about Martin and his letter from jail. It inspires you to write your own letter. On Facebook, of course.

10 Things I Hate about Yale and New Haven

You forget most of the things but you remember one that warned *I'll scream if I meet another fake-ass whack-ass black person* and another that said something to the effect of *I'd rather be a dead rotting cow in a ditch in Oklahoma than to have to live in Connecticut.* The letter works. Almost everybody hears about it. Even fewer people talk to you now. One of the few, Daniel, is a lot like you, except that he's from Gary, Indiana, and his parents are lawyers, and his sister went to Yale. But he sounds like a version of you that could be from Gary, Indiana. And he plays football. And he thought the BSAY meeting was a waste of time, too. And he lives across the hall. He comes to discuss your letter.

Casey, you should chill out, man. Maybe if you talked to people, you wouldn't have so many problems.

Fuck you, Daniel.

You don't talk to Daniel anymore. In part, because it's spring and he is pledging a fraternity: Omega Psi Phi, like his brother and father, and like the coaches at SOC. Everybody on the football team—everybody you know—is pledging a fraternity, either Delta Kappa Epsilon or Zeta Psi. You've never heard of either. Thank God you know one upperclassman who is a brother of Kappa Alpha Psi, a Nupe, like lots of boys where you're from. You don't know this boy is about to drop out of Yale, so you listen to his advice. You go to an interest meeting. You meet the other brothers. There's one who is tall and cute and crazy-looking. Wouldn't be bad to spend some time with him. Ev—that's his name. *Hey, Ev.*

Ev tells you to show up at a certain house on a certain day at a certain time. You do what Ev says. Two other boys are there to pledge with you. They go to University of Bridgeport. Nice boys. A little slow, it seems. But they'll be your brothers soon.

Ev blindfolds you. You let him. Ev tells you to eat what he puts in your mouth. You do it. It's an onion. Ev insults you. You take it. End of set. Come back tomorrow.

Tomorrow: Ev makes you stand with your back against a wall. You stand there. Ev blindfolds you again. Ev tells you to hold your arms out straight. Ev tells the boy from Bridgeport to spell a word. He can't. Ev strikes your chest with the palms of his hands. Ev tells the boy to spell something else. He spells it wrong. Ev strikes you again. Ev asks the boy a question. The boy doesn't know the answer. Ev strikes you again. Again. Again. Ev sees a few tears fall from your eyes, beneath the blindfold. Ev asks you if you can't handle it. If you don't want it. You tell Ev that you do want it and you can handle it. The Bridgeport boy can't spell to save your life. Your chest is swelling. Taking the shape of Ev's palms. He stops. Tells you that you did a good job. Drives you home. You realize that you could handle it and you did want it, but if you're going to let Ev break you, he's got to give you a lot more than some Greek letters and a brother who can't spell. You quit the next day.

You've got to stop this stuff. Stop letting Ev hit you for somebody else's mistake. Stop laughing at things you don't understand. Stop talking so fast and get that mush out your mouth. Stop buying those snacks you're about to run out of money. Stop eating the snacks in your dorm room alone. Stop wearing your hat when you meet Doris Archer.

First of all, Casey, take your hat off. Thank you.

You've made it to the last month of school, and Coach Reno has sent you to a new academic advisor—the best one, the university president's chief aide, the holder of three Harvard degrees, the wearer of a crisp brunette bob and a Yale football necklace. Doris Archer. Don't call her Doris. Call her Dean or Master. She's not here to be your friend, so take off your fitted when you walk in her office.

Do you wear those things around campus?

Yes, ma'am.

Oh, no, Casey. It's just so . . . stereotypical, you know? You're at Yale now. You don't have to do that anymore.

You want to tell her she's a racist. You want to cry. You want to go home and stay there. But you can't do that. This is jail—act like it. *Change.* At least she gave you some instruction. At least your words still work and Professor Ehrgood gave you an A in English. At least Coach Reno gave you a shot at a starting spot on the varsity in the fall. At least Yale gave you money to fly home for the summer. Hurry up and go. Rest. You have three more years to survive.

chapter **TWELVE**

Time's up. You have one night to survive.

Was it a summer night? I believe so. Fall seems too early, since if it had been Thanksgiving break of my freshman year, I would not have dreaded going back to Yale as much as I did or been as eager to come back home as I was. It could not have been winter, if only because I don't see a Christmas tree when I recall that night and I know how much those trees meant to my sister. To us both. And since I have told the story of this night many times as being a *winter* night, then I also have to accept that I have not told the truth. This does not surprise me. I wonder, though, whether I lied because I did not remember or because it was convenient to do so. I don't know. All I know is that it happened.

I know that it happened at night, after winter 2005 but before fall 2006 (we lived in a different house by then), and that my niece, born July 2005, was old enough to sit up on her own but not old enough to walk. So she sat there—or she sits there in my memory—on the carpet, a few feet away from her mother and my mother and me. She was the only one not tied up. Who would tie up a baby, anyway? Especially in the summer.

She was so sleepy. Maybe that's why they didn't tie her up, because she was still half-asleep or more. She had been fully asleep just a few minutes earlier. Her mother had been asleep next to her in bed. My mother had been asleep in a room on the other end of the short hallway. I had been awake, sitting at the kitchen table, writing a speech that I was to give the next day. Then I heard a knock at the front door.

It wasn't a knock, really, although I've always opened the story with a knock at the door. It's just that I can't describe the sound, since I felt it more than I heard it. It felt like that instant when lightning cracks the trunk of a tree and splits it in two and leaves all that smoke behind. Never seen that? Neither have I. And I had never heard whatever sound that was at the door, and hope you never hear it, either, because if you do, somebody is likely about to try to kill you.

I felt it again. Stood up from the table, almost as a reflex. I wanted to get away from the sound. I wanted to sneak across the living room, past the sound at the front door, and into my room, where I was going to hide. The walk couldn't have been more than thirty feet—maybe twelve feet from the kitchen table to the front door, then about eighteen more from the front door to my room—but it seemed like a long walk. A long hard walk because I felt real heavy all of a sudden, like a few thousand screams were trapped in my belly, bursting out one after the other. The screams were so loud that I was completely silent as I tried to make that thirty-foot walk, starting with a twelve-foot tiptoe past the front door, if the door would do me a big favor and hold on.

The door didn't hold. I was tiptoeing past the door when it gave up, right when I needed it most, gave up like a man falling backward off a cliff. Then I saw them—the two men, more like two big orbs of darkness, coming over the place where the door had stood, coming after me, with their arms pointed at me, with something in their hands, death in their hands, trying to catch me, trying to give death to me. If you joined me in my dreams, you could see them much better. They're still there. Still chasing me there. They catch me sometimes.

I ran like I knew how to run, to my room, and slammed the door behind me, and stood with my back against the door, silent, hiding, thinking, hoping, fooling myself that if I was quiet they would leave me alone. There were two women and one infant in the house, asleep, and I did not try to save them. It did not occur to me to save them, or to alert them, or to think about them at all. My gut instinct was to run and hide and save myself. Some people have the instincts of heroes. They fight back. They save others. They protect the women and children. They die. Some people have the instincts of cowards. They run. They hide. They stay silent. They also die. Some people are asleep and don't have the luxury of instincts or choices. They die, too. There is no moral.

Come the fuck out before I shoot your bitch ass.

That's what the man said to me from the other side of my bedroom door. Did he push the door or did I move voluntarily? I don't know. And I don't know what he looked like because I clenched my eyes shut and showed him my clenched eyes so that he would know that I had not seen him, so that he might show the blind coward some mercy. He pushed me to the floor anyway. Pushed my head against the carpet and made the skin come off my cheek. That was unnecessary. I was going down willingly. He put his knee to my back, I think. I know that my back felt heavy and I couldn't move, so I figure it was his knee, which was also unnecessary because I was not trying to run away. Then I heard that tape. It was so loud, must have been duct tape, and he pulled my arms behind my back and wrapped all that wide thick tape around my wrists. I felt that this, too, was unnecessary, because my arms had been limp and I hadn't been moving my hands and that tape hurt. Right below the crown of my head, close to my right ear, since my left was against the floor, I felt a heavy metal something—his gun, I guess, since I couldn't see it myself and now it's been so long that I can't be sure he held his gun to my head at all.

Where's the fucking money?!? his colleague kept yelling.

I could hear my mother next to me—*What?*—biting off her *t*s like always. I could hear my sister—*What are you talking about?* I could hear the baby crying softly—*Mama*—or maybe that's just what I would have said if I had been her. I didn't say anything. I didn't cry. I just lay there silent, all those screams trapped in my belly, running away like a paraplegic. I opened my eyes and scanned the room for the final time. I saw my mother there, tied up. And the baby, old enough to sit alone but not to walk away. And my sister. I rested my gaze on her.

I closed my eyes to pray. It had been a good while since I'd talked to God. For most of my life I had not really *talked* to him but beseeched him, begged him for stuff, blamed him for stuff, tried to make him explain everything to me. But for the first time, I didn't go to God desperately. Didn't have my hat in my hand. We had our first honest chat, me and God, two old friends sitting on the porch on a summer afternoon sipping some lemonade before they take a ride. *You ready to go? Yep, I'm ready.* That was the gist of our conversation. I meant it. It's so strange how we spend so much of our lives running from death, turning into heroes and cowards because of it, giving death grand dimensions with the stories we tell about it. But death comes and it has no real meaning and, even still, it feels simple and right. Feels so much better than most of life. At least, it did that night.

I wanted to smile. Or I think, now, that I should have smiled. There was something so beautiful about it all. Something silly about being tied up like a hog on the floor, something *just* about the baby seeing death so early, and my mother seeing what it's like to lose somebody, and my sister seeing her little brother's murder, since she was the one who caused it. Yes, I should have flashed a big grin at my sister, to remember me by.

She could remember me when she thought of her child, of her child's father, whom she loved despite his illegal line of work (for which he's already paid his debt to society, to the extent that he owed society anything), loved enough to hide his money, enough to let those men kill us all before she told them where the money was, enough to offer her baby brother as a sacrifice. And maybe I owed her that much. She had given up so much of life for me that perhaps she deserved mine in return. I don't believe that at all, though it's possible.

But then she didn't take it.

The man holding me down suddenly yelled to his colleague—*C'mon, nigga!*—and removed his knee from my back, and his colleague dropped whatever he was looking under, and they both ran out of the house. I don't know if they found the money.

I lay there, still tied up, unable or unwilling to move. Mama scooted across the floor and untaped my wrists and helped me up. She was standing closest to the space where the door once stood, when two police officers came through. I figure someone in the neighborhood phoned them. In my memory, it seems that the officers tossed a lot of questions in the air and just waited to see if somebody would catch them. Nobody did, so they left without offering much help.

And once they left, my mother did the lecturing, if you can believe it. *Natashia! What?! Why would you do this? You need to get it together, girl!* And just like the good old days, I took my mother's side.

Leave her alone, Mama! If she wanna get killed behind some nigga, let her!

We picked the door up off the floor and put it back in its space. My sister and mother and the baby went back to bed. I sat back down at the kitchen table to finish the speech I had been writing—not exactly like nothing ever happened, but close enough for my sister to never say *I'm sorry*, for me to never ask *why?*, for us to never even talk about it with each other, ever.

I should have said something, though, even if it was just the only honest thing I had to say then or now about that night. *Dang, Tashia. That hurt.*

Not the death part. Not being burst upon or thrown to the floor or tied up or cursed or knelt into or threatened or embarrassed. All that was pretty bad, but I won't lie and say it was the worst thing to ever happen to me. Nor was it the best, though I decided to spin that story many years later—said that facing death had made me a nobler person, a person with a purpose and without fear, ready to give his life for Causes and to Others. But none of that is true, either. I did not *face death*—nobody has ever looked Death in the face. Surely not me. My eyes were closed.

All I know, or what I believe, is that Death itself matters much less than the terms on which death is offered, the circumstances by which death comes. What those terms, those circumstances, do to us. And so I often wonder whether actually dying would have been better than lying in the presence of death on account of my sister. She was the only proof I had and needed that there was always a place in the world where I was safe, where things would be okay, a place that I could always hide behind or stand on, always believe in—even if that place was not a place at all, but a person.

I miss that place. Don't know what else to tell you.

PART THREE

And the earth was without form, and void; and darkness was upon the face of the deep.

Genesis 1:2

chapter **THIRTEEN**

I should say—or maybe I shouldn't, but I will—that I do not recommend this life to anyone. Not that mine is worse than any other, just that it is the only life I know well enough to speak on with some authority and so I say: *Don't do it.* That is also what I would have told my mother and my father when they got the idea of me in the first place but, of course, no one asked for my opinion (or yours, as you are here with me). Now the milk is spilled and we can cry over it—we *should* cry over it—but we can also find some use for all that milk down on our floor.

If, for example, you find yourself in a dark confusing period of history, *when the gods have ceased to be and the Christ has not yet come and man stands alone,* you will have some sense of how things fall apart and a dim view as to how they might be put back together. You will know that it is hard to draw a clear line between this falling-apart and that putting-together; impossible to stop the one or to prophesy the other. You will know, when you look back on the other times you stood alone, that the question is not whether you are alone but whether you are standing. You do need a place to stand. At least I did. And it struck me not long after I got up off my sister's floor that Yale was as good a standing place as any other, so I went back for my second year with greater interest if not hope, and I signed up for Professor Ehrgood's sophomore English class because: *In the beginning was the Word and the Word was with God, and the Word was God. In him was life; and the life was the light of men. And the light shineth in darkness; and the darkness comprehended it not.*

By which John meant, perhaps, that we have to say *something* because the words make us feel less alone, and the words help us tell the difference between standing and not, and the words help to guide the first few steps from our place in the dark.

It's plausible.

What's that?

It's "plausible." That's what you mean, Casey. Not "feasible."

Oh.

Ehrgood hovered around the oval oak table that sat sixteen students and filled most of the small classroom, made to feel smaller by the walls: one lined with narrow windows that did not open, the other three covered with palimpsestic chalkboards. In front of the chalkboard closest to my seat, Ehrgood stood. He stretched to write the two words and slashed a line between.

Feasible means that something can be done, he explained. *A plan is feasible. Plausible, which is what you intend to say, means that something is, at least on the surface—and it could only be so on the surface, understand—reasonable. Believable. You don't say an argument or an idea or a theory can be done. You say it could be true, even if it's not clear that it is true. That's plausible. Plausible.*

Ever since I'd learned *feasible*—apparently I had not learned it, after all—the word had been my favorite weapon. I brandished it to feign intelligence. I lobbed it as a flash bang to escape overwhelming ideas. When I felt petty, I used the word to maim a self-assured classmate who would be insulted if I said that his argument was only *feasible*, not *true*. Ehrgood was not fooled. He faced me now, massaging chalk residue between his thumb and forefinger, blinking.

Okay. Try again.

I think what you say is plaus—

No no no.

He scurried to a barren chalkboard and scrawled: *I THINK*. Drew an X through the phrase.

I know you think it. You wouldn't say it if you didn't think it. Try again.

Clearly, it's plaus—

Ah. Too strong.

On the same chalkboard, Ehrgood wrote *clearly* and, next to it, *obviously*. Drew an X through each.

Now. If it were clear. If it were obvious. You would not have to tell me. I would already know. Everyone would already know.

His face—at least the mouth and cheeks and corners of his eyes—held the early signs of a snicker, of joy, as if somewhere inside him, the right word, the precise phrase, led to ejaculation (another word that he would hate because it ended in -*ion*). He fluttered his hand at me without saying the *go on* that the flutter implied.

It's plausible.

Yes. Exactly. Good.

Ehrgood hardly ever said *great*, rarely said words like *amazing*, and never, as far as I can remember, said *perfect*. To him, confusing something that was *feasible* with something that was *plausible*, something that was *good* with something that was *great*, was damn near as bad and just as dangerous as setting out for spice in Asia but, instead, landing in the *new world* (another misnomer). And with so much lost language all over the place, he could not imagine anything being *perfect*.

Do you understand?

Ehrgood again, later in the semester, opened class with this question. He had assigned a text by the German philosopher Jürgen Habermas and now he stood, arms outstretched—chalk in one hand and Habermas (the text, not the man) in the other—asking a student if she understood. The classroom was small enough to hear a low voice, an uneven chair, a giggle at the word *philosophize*, but Ehrgood kept sliding toward the girl, leaning his head at an angle that drew a sandy tuft of hair down over his brow.

What's that? I can't—I can't hear you.

I can't tell you what the girl said, but I'm willing to bet my rent check that Ehrgood had already stopped listening.

When you are unsure—he slid back toward the chalkboard, chalk-hand and Habermas-hand now clasped at his chest—*you get quiet. Psst psst psst . . . umm . . . psst psst. The longer you speak, the more unsure you become. By the end of your point, you have lost all faith. And worse—and worse—we have lost all faith in you.*

He blinked and smiled and took a brief glance at the ceiling.

Don't do that. Don't do that. When you are unsure, speak louder. Sit up straight. Look into our eyes and say it. Whatever it is—SAY IT. Okay? Yes. Now. Do you understand?

He asked the girl again. He went around the table and asked each of us. For the first time since I arrived in New Haven, I was not the only one who did not understand.

Of course you don't understand. Of course!

He wafted around the oak table reading a passage of Habermas in a tone that made you wonder whether, at some point years ago, Habermas had said a sideways word about Ehrgood's mother. He laid Habermas to rest on the table.

You have to know that if you don't understand, it is the author's fault. Not yours. It's not your fault.

This is not altogether true. It is helpful to believe, though, when there are many things you do not seem to understand and you have waited many years to point some fingers. My wait was over now that I had learned this lesson, taught to all the boys and girls who, for three centuries, had come to Yale and been informed that we were in these halls to learn to *think* (not *do*), to think like this: like something more than simple men and women. Like gods? Were we—was *I* to be the god that was the word and life and light of men? The light that shineth in the darkness though the darkness comprehended it not?

Ah, no. I was the darkness.

But for once! Somebody gave the Darkness a chance to do it his way: to choose the words, to say what could be done and believed, to walk his path without the light breathing down his neck. Ehrgood did with my mind what Coach Walton had once done with my body—and this new instruction, just like the last, carried me a long way from where I started, right up till I realized that I'd left myself behind. Hold my hand . . . I'll show you.

chapter FOURTEEN

No, really. Hold my right hand. It is broken.

I did not know that it was broken, at first. I knew that it was the third quarter of the ninth game of the 2006 Yale football season, that this game was our second-to-last chance to clinch the Ivy League championship, and that this championship would vindicate the band of boys, myself included, who had staged a coup (I suppose you could call it a *violent* one) over the past year, intent to overthrow our leaders and make this team our own. Not that they resisted much.

The coup began in Philadelphia, on a dark doomed cold wet Franklin Field, the oldest football stadium in the country, 22 October 2005, during a game against the University of Pennsylvania Quakers. I won't bore us both with too many technicalities, because a game is simply the sum of one hundred or so plays, with eleven boys from each team on the field at a time, each with one primary job—quarterbacks, to throw; wide receivers, to catch; cornerbacks, to stop the wide receivers; etc. etc.—along with a few support jobs, mainly blocking and tackling. All these jobs are designed to help the job of the offense (to score points) or the job of the defense (to prevent points from being scored). The offense and defense support the job of the team (to win). And all this, even in a small silly way, supports

The Job that humankind has always wanted more than any other: to live forever. And if you know this, you can boil down the many zigs and zags to a simple human drama on the field.

That is all we had to do, we twelve freshmen who had been invited to travel with the varsity to Philadelphia. A dozen eighteen-year-olds from many nooks of America, most of whom had no business at Yale and who, knowing this, had no delusions about our intellects yet had enough sense to know that nobody on the field for Yale was very good at their job(s). Didn't take a Yale degree to know what an ass-kicking looked like.

By the end of the first half, our offense, led by the team captain, a future Dallas Cowboys quarterback, had negative-six yards. And our defense, anchored by the two boys, now seniors, who had hosted me on my recruiting visit, had given up almost thirty points. We twelve stood on the sidelines in the apocalyptic gloom, the oversized stands of Franklin Field nearly empty yet offering, thanks to the rain bouncing off aluminum bleachers, more noise than any crowd would. Under his breath, one of the twelve put the scene in words both typical for the sport and inappropriate: *Goddamn we're getting raped out there.* The worst was yet to come, at halftime.

One of the senior leaders, a loud man-child from Manhattan who always taunted underclassmen and preened in practice and had (I heard) once been a great player, suffered from some condition that made him weak and fainty during games—so much so that he often needed an emergency IV to stay alive enough to run up and down the field. I would call this condition *being out of shape,* but the doctors felt it was more serious.

Shocker—this was his nickname, likely self-styled; he wore number 1, which he passed to me when he graduated (we really did and still do like each other, I just have to tell this story)—had given such a valiant non-effort that his health was in grave danger by halftime. His long hair was strewn down his back and over his face and dripped water—rain and sweat—over his uniform and down his arms, at least one of which was already hooked up to an IV. As the team entered the locker room, we freshmen huddled in a corner, staring out at our leaders hunched over on rows of old wooden benches, the screaming coaches kneeling before them. Beyond this, we saw, in the opposite back corner of the room, a naked body in a cloud of steam. It was Shocker, taking a shower. And out from the mist of that shower-tomb, we heard his voice crying out: *Don't give up, fellas! Don't give up!* as he shampooed his hair.

The second half was only less disastrous for Yale because Penn removed their starters, then their backups. Only then did our future Dallas Cowboy score a touchdown, against the third-string Quaker defense. When it was all over, we showered in silence and processed to the freshman bus, which trailed the two upperclassman corteges up I-95 back to New Haven. By the third hour of that sad ride, we had decided to call a meeting the next day: a freshmen-only meeting, a rare event if only because freshmen hardly ever have anything important to talk about.

Word spread throughout the night and early Sunday morning, from the twelve to the rest of our class of thirty, which would become notable not only for its wins but also for the fact that not a single member quit the team over four years, perhaps out of fear. After the Sunday morning workout we huddled in the varsity film room and waited for Grant McKay to close the door in the faces of the upperclassmen, who had been walking by, peering in at us, confused and offended by such a blatant violation of social mores. Grant was one of the larger of us, six feet, three inches or so, maybe 250 pounds, with a head the shape of the old G.I. Joes and the personality of many boys I'd come to know at Yale who wanted deep down to be president, but would likely peak at, say, governor of Maine.

I know some of you weren't there yesterday, but we decided to call a meeting of our class because these guys—he pointed out to the hallway at the upperclassmen's shadows—*suck. It was embarrassing to be a part of what happened at Penn.*

Tommy Downing—who, had he not be born in New England with a football in his hand from an early age, could have easily been a terrorist or any number of other things that require blind faith in a simple cause and a deep hunger for physical violence—could not wait for Grant's peroration, so he stood up. The room fell silent. I'd like to say there was spit foaming around Tommy's mouth, but that's too dramatic and probably not true, although I did in years to come see this foaming business a few times.

This has gotta fucking change, fellas. Starting today. Fuck these guys. Yesterday—never again. Never a-fucking-gain.

Tommy didn't speak for much longer, and his portfolio of words quickly pared down to *fuck*. It was more than enough. We who had been there knew. And those who had not been could feel the shift: some collective trauma had transformed the collective itself, had created, within a team of one hundred twenty people, a new team yet unborn—a *we* to come.

We struck in the spring of 2006, when the current class of juniors had all but assumed their roles as senior leaders. They bossed us freshmen around, chose the best jersey numbers, stood at the head of lines, tried to negotiate a hard and bitter peace with the coaches. The leader among these leaders was a pretty Californian who, even after a three-hour game, might not have a single hair out of place. He raised a grave concern a week or two into spring training, via an email that I've lost but still remember, more or less:

Fellas,

We are here to be student-athletes, but the current spring morning workout regimen makes it hard for many of us to be good students at all. We leave morning practice so exhausted that the rest of the day is a wash. And with the cold weather, guys are getting hurt more often, which means we will be coming into next season still trying to recover. Many of the rising seniors have

discussed this and agree that we should talk to the coaches about
lowering the intensity, which will be better for everyone. Let me
know if you have any thoughts before I talk to Coach.

—DB

I'm almost sure none of us freshmen responded. Each of us, except perhaps Tommy, hated waking up at six a.m., hated the nauseating wind sprints, the pneumonial cold. But more than this, we hated the upperclassmen—not for who they were but for what they symbolized: weakness, defeat, yesterday. They wanted less intensity. We gave them more.

We showed up every morning and outran them. Out-hit them. Out-taunted them. Out-led them, too, since we followed one another's orders before we yielded to theirs. And as the mornings summed to the final spring tally, the team was, in spirit if not in fact, *our* team—not least because seven of us had earned starting jobs going into our sophomore season. And what a season it had been.

After falling to the University of San Diego in the opener, we had not lost again. Destiny and dumb luck drove us on from one game to the next, all the way to this second Saturday in November, the ninth game of the 2006 Yale football season, fifteen minutes away from our seventh win in a row and an Ivy League championship and history. If only we could beat Princeton.

We had reached the holy moment that comes in some games, when you stand on the field and spin around to look out and up at fifty, sixty thousand bodies smashed together in the stands—when what was once a dean, a senator, a dining hall worker, your mother, is now a blot in a great sea of blues and tweeds and fur and orange or crimson. When the noise is so loud and varied that the thousands of voices become one voice, and the cold wind blows across from a sliver of the North Atlantic to make the flags atop the stadium all wave in one direction, and the forty practices and hundred hours of film and thousand plays have turned eleven boys into one body that looks at itself in the mirror and asks *What am I about to do?* And knows. And knows. In the midst of all the chaos comes a moment when it is still and quiet down on the field. We had reached that moment in this game against Princeton. But we were tired. And we knew—or at least I feared—that we were about to lose.

The Yale defense, half of us sophomore leaders of the coup, was pinned in the northwest end of the Yale Bowl field. Princeton had just scored a touchdown to almost close a deficit that had been so large earlier in the day that even the insufferable Princeton band had hushed for a while. Now all that was left was a short kick to add on an extra point—a play, like some events in life, that is so routine, so dull, that you notice the smallest difference with the kind of shock reserved for mass atrocities.

From my position on the right edge of the defense, I had the best view to watch the play unfold: ball snapped from center, caught by a small Princeton player kneeling on the ground to hold it for the kicker. I loafed from my edge toward this boy. Then I saw it: his eyes bulged, as if a mug of scalding coffee had just slipped out of his hands. Instead of holding the ball for the kicker, this selfish bastard kept it for himself. Shot up from his knees and started running. *Shit.* I got my ass low and turned my loaf into a sprint just as he tried to scamper around me into the end zone. We crashed into each other, my arms wrapped around him, my hand between his back and the tall muddy grass. We fell. The thousands of Princeton blots in the stands shut up. The blots in blue let out a wail. Princeton 20, Yale 28.

We eleven Yale defenders fled the field, accepting hind and helmet slaps, searching for water and a seat on the bench. I found both, and looked down at the hand on my right thigh. I felt it then: not pain, but curiosity. Tried to jam the thumb into the socket. Turns out, thumbs don't have sockets. Coach Reno came yelling for the defense to go back on the field, so I rushed to present my hand to one of the trainers, who wrapped tape around it like a mummy paw and made the thumb keep still. This worked for a few plays, but I eventually just let the whole arm dangle at my side. It surprised me—how personal the pain felt, how it turned my thoughts and feelings and words into *wow*. Ecstasy . . . Maybe that's what it was.

While I winced on the field and downed aspirin on the bench, Princeton scored points: 34 to our 31, in the end. Tens of thousands of Yale fans, still stunned by the day's reversal, emptied the Bowl slowly. Many men and more than a couple children walked through the tunnels to their cars and looked back over their shoulders every few steps, back down at the field. Some of them felt, even if they did not admit, that their Yale men had a better chance of winning this already finished game than beating Harvard the following Saturday in Cambridge. It wasn't that the Harvard team was that good; inferiority complexes often produce this kind of irrational pre-doom. This pre-doom was now on the minds of these men as they walked through the tunnels to their cars. It was on the minds of many of the players, who hid in the showers for a long time. And it was on the mind of the team doctor, himself a former Yale football captain, when he looked at an X-ray of my right hand.

Well, Casey. He sighed. *It doesn't look too good.*

He snapped the X-ray into a light box outside the locker room. Used his pen to show the first metacarpal floating alone, ligaments shredded in the void.

We're gonna send you to a specialist on Monday. But I'll warn you now . . . I'm not sure you're gonna be able to play next week.

I would have cried if I had not then felt a strange relief.

On Monday morning, I walked up Science Hill to the campus hospital, my right hand in a make-do cast. Coach Reno met me there and stood next to the exam table like I imagine parents do when they go to the doctor with their sons. The specialist was an old man who was said to have invented thumb surgery or something. He had his own light box and snapped my X-rays into it, squinting at the image for a moment before a chuckle snuck out of his closed mouth. He shook his head and turned to me and Coach Reno.

See this thumb? The bone is broken off. Your ligaments are all torn. You need to be in surgery right now. Any delay could cause irreparable damage, I'm afraid.

A day passed, it seemed.

We got a big game next week though, sir. Harvard. For the championship.

Ha! Well you won't be able to play with pins in your hand. It's impossible.

The room was silent.

We really need you, Case.

If Coach Reno said much more than this, I don't remember. It was all I needed to hear. And maybe it was all the doctor needed to hear, because he suddenly specialized in things that seemed impossible.

Would you like for me to give you something that will calm you down and make you play like a champion?

That's what he asked. Not this doctor but the man who found my father right before the 1977 Orange Bowl. You've got the basic facts—Daddy was a sophomore . . . twenty years old . . . had been sidelined with a broken back for the last four games . . . Woody calls him off the bench . . . Comeback, legend, etc. etc. But what you do not know, what I did not know until recently, is that prior to that call from the bench, Woody had called Daddy into his office as the team prepared to face the University of Colorado.

Roderic, we need you.

And before the game, when meeting Woody's need still seemed too hard a task, an Ohio State alumnus showed up with an envelope for my father. Inside, Daddy found cocaine. He had never tried it. He would not play again without it. And when he was done playing he still needed it, and when he couldn't afford it, there were cheaper substitutes, and . . . you know the rest of the story.

He wrote of that 1977 day—

The events of the next few hours are clear and cloudy at the same time. I remember the bus ride to the stadium, the pre-game taping, Woody's pep talk, things I had come to know so well, but this time everything was different. Everything seemed magnified out of proportion to reality. I felt like I was watching some kind of drama from the outside, as if I was there, but I wasn't really there.

He was there, as we know—present enough to bring the Buckeyes back and to be named Most Valuable Player and to receive two mementos: that scarlet felt banner that hung in the living room of our Columbus apartment, and a heavy gold ring with an amber stone and his name engraved on the side. Coach Reno handed me a similar ring during a ceremony at Payne Whitney Gym, after we beat Harvard to win the 2006 Ivy League championship.

But instead of offering me cocaine—which, if I had known as little as my daddy had known, I might have taken to step on that field in Cambridge—the surgeon and our team doctor offered to deaden the nerves in my hand so that I could endure a full game.

It's still gonna hurt like hell, Casey. But once we're done with the injections, we'll put your hand in a big cast and give you as much Tylenol as we can to help you make it through.

I remember the bus ride to Harvard Stadium, the pregame taping, Coach Reno's pep talk, things I had come to know so well. But aside from one good play I made at the beginning of the game, the rest of the day is lost to me. So the ring I have—silver with a blue stone *Y* and my name engraved on the side—helps me to remember what I did.

It also replaced my daddy's ring, which he had given to me just after he got it back. For not long after Woody handed him that Orange Bowl ring, Daddy pawned it. A pharmacist bought it in a Dallas pawnshop around 1980 and held on to it for nearly twenty-five years, until he died. The man's widow found the ring in his personal effects and asked her pastor to track down its rightful owner, who welcomed the pastor (and the *Dallas Morning News*, of course) to his Dallas County office for a reunion ceremony, in 2002.

As the *News* put it:

The return of the ring, representing [Rod Gerald's] greatest gridiron moment, seems an irresistible symbol of renewal and redemption, of a life coming full circle, bent but unbroken—like a ring itself.

You're kind of a miracle . . . the pastor said.

The circle kept going: Daddy gave his ring to me, still bent but unbroken and, finally, stolen one afternoon out of the car I brought to New Haven for my sophomore year. I lived all those years in the American ghetto but had to wait until I was a student at Yale to be robbed.

Daddy wasn't mad, though. He still remembered what he'd accomplished at the Orange Bowl. So did loyal Buckeye fans. It was a group of alumni who, almost forty years after his heroics, raised enough money to pay for surgery to repair his spine. The nerves were pinched, his disks had disintegrated, his foot dragged, his leg went numb, and he ached. A bit like my thumb aches when I hold this pen too long. But I still have my ring and more: at the Yale Bowl, in a rooftop lounge called the Champions Room, which is off-limits to anyone who has not snuck in or contributed at least $1,500, canvases adorn the walls—images of all the great teams in the great history of Yale football, going back nearly a hundred and fifty years. The latest canvas is of the 2006 Yale team in white on a late afternoon in Cambridge, the sun climbing down the back side of Harvard Stadium. A few minutes have passed since these Yale men were crowned champions. There, in the center of the canvas, the camera has focused on one boy: me—facing the camera but looking beyond it to the stands, my left fist raised in triumph, my right arm hanging at my side. Another hand is grabbing my right shoulder. It's Elijah. He was a freshman then. Now he's gone, and Daddy's worn, and I am left here holding the bag and the story. But all I wanted was to hold your hand.

Well, the truth is that I was nineteen, so can't be too sure what exactly I wanted. Not even Jesus knew what He wanted when He was nineteen, which may be why there's nothing in the Bible about that time in His youth. Hard to give your life to save the world until you know deep down you want to do it, I bet. Should probably be just as hard to give your life for a game, but it's not.

Around eight years old, your daddy drops you off at Little League football tryouts without you even asking. He sits on the hood of his car to watch you, claps when you do something right, shouts *C'mon, Scooter!* when you do something wrong, and even when he's gone there is somebody, kin or stranger, there to clap and shout for you. This arrangement holds, and by the time you can legally drink, you have played thousands of plays and watched hundreds of hours of film and eaten extra meals to stay fat and taken extra medicine to stay healthy and had the support and attention of countless coaches and scouts and fans and newspaper articles and television shows and cheerleaders and water bottles and strips of tape and fight songs, all designed to help you in your epic quest to do something you were never even sure you wanted to do. You do it anyhow—you put that powder in your nose, put those pins in your hand, you make whatever sacrifice is asked of you, and in return you get some rings that people steal and felt banners that you lose, and in a room you can't afford to enter, you get a picture of you and your friend, whom you'd rather see again in real life. But when it comes to the things you want deep down, the things you need to live, like love, or to become, like yourself—where is all the sacrifice? Where is the instruction? I'm not complaining, just trying to understand.

I gave so much to win a football game for a team I had not even known existed two years prior. But the winter of 2006 came and for the first time I got something—someone—that I had wanted, perhaps more than anything, with little if any doubt whatever. And if I had been willing to make one iota of sacrifice or been given one hour of instruction, then maybe I would not have made such a mess of it, of him, of us.

chapter FIFTEEN

It all started when he made me wait.

Well, some of it started when he sent his first message.

Sup?

I'd kept that message open for a long time, though it didn't take long to read. Kept it open until Joan walked toward my station at the back of the South Oak Cliff computer lab, almost in time to see his message on a dating portal that also sold pornography. I later learned that this was called *synergy*, a great thing that exists because two lesser things combine. I wish I had known that then. I would have said: *River, we could be a synergy, baby.* But I didn't know.

So there was his short message and his face that resembled my mother's, at least in tone and peculiar beauty, and his eyebrows. Each brow looked like one half of an old ice-block tong, made of wool. I wondered if they came naturally like that, if *he* came naturally like that. I wondered if this was what they called *love at first sight*, though now I know it was not love. It was just the birth of my want for this boy—not to lie with him, not to speak with him, but . . . to be the only survivor of a nuclear holocaust, with him. No one else would ever see or touch him again. And we'd both have a natural glow, forever.

It took only a few months of phone calls and online chats for this want to grow into, or maybe *from*, a need to pour myself freely and fully into something or someone—or, at least, into River. And the need was so great that it was as if I tried to channel all the Big Bang's noise through a single small speaker, through him. This, I understand, is not healthy, for a speaker or a teenager, nor did it make much sense. But I figure we all have a person in our lives who takes up more space than good sense would allow, than we ourselves want to allow. So there they are, there he was, in the space beyond reason, where I wanted to be.

But then he'd made me wait.

Sure, he had a good reason: At sixteen I was illegal, according to the state of Texas. But I'd never met a boy who made me wait, and had never met a nineteen-year-old who was afraid of the law. So either because I was intrigued or because I was insulted, I waited.

Two more years passed. Red came, and others. And in that time River became, for me, less of a person, more of a mission unaccomplished, never failed. Maybe that's what love is. Probably not.

Whatever the case, I turned eighteen and went—was allowed to go— to see him in the flesh. He was my prom date, I guess you could say.

I had to do a lot to get to him that night. Had to stay up late, and plan, and lie. None of this was out of the ordinary. But I also had to steal a car. That was new. *Steal* might be too strong. Let's say I had to *disappear in a car that was not mine.* A town car Tashia had rented, just like the one Daddy used to drive. By midnight, long before the prom was over, I was on I-35 headed south to a town called Carson, driving fast. I worried that my prom suit made me look ridiculous, all orange and pinstripey, with that clown- ish paisley tie I borrowed or bought cheap. I worried that my eyes were puffy. I would not have worried about any of this if I had known how dark Carson would be, nothing but long strips of dimmed shopping centers, small shadowed churches, a 7-Eleven, an old high school, a park, a few hills, and River. I've been all over America since then and I have come to believe that some towns exist solely to create beautiful strange boys. I am thankful.

I pulled up to his parents' two-story house, on the corner, in the dark. Took that walk I came to know so well: from my car across the street to the front door, no porch light, no light inside the foyer, to the wooden bannister guarding the stairs, up four steps to a landing, left, up four more to the upstairs hallway where there was no light, turn right, walk softly, *door's right there.* He had to guide me that first night but by the end I could handle it with my eyes closed.

In his presence for the first time I was afraid, of what, I do not know. Under the ceiling fan light he stood taller than me, but that would not have frightened me. Maybe it was his voice: despite having lived in this small town his whole life he sounded like he might be from the Bronx, even when he was tired or angry. Maybe it was those tattoos covering his veined forearms. Maybe I was just insecure.

He sat on a chair in a small lofted space, where a desk and some shoe boxes and a television were, separated from the larger lower space where his bed was. I sat on the bed, looking up. We sat like this for a long time. I thought I might be sick, so I just stared at him, said stupid stuff like *Dang, you live far.* He laughed and looked away. When he looked back, I was still staring, so he turned off the light and told me to come up to where he was. I reached out to grab his arm and climbed the two little altar steps, ducking so I wouldn't hit the ceiling, keeping my eyes open so I could see as best I could and know that it was real.

When it was finished, I had to leave. That's what he said. It was nearly five a.m. and he had a flight to Los Angeles in a few hours, so I had to go and he had to go and we had to pretend this did not happen because he had a boyfriend.

Oh, aight. That's all I said.

And all I said later that morning when Tashia barged into my room demanding an explanation—*Where have you been?*—was: *I went to a party,*

Tash. She replied, softly, *You could have called.* Closed the door to let me get some sleep. She's good at keeping words trapped inside her head, too.

And all I said later that summer before I left for college, when River appeared in Dallas without any notice, was *Where do you want me to pick you up?* And when we were done, lying there watching some boring anime cartoon, when I accidentally held him and he asked *What are you doing?* like I was taking money from his wallet, all I said was *Nothing,* and scooted over to the other side of the bed. I wonder if that's what he came to love— that's not the word, I know—about me. How well I kept my mouth shut. I wonder how I came to believe that silence was better than uncomfortable words.

How about we blame that on my daddy? Not to pile more on the poor man. It's just that he forgot my nineteenth birthday. Perhaps he did not forget—nonetheless, I did not hear from him, and this bothered me. It also bothered me that my father could still bother me, and *now* it bothers me that I wrote in a journal I kept at the time: *I guess when you're a man you don't need a daddy no ways,* like I was Tupac or something. Anyway, I was on the phone with River that night, at the exact moment of my birth. I knew the time because I had been told it repeatedly as a child (Granny was certain it was yet another sign I was the Antichrist); he knew because I told him, repeatedly. I wanted to see if he remembered.

What time is it, River?

Lemme check . . . uh, it's 12:06.

Cool.

I held the phone, silent, waiting for him to say it. He didn't say a thing.

We hung up and I went right back to the journal, to write River out of my life, which is what he deserved for failing a test that meant so much to me that I hadn't even told him about it.

Then he called, sometime before two a.m.

Hey, River.

Oh, yeah. Happy birthday. He laughed.

Ah, thank you.

That's all I said, in the voice of a man who always says *thank you* as if someone has just picked up his handkerchief, even if, in fact, someone has just pushed him from in front of a speeding car. River laughed again. I wondered what was so goddamn funny.

You're crazy. It's hilarious. You got this nonchalant-ass facade, like nothing bothers you. But I know I do shit that pisses you off sometimes.

Whatever.

Yeah, whatever. I just be playing dumb. That's probably fucked up, huh. But I'ono. It's just too much responsibility. You're too much responsibility. Say we got in a relationship. And that's it. Or if we broke up . . . we wouldn't be friends anymore. You know? So . . . I'ono . . . I just ignore it.

It's all good, River. Appreciate the birthday call.

Mmhmm. Anyway, have a happy birthday, boy.

I sure felt like a fool, though I was skeptical of this whole *you're too much responsibility* business. But if I had realized that he could hardly even handle himself, perhaps I would have believed. That became clear enough in the summer of 2006, the first time he let me hold him, the last time I had to wait.

I had gone to Carson in the night, and when I woke up the next morning, River was clinging to me, grasping the back of my tank top. I saw him before he knew I saw him, just watched him for a moment—eyes darting to the corners, the bottom of his comforter, his hand, my face.

Are you okay? I whispered.

Look at my hand.

His hand was shaking.

What's wrong?

I don't know, Casey.

He stretched his neck back, clenched his eyelids when the light hit them, tucked his head into my chest. I thought he might die right there in my arms, which was, I admit, an incredible thought—not him dying, but us being part of something big and tragic, like a famine or a real bad storm. You know, one of the reasons the world will never be rid of tragedy is that it keeps half of us employed and the other half entertained, and as sad as we feel when things are going wrong, can you even imagine, my lord, what it would be like if we had nothing to fear or complain about, no animals to rescue, no days to commemorate, no stories to tell for a little sympathy on a night we could use some attention, no one to hold in their time of need after waiting forever to hold them? Here was this boy, helpless, flailing about in his head, unable to set his eyes on one thing, holding me like I was the last mooring post in the world. And his helplessness was the most extraordinary thing I'd ever witnessed of him, if only because it made me important, if only for one morning, if only because he was out of his mind.

I'm so stupid. So fucking stupid.

Huh?

I took some ecstasy yesterday. I don't even know why. I've just been feeling like shit. And it was the last pill I had. So I just took it.

I held his head and rubbed his wooly hair and murmured in his ear *It's okay. You'll be okay* until he fell asleep again. But, as is almost always the case when someone says *You'll be okay*, I did not know whether he would. I didn't know he had taken ecstasy before, or why. I didn't know that he'd been having a hard time, or why. I look back on that morning and realize there was so much about him that I did not know, that I should have asked, instead of just lulling him back to sleep.

I say that because I met a man—not like *that*; it was a serious meeting— a few years after this morning with River. A man who had gone to prison for murder, a long time ago. I'll share more details later, but what matters now is something the man told me that afternoon in his office: *There are no excuses for committing a crime*, he said. *But there are reasons.*

I sure do wish I'd met him sooner. It seems that I have always been tied up with folks—not all the people I've known, but enough—who were tied down by the mess of life, by vice and sickness and shady dealings. Not that

I cared that any of the things they did were against the law, per se, just that they seemed pretty reckless and caused me a lot of trouble. I spent all that time with them, building up resentments, adding more guilt to their tabs. And justified as my calculations may have been, I never considered that maybe, just maybe, there were *reasons* behind the things they did. Never took into account what it does to a boy or girl to be abused or neglected, and to carry that all alone, in silence, in the dark. You never know what you need to know when you need to know it, you know?

All I knew is that things changed that morning: we shifted from one foot to the other and it felt like moving forward, into a new chapter where River had the need and I had the power and I called this power *love*.

Or maybe things changed when I slept with his friend. Well, his ex-friend. I didn't know, at the time, that they had been friends—that's my story. River found out, yelled at me, berated that other poor boy. That wasn't right. It was wonderful to see him angry, though. I especially liked one of the more overwrought parts of the tongue-lashing he gave his ex-friend: *Casey is the love of my life. I just had to get myself straight before we were together. I'm good now.* Who knew he'd ever fight for me? If I had known this was all it took, I would have slept with someone he hated, years before.

Whatever it was that made things change, three years after it all started, as we approached the winter of 2006—the winter after I had offered my hand as a sacrifice to Yale football—River decided that the wait had been long enough. Tried to rush me, even.

What do you need to think about?

I don't know, River. I just need some time.

That's ridiculous, Casey. When somebody offers you real love, you shouldn't turn that away. You should be grateful.

I was not grateful, but afraid. A bit power hungry, too. I can't tell you how lucky the world is that I have not gotten many chances to give some tits for all my tats. *Oohwee.* It felt so good to be the oppressor for a change.

But I couldn't hold out long, if only because River sat on my damn hand when I visited him that winter break, with all those pins still holding my bones together. Then, something strange, he grabbed my hand and kissed the cast and said *I'm sorry, baby.* No one had ever apologized to me before, that I can recall. My advice: Apologize today, for everything.

I surrendered. And so began our 259 days, perhaps the most important days of my life. Definitely the most important that no one knew about.

We eloped to Austin, to a small hotel—not a Motel 6 but something nicer, with a comfortable couch we both could fit on, my back to the cushions, his back to my belly, my arm around him, reaching for pizza. We'd gone to Austin to . . . eat pizza and watch cartoons. That's all we did, if I remember correctly.

We had decided not to do anything else until we'd seen a doctor. Well, I had imposed this rule because I assumed that he had been a whore before me and I did not want to suffer the consequences of his happy days. Even went so far as to stop at the little hospital at which he was purportedly tested so that he could show me the papers. I sat in the waiting room while he tried to retrieve them, but he came back empty-handed with that *Will you drop this?* look on his face and so I dropped it, for many reasons or none at all aside from feeling it was time to get on with things, which we did.

By the time I made it back to Dallas the next day, I had a fever. And by that evening, when I tried to swallow, it felt like a tiny cactus was being forced down my throat. I lay in bed and my jaw clattered from the chills. My sheets were damp from sweat. A few doom-tears rolled down my cheek. *Can you bring me some orange juice?* I called out to Tashia. I also wanted to tell her to pick out a nice dress for the service, and to remember me in my better days.

Baby, I'm clean. I'm telling you. Excruciatingly honest.

I think that was the first time River used that phrase—*excruciatingly honest*—which became the slogan of our relationship. Regular honesty was not enough. His phone records were not enough. Excommunicating my friends was not enough. We needed *excruciating* honesty. And on this first trial, he was right. I just had strep throat.

I do regret overreacting, but I had my reasons.

I had been just a boy, seven years old, the night Daddy drove us all the way from Columbus to Dallas, trying to make it to St. Paul Hospital in time for Easter Sunday, in time for his brother to die. I did not yet know my daddy's people well, so I sat in the ICU waiting room minding my business, until Tashia stood up and said *C'mon Casey* like I had asked her to take me somewhere. I had not asked her a thing and I did not move, so she grabbed my wrist and pulled me from my seat and *c'mon*ed me down that fluorescent death-way—*You gotta see Uncle M.* I didn't need to see nobody, didn't need to see an uncle I hardly knew, didn't need to see a man a few hours away from death. And Tashia, at eleven, was just a girl herself—why was she so adamant? Why me?

I won't paint a picture of what I saw. We should all have somebody's image in our mind, if not someone we knew—our blood, our child lover friend—then someone we read about, heard about, *somebody*, for Christ's sake, who died in the plague.

At Uncle M's home-going service the following week, there were times when I was the loudest one crying, which makes no sense since I hardly even knew the man, and dramatic as I am, I've never been *that* dramatic, not even at seven years old, even though there was a plague that my sister seemed to believe I needed to know about. 32,329 other people, that we know of, died of AIDS in America the year my uncle died, I read.

Twenty-one years later, I had a scare. Not the monthly persistent-cough, random-fever, swollen-gland kind of scare but the kind that comes with a long and serious conversation, that punches you in your spleen and says *I told you so* and puts that zombie stare in your eyes. Twenty-one years had passed and we were still dying, still walking around with the specter of doom, sleeping with it, sharing it with our friends. But now there had also arrived, I'd heard, some medicine that I could take to prevent the virus from taking hold, as long as I started within three days, like my own private resurrection.

I'd heard this on the night of the second day. The next morning, I taxied to a sketchy emergency clinic, where I told the nurses of my situation—a situation that, based on their damning eyes (perhaps I was imagining this), I deserved. With a prescription for two medications that could possibly save my life, I rushed to a pharmacy an hour or so before it closed. The pharmacist called my name from the counter a few minutes later, looked at me like he'd just found out my mother was dead.

Sir, are you sure you want to fill these? This one is, uhh, twelve hundred dollars. And the other is, let's see, thirteen hundred.

Twenty-five hundred dollars to *possibly* save my life, not even a guarantee. With all my great fortune and health insurance and credit cards, those two prescriptions wiped me out, and I'm amongst the lucky ones. I got the first dose in right at the seventy-two-hour mark, the beginning of a month of all those side effects, and then two more months of waiting, wondering whether my life had been saved.

I learned a lot in those three months. Not only that the plague is still with us. Not only that somebody in charge of health in this country has got some real explaining to do. I also learned—just by stewing in my situation—that either all the queers of the world are going to have to become John D. Rockefellers, or some pharmaceutical magnate is going to have to become Jesus H. Christ, or a day will have to come, and soon, when we realize that we gain nothing from carrying this shroud of death, that living in fear of ourselves and the people we're trying to love will destroy our hearts and minds as surely as the virus, unchecked, may destroy our bodies.

I did not understand that when River and I were together, though, so I still needed that *excruciatingly honest* as we began our 259 days together in December.

By Valentine's Day (day 75), we had not given each other disease and we also agreed not to give each other gifts. But River kept asking me to check my mail and, being generally ornery and particularly busy that day, I kept refusing, until finally I went and found that he'd sent a whole case of my favorite Starburst candy, a flavor they've since stopped making. On top of the rows of Starburst was a plastic bag with a pair of his boxers, the ones with The Jetsons printed on them. I had asked River to give them to me, off his body, when I'd seen him last.

Casey, that's gross. I've been wearing them all day.

So.

Here they were at last, crumpled and unwashed.

I didn't send anything, per our agreement. River was my first valentine, how was I supposed to know he wasn't serious about the gift thing? Now I had all this candy and his boxers and my shame. So in a panic before midnight, I went into my dorm room closet and closed the door to record a song for him, by Musiq Soulchild, who guided me so well in the days of Red.

The way we are is how it's gonna be
just as long as your love don't change

I hoped he could hear me clearly on that recording, not only because I went through the trouble of switching the pronouns, and sang louder than I wanted to (Daniel still lived across the hall), but because I meant the words I sang, even though I did not understand how impossible the lyrics were—how, in fact, our love had to change; how *we* had to change for our love to exist at all.

We were changing. I just didn't notice.

Day 100 arrived along with spring break. While my classmates went to Cancun or Miami, I flew to Carson. River stood in the lobby of the small plane depot, waiting for me with a du-rag on his head. He never wore du-rags, so that was weird. Not as weird (at least to me) as the Cheshire grin I had on my face in the middle of the airport, so I looked down at the floor and handed him my bag.

Hey, boy. He chuckled.

In the car, he explained the situation on his head: He had grown his hair out, the crinkly chestnut hair that came from some mix of his Mississippian father and his Dutch mother. When it got too unruly to deal with every day, he had let a friend braid it—well, that's what they'd *called* themselves doing—and here, hiding under the du-rag, was the disappointing result, which he showed me once we reached his parents' house.

Oh, babe. Want me to help you take it down?

We sat up on the altar in his room for an hour or so—me in a wooden chair, him on the floor between my legs. I had never taken anybody's hair down before, but I had seen Granny and Shon do it many times. Used the same kind of rattail comb they used to untangle the strands, tried my best not to bruise his scalp. Just as I was feeling accomplished, he mumbled *You notice anything?* in a way that made me instantly know that I had not. He turned around and forced a smile.

Wait . . . you got braces?

We had been together for at least three hours, in the light of the plane depot, of the grocery store, of his room. I had stared at him the way I always stared; had kissed him, even. Somehow, I had not noticed all that metal in the boy's mouth. He turned back around, said nothing else about the braces or my blindness, but I knew—now I know—that this was a hard blow, that even or especially the most beautiful among us need someone to notice them, to truly *see* them as they are and as they change. I could only, hardly, see myself.

At Yale, the clothes that had helped me win a best-dressed award in high school only helped lose me the respect of my classmates. So on the second day of my visit, River drove me to the tired mall one town over to buy new jeans. We walked past the stores like distant cousins, accidentally brushing each other's arms. In Macy's, I tried on a size 34 pair of Levi's, which felt like Spandex, since my usual jeans were size 38, even though my waist was just a 31. I called out from the dressing room.

River . . . these jeans make me look gay.

He stood a few feet away, tilted his head, looked at my smothered legs. Laughed.

Hmm. Yeah. Gone and get 'em, though. They're on sale.

This exchange still cracks me up, but it marked an evolution, one I can best describe via this exchange I had in an Atlanta gay club, a year after River and I bought my new jeans.

I was leaning against the club's mirrored wall when my friend Kenny, who had been a track star in college and had become a star of another sort in the clubs of Atlanta, rushed over to me.

Say, Casey. C'mere. Act like you're my boyfriend.

Huh? Why, Kenny?

Man, some fucking faggot over there tryna be messy.

Oh dang, aight.

I haven't talked to Kenny in years, but I hear that he's gone on to have a nice career as an escort, so perhaps he has changed since that night in Atlanta. All I know is that I was changing that day at Macy's, and River must have been, too, since he supported me wearing those jeans even though they seemed so *gay* to us both—just as some of my friends' voices seemed too *femme*, just as going to the clubs seemed only for queens, just as we sometimes went to a park to throw the football back and forth as hard as we could, not because it was fun but because it was proof that we were real boys. And so with me and River, as it has always been in this country, jeans were a symbol of progress.

But I didn't notice this, that afternoon at Macy's. I blame River's mother: on our way back from the mall, he remembered that his family was going to dinner that night in honor of her birthday.

And you're just gonna leave me at the house all that time?

Casey. It's my mom's birthday. I have to go to the dinner.

I was silent.

Do you wanna come?

Do I wanna come?! I thought.

Gone, River, I said.

It was an empty offer, I decided, given that I'd been sneaking into the woman's house for three years by then. So I let him go alone and I let him return to find me in his room, watching *The Pursuit of Happyness*. I didn't say *hey* until long after the movie ended, when I looked over and saw him sitting on the floor with his head between his knees. I hugged his neck and said *I'm sorry,* even though I can't remember whether I truly was.

I do remember that he was sick of me.

You ready to go?

That was the first thing River said when we woke the next morning. He grabbed my bag as soon as I finished packing and flung it in the trunk of his Ford Bronco. Took off driving up I-35 like Dallas was something worth racing toward. We said nothing for the first thirty minutes or so, only noise was the radio and the cars passing and the tires on the road and then the Bronco's engine.

Fuck.

River's jaw had slacked a bit. He turned the radio off.

Fuck.

He studied the instrument panel, glanced at the smoke rising from the Bronco's hood, then slowly guided the dying truck off the highway and onto the gravel shoulder that separated it from seemingly endless acres of weeds and wildflowers. He got out to pop the hood and I got out to sit in the field, away from him.

The hood crashed back in place and River walked over to sit down, not right next to me but within earshot. The sun had been hiding behind clouds, but when I looked at him, it shined its light on his face, squinted and freckled as only it ever was in the sun.

Guess you won't be getting rid of me so soon, huh.

He tried to strangle a smile.

Guess not.

We sat there in the grass and gravel, silent, picking at pebbles. We laughed at the same time, or close behind each other, though maybe not at the same thing. He was so beautiful, blinded by all that sun and rage.

You know what's wrong with it? I asked.

Nope. And all I got is gas money to get to Dallas and back. I'ono what we're gonna do.

I could lie and say I felt some sympathy for him, but I didn't. I was always annoyed by this—his constant lack of money or well-developed plans, or other things I thought twenty-three-year-olds should have. Now I know that twenty-three-year-olds don't hardly have nothing, ever.

Like the deus ex machina she'd always been, whenever she wasn't trying to get me killed, Tashia prevented us from being stuck on the highway like day-old armadillos. She kept money in an account for me, to make sure I had food and a little pocket change at school. There was over two hundred dollars in the account that day, so we called AAA and got the Bronco fixed. River drove the rest of the way at a decent person's pace, and at some point in all this, one of us said *I love you* and this stood in for all the things we had not said, did not know how to say.

If only we had found more words. Instead of pinning me down and making me bleed, he could have said *You hurt my feelings.* Instead of waking him out of his sleep, choking him like that, I could have said *I don't want you to leave.* We had learned so well as boys to keep our mouths shut and now, as boy-men, we knew no other way. Perhaps we would have tried harder during those 259 days, if there had not been so many moments when our silence was worth a thousand years of noise, when our cloistered world felt like a perfect hiding place, as it did that final summer.

On summer nights in Texas, the cruel overseer-heat of day goes in for some shut-eye and sends out the sweetest breeze you'll ever feel in your life. Not a cool breeze, but a breeze that feels like the warm hand of God come to wipe away all tears. In a dim-lit town like Carson you can close your eyes and see a trace of stars through your eyelids. You open them and it takes four seconds to find Orion's Belt. *There it is, River.* He looked and saw it, too.

We sat in that night-star silence, in my car with the sunroof open, on a park bench under giant live oak trees, and our lungs felt twice the normal size, filled with that breeze and each other's air. Our hands lined up so that it went my finger then his then mine then his, from thumb to pinkie. And I played the same song over and over, or sang it to him.

> *I hope that you're the one*
> *If not, you are the prototype*

I did not just hope. I believed. And though River sometimes rolled his *How many times are we gonna hear this* eyes and laughed when the song came on, he too must have been a believer, because as the end of summer neared, he suggested moving to Connecticut, *living together*, introducing me to his family and such.

These plans, these feelings, this belief . . . all of it became, almost suddenly, a terrible problem for me, though it took a long time to understand why, and even longer to admit.

I could blame God—at least the God that I had been given. I could still remember all the sermons and scriptures, like Papa's favorite: *What would it profit a man to gain the whole world and lose his soul?* But for better or worse, I had already accepted my godlessness—or god-apart-ness—and River seemed a decent consolation.

I could blame the society in which I had been born and still lived. Could say that I was unable to bear being cast out of my family (who, as far as I know, have never cast anybody out, for anything), or accept the scorn of my peers, or endure the stares and sneers of strangers. Perhaps this played a role, even a small one, especially since I was in the early stages of crafting a new life, or a new story, in the image of perfection. But while it was not clear how River would fit into that story, I did not think it impossible.

I could definitely blame River, which I did at the time. Could say that there were *irreconcilable differences*, whatever that means. I may not have mastered many interpersonal skills in our 259 days, but I had developed a virtuosic gift for placing blame, so I blamed him for everything. Even found a way to interpret his offer to move to New Haven as a sign that he was not trying to be serious about his life.

But the truth is that I was the one unwilling to try. Perhaps *unable* to try because I could not love him, after all.

By *love* I do not mean the strong dramatic feelings that we see on television, or hear in songs and from people who act like they know what they're talking about. What I mean is something that I read many years later in a book by bell hooks, conveniently titled *All About Love*.

Love, she defines, via M. Scott Peck and Erich Fromm, *is the will to extend oneself for the purpose of nurturing one's own or another's spiritual growth.*

If I had known this then, I might have stopped saying *I love you*, or I might have tried to make the words mean something, or I might have realized that the terror I felt had less to do with River and more to do with the fact that, by twenty years old, I no longer believed in people. I found the prospect of needing a human being, trusting them, *extending myself* for them, to be more horrifying than being abandoned, or almost killed, or damned for all eternity. People seemed to be the most dangerous things in this world.

And so what I felt as my days with River rolled toward Something Major was a bit like what I felt when I started to tell you this story. It was as though I stood atop a very tall building and gusts of wind were whooshing all over me and I was trying to decide whether to jump—not to my death, but into this vast unknown that was calling out for me. I knew, or felt strongly enough to consider it a fact, that the work could not be done unless I jumped, unless I gave it all or none, unless I was *placed into the dipper and poured back down on the world.* Luckily, I could not stay up on the rooftop of that life I was living before I sat to tell you this story, so I took the plunge and here I am. We'll see what comes of it.

But back there on that rooftop with River, I could not jump. For one, the rooftop seemed too safe to take a chance. Even more, so much of my experience had been not jumping from rooftops, but being pushed off without much notice and against my will. And part of me wanted to prove, if only to myself, that I could do some pushing for a change. So I did.

When August came and I returned to New Haven, I made what I'd decided would be my final call to him, one afternoon.

I don't think we should be together right now, River.

He held the phone.

So you're saying we're breaking up?

I looked at my fingernails for a long time.

Yeah, I guess.

He suggested that we take a break, not talk to anyone, not sleep with anyone. See if we could work things out. I explained that this made no sense, that we needed to be adults. Adults!

And that's when he told me how long it had been.

From December to August 17, nearly 259 consecutive days of "I love you," "you're the only one I ever wanna be with," and "excruciatingly honest." A man who took you from not expecting anything of him, to showing you that you can trust and depend on him to be there for everything . . . Congrats on dissolving this.

Saying *thank you* didn't seem appropriate. So I said nothing, for months. Kept my word and refused to call, except for the few times I called from an unidentified number and held the phone in silence, just to hear him say *hello*.

This, you see, is why I say that these days were perhaps the most important in my life: once I ended them, I had no doubt that I could do anything, no matter how vicious, how hard, how painful or implausible. So although the Apostle Paul wrote in that same letter to the church at Corinth—*Though I have the gift of prophecy, and understand all mysteries, and all knowledge; and though I have all faith, so that I could remove mountains, and have not love, I am nothing*—he did not tell it all. Paul should have added what I came to learn: that without love, you *are* something. You are a danger to yourself and others.

Yet somehow, after breaking this one black boy, I was put in charge of building all the black boys at Yale.

If you catch a whiff of confusion when you read that I, Casey Gerald, one of the most bitter reclusive boys to ever attend Yale College, evolved almost overnight (two years of nights, actually) into a *leader* of anybody, then you are not alone. Most of the students were shocked, too. A decade has passed and I still struggle to explain—to understand for myself—not *how* it happened (that's simple enough and I'll let you in on most of it), but *why*. So let's just start with what I know for sure: it wasn't my idea.

There had been, for over a hundred years, the black fraternities, and the Freemasons, and the Boulé, and the many local and regional associations, and the black men's college at Atlanta, and, of course, the prisons, which have stood since Emancipation as the most sincere national effort to gather black men in one place, even if you consider the Million Man March. But aside from all this, founding an organization to support young black men was not my idea because it came as a suggestion from two boys at Cornell who, early in the summer of 2007, proposed that all the black boys from all the Ivy League colleges unite to form a Men of Color Council—a forum to share our wisdom, our connections, and our lives with one another. To *network*: a word that, having hardly heard it before going to Yale, and having heard it over and over again ever since, I have come to believe defines today the way *repent* defined the days of my youth and *discover* defined the days of Columbus and Cortés and Drake, with the same promise of glory for some, of ruin for others, and of a new world, like it or not, for all.

What you think about this, Casey? Daniel asked through a phone somewhere after speaking with the Cornell boys, assuming they had also contacted me since they claimed to have tried to track down every black boy who attended one of the seven other Ivies. Apparently this had taken only a week.

All these niggas wanna do is get together for some mixers and galas. Fuck that.

He cackled—*Yeah, man, you probably right*—but he knew that I was serious. We had gone nearly a year without speaking on account of him trying to get me to like the people at Yale, to give them a shot, make some friends, ingratiate myself. It had not worked. I missed my people too much, though I could not say for sure what I meant by that.

From roughly ages eight to eighteen, I had understood *my people* to mean black people. There was little reason not to. We had in my corner of Oak Cliff something close to what sociologists call *institutional completeness: The condition of a group within a larger society where the major institutions—economy, politics, family, schooling—are reproduced, thus enabling the smaller group to have little social connection with the larger group.*

In practice this meant that the teachers were black, the bank tellers were black, the tax man and the trash man and the mailwoman were black, and even (until recently) the yard workers were black. The dope fiends were black, the dope dealers were black, and (for the most part) the cops who arrested them were black. My best friends and sworn enemies were black, all.

There was a great gift in this: it never occurred to me that I was inferior because I was black. I was informed that white people were racist.

That America was racist. That black people in America had been knocked down for four hundred years—the number was always four hundred years; even today, thirty years after my birth, it is still *four hundred years*. But I was assured that this was because there was something wrong with white people, not with me. Some said that white people were the devil. Some said that white people were mean. Some said that white people just didn't know any better. Well, I knew at least one black person who seemed like the devil, and had met a fair number who were terribly mean, and was the offspring of two who didn't seem to know any better. In fact, it did not seem to me that anybody ever knew why they or anybody else did anything, so I didn't spend a whole lot of time trying to figure out the motives of white people. All I knew was that I was not white and that I would have been heartbroken if I had been born white.

But this institutional completeness was a bit too complete, since it wasn't until I arrived at Yale that it dawned on me that the defining trait of *my people* was not only that we had so much pigment in our skin but that we had so little money in our bank accounts, so little food on our tables, so few books in our classrooms, that we did not take family vacations, that we did not go to the museum, that we did not pay for our lunch at school, did not buy our toys at Toys'R'Us, did not order steak in restaurants, if we ever went, did not go to the dentist for our six-month cleaning, if for anything, did not have vision exams to know we needed glasses, which we could not afford anyway. And we did not add all this up and call ourselves *poor*—perhaps because it was so obvious that it did not need to be said, or because it was so common that we found more interesting language for each other, or because we were ashamed. I'm not sure. Whatever the case, the black students at Yale were a mighty rich discovery—not only because they had so much more or had lived so differently than I had, but also and especially because they looked at me as though they were itching to pose Du Bois's question: *How does it feel to be a problem?*

Quickly and surely I began to suspect, as perhaps the coolie suspects when he first encounters the Brahmin, that these elect were invested in the distinction between their kind and mine, between the *blacks* and the *niggers*, began to suspect that those of us who spent our lives in the Left Behind had been kept there, in the dark, blind to these other worlds, these higher reaches, these *possibilities*, for a reason. I was not sure what the reason was and I did not have any proof, but I sure felt that this was all too fishy to be a simple coincidence. And the more time I spent in their midst, the more I became convinced that *they* were the problem—not any individual boy or girl or mother or father but the idea that they represented, of a class apart, and all the trappings that came with it: the mixer, the gala, the networking reception, the panels to discuss blackness in theory when actual blackness was having one hell of a hard time right down the street—when *I* was having a hard time right under their noses. My desire to overthrow them was personal, I admit. It had to be personal.

Above all, Che Guevara wrote to his children not long before he was executed, *always be capable of feeling deeply any injustice committed against anyone, anywhere in the world. This is the most beautiful quality in a revolutionary.*

I had not heard of Che at that time and now that I have, I want you to know that I do not agree with everything he did—but I do thank the man for helping me explain and understand myself: the retching stomach knot and threat of tears at the sight or sound of something, anything, that struck me as unnecessary or unfair human suffering (especially if it was *my* human suffering)—this was the most innate quality I possessed, beautiful or not. I don't say that to sound tough or brave or even to take any credit, because I never did anything to call it up or make it stronger. It was a *gift*—just sitting there waiting for me, as early as Halloween 1992, and was, now that I think about it, almost revealed to the world, or at least my little Oak Cliff world, in 1999.

The incident I'm remembering involved, of course, a speech. Don't remember what it was about but I do remember that a passel of adults liked it so much that they decided to send me to Australia, which I'm not sure I had heard of before 1999, as part of some "student ambassador" scheme that Dwight Eisenhower had cooked up before he died. I didn't have any problem going to Australia but I also didn't have any money, so Ms. Davis or somebody decided that I should say my speech once again, before a larger group of adults—all men, for some reason. Two of the men in attendance were politicians, an elected judge and a state senator. I gave the speech and the adults clapped. The state senator bowled his way to the microphone and announced that he was going to write a thousand-dollar check for this great cause. *Judge, you write one, too!* he cried. The judge, dragged into this honorable swinging-dick competition, jumped to the microphone and retorted—*You got it, Doc!* And all the men clapped for the judge and the senator and somebody took a picture of them and then they all went home, feeling good, and I went home, too, also feeling pretty good. This had to be shortly after Martin King Day '99.

Well, March came and, with it, the *News* story on my father. Then I discovered the medical malpractice that the Facilities were passing off as care. Then the end of school approached and something *had not* come: my money. And I guess the string of events had convinced me that people suffer—children suffer—when those in power do not do their jobs. What I had not yet learned is that those in power always get away with it. And so I planned to mete out justice myself.

Thanks to Granny, who never threw away any of my belongings or traded them for money or lost them in storage, I still have the letter to the senator that I composed. I present it to you, unedited (except for the senator's name, because people are very litigious in America these days):

May 13, 1999

Dear Senator Blazzy Blah,

   Coming from a very religious family, it has always been instilled in me that a man with any honor is to keep his promise—especially to a child, and when they don't, it is known as a lie. However, it has been brought to my attention from a very loving principal and teachers that you didn't uphold your promise—a very disappointing discovery.

   Whatever happened to vows that are said to be kept? Not only am I preterbed, I am utterly disappointed at such a tawdry performance of disregard.

   Whatever happened to "It takes a village to raise a child," when in my village, such so called "distinguished" authorities have showed that lies are their main priority. You know, I have had serious thoughts about being a politician, but after I've seen that you must lie to be the best on the voting ballot, I've now altered my decision.

   When I spoke at Paul Quinn College, the M.C. said that you paid for my trip, but my wonderful PTA, who stand by their promises with the utmost of respect, they might just want to give the Dallas Morning News a ring. Not only are you and your mouth a disgrace to this community, but to this state. Galatians 6:7,10 says, "Be not deceived; God is not mocked: for whatsoever a man soweth, that shall he reap. As we have the opportunity, let us do good unto all men, especially those of the household of faith." I say to you, not only am I of the household of faith, but God is a close friend of mine, and of course, he will prevail. You don't have to give me the money you promised, I don't have to go on my trip, you don't have to win the next election—nothing for you is carved in stone, for it is all up to you. Now I don't mean to be disrespectful, but I'm very appalled at the oblivion of your character. I know you might think this letter is nothing, but when the black community finds out that one of it's prominent black "leaders" show less leadership qualities than a 12 year old child, you might just be convinced. Phillipians 2:3 quotes "Let nothing be done through strife or vainglory; but in the lowliness of mind, let each esteem other better themselves." May god bless you and touch you much needed spirit

Truly Disheartened,
Casey D. Gerald
6th Grader at R.L. Thornton Elementary School

Ms. Davis had stopped her class to help me choose impressive words to attack the state senator. Stood at her desk, me on the other side of the room reading draft sentences aloud, and shouted back—*Ooh! You are not mad you are perturbed! Yess*—which sounded great to me, though I wasn't a perfect speller, as you can see.

Shortly after I wrote it, as preparations continued for its effectual release, my letter fell into the hands of another teacher who, of course, ran straightway to the principal, who then summoned me to her office. I strolled down to this meeting with hopes that Dr. Jones, who reminds me now a bit of Lena Horne, was going to offer a few suggestions and maybe a stamp.

She sat calmly behind her principal desk. The Gestapo official who confiscated my letter sat on a couch. I sat on the couch, too.

Now, Casey, Dr. Jones cooed. *You know we cannot send this letter, right?*
I did not know that.

I sure do understand you being upset, she continued. *Certainly. But I'm gonna tell you just what my mother always told me when I was a little girl.*

She'd say, "Aretha, you can catch more bees with honey than you can with vinegar." You really can, darling. Just trust me. All right?

Yes, ma'am.

Dr. Jones was so wise and so good to me—she wrote two traveler's checks to replace the politicians' missing money—that I didn't put up a fight, just filed the letter away and placed my grudge against the senator on the shelf with all the others I was collecting at that time. And it seems that, with much else on my mind, my gift went into hibernation as the new millennium began.

But then I got to Yale and discovered that all (or at least *some of*) the hell my people and I had gone through was not an act of God but a highly sophisticated scheme, an *okeydoke bang-bang*, carried out by a whole chicken coop of Senator Blazzy Blahs. And there it was again, my righteous fury, untempered by time and unchecked at last. Granny was not there to chase me. Ms. McLemore was not there to bargain. Daddy was not there to whip me. Dr. Jones was not there to intervene. And if she had called to assure me once more—*Casey, darling, remember . . . you can catch more bees with honey than with vinegar*—I would have smiled and said (respectfully) *Yes, ma'am, I remember . . . but I don't wanna catch them. I plan to smash the whole nest this time.*

Thanks to Yale football, I knew how to do just that.

If the game of football sat at the top of the social order in Texas, at Yale it scraped the very bottom—the closest thing the college had to a ghetto. But like every ghetto, Yale football gave me a great advantage, a hidden workshop where I could tinker with my inner man and outer appearance, where I could *laugh and eat well and grow strong*. So although some wise man said *One must wait until evening to see how splendid the day has been*, I'm here to tell you that it is in the evening, in the back of a bus from Philadelphia, in a cell-like dorm room all alone, *in the darkness*, where plans are made and the makers of plans become the saints and monsters that we witness or endure by day. Two years of night was all it took for my eyes to adjust to total darkness, enough to see the outline of my hand, to reach and grab whatever was in front of me or knock down any fool who needed light. And that first coup had taught me well that sometimes all one has to do to conquer is to try. So I did.

Besides, I wrote to Daniel once we hung up, *we shouldn't be one of the thirteen colonies. We should be America.*

We would not join the Men of Color Council or anything like it. Daniel and I would found our own institution, not to network but to . . . We'd get to that.

First, we needed a name.

What about Association of Yale Negroes?

Daniel, that's the oldest-sounding shit I've ever heard. Is that what they call y'all in Gary . . . negroes??

Ha . . . shutup, nigga. We gotta think of something fresh.

Yeah. That ain't it, though. You think we can call ourselves colored? Like, Yale Colored Men's Forum?

Hmm . . . I'ono if it's okay to call black people colored no more. Let me ask my daddy. Daniel's father was a civil rights lawyer. *Yeah, man. I kinda liked "colored" but my daddy said it's not okay.*

Damn.

We spent at least half a week auditioning names for our new group. We knew *Yale* would be in it. But we needed a term for our race, our gender, and our structure. Of course all these things are social constructs, but we were twenty and it was a simpler time.

The only term we nixed immediately was *African-American.*

It had always seemed strange to me that an Irishman could show up at Ellis Island in 1912, or a Hungarian Jewish family could show up in 1940, or an Afrikaner could arrive in 2006, and before the next census was taken they could all just check *white* and the newspaper would call them, simply,

Americans. But somehow, some relative of mine could be kidnapped from Africa four hundred years ago, kept in America for all that time, stripped of name and gods and family, forced to work and build the land, and I—who had hardly been to Oklahoma, let alone to Africa—was given this hyphenated title, this other continental allegiance that I had not asked to have taken from me in the first place and had not asked to be branded with, either.

I would not argue with someone who claimed that my pose was tinged with anti-African sentiments, but I would ask them to consider that any attempt to dilute my Americanness must be tinged with anti-blackness . . . anti-*meness.* Besides, my mother and father and sister had been the first somebodies—on the same day, no less—to stick a name on me that I did not choose myself and had to carry around for the rest of my life. They would be the last, if I had anything to do with it.

Black. That's what we would be.

We would call ourselves *black.* We would call ourselves *men,* since *boys* was inappropriate as a title for serious people (in practice, I called most males, myself included, *boy,* and still do). We would call the group a *union*—*forum* was already taken by our counterparts at Harvard, and we had already stolen their constitution and one of their events.

We had then to discuss
Whither or where we might travel, with the second question being
Should we have a purpose

It makes sense that we spent more time choosing a name for this new institution than deciding its purpose, since every grand purpose grows from personal pain. It is not until some meaning is grafted onto the bone of the pain—sometimes not until centuries have passed and somebody makes up a nice story about those early days—that ideals and causes and manifestos are added to what was, at base, a simple human problem. Remember that God made Adam only because He was alone, then made Eve because Adam was alone, then told them to multiply so that they would not be alone. And all these millions of years later we are still creating most of the good and evil things that we do because we are, so often, alone. So it was with the Yale Black Men's Union.

Yale, for me, had been the loneliest place in the world. And though Daniel was not as theatrical about the ordeal, it had not been much better for him. Our friend Brian, whose family's Great Migration had taken them to Lima, Ohio—which paid off, they thought, when their progeny migrated to Yale—had been miserable, too. We knew one boy—a math genius from Mississippi, if you can believe it—who dropped out after his sophomore year, not long after he recruited me to join the Kappas. Then somebody messed up and let me find a statistic: only 92 percent of black boys that enrolled in Yale College graduated, compared to 98 percent of everybody else. I was not sure where this statistic came from. I am not sure whether it was even true. But if Twain was right that *there are three kinds of lies—lies, damn lies, and statistics*—then he failed to mention how useful all three could be. *There's a goddamn plague around here.* We would do something about this.

We also knew, Daniel and I, that as bad as things may have been for us, they were much worse for boys outside the tall iron gates of Yale. Every week our first two years, or at least every month, or maybe it had only been three or four times, we went to Bridgeport, forty-five minutes south of New Haven, to mentor high school boys, at the invitation of the only upperclassman on the football team who made sure we earned good grades and did more than sit around staring at our navels. However many visits there were, each made me grateful to have grown up poor in the South, where at least we had some grass and the winter was not so harsh. It also made me—Daniel, too—angry at how comfortable and self-concerned so many of our classmates seemed to be. There were over two dozen groups headquartered at the Afro-American Cultural Center—"the House"—at that time, yet one of the most respected black upperclassmen lamented:

The black community at Yale has failed because it doesn't do anything serious. We would do something about this, too.

The last piece of purpose became the most controversial. It made no sense to me that a black boy would come to Yale and spend four years at the House or, more to the point, only with people who were just like him. Some of this impulse was the toxic waste of my war with the black bourgeoisie, for sure. Some of it was a naive commitment to integration. But it was also why I loved when Maya Angelou quoted the Roman slave-turned-playwright Terence: *Homo sum, humani nihil a me alienum puto.* And for those who, like me, don't know more than a lick of Latin: *I am human, I consider nothing human alien to me.*

If these boys were going to go through the trouble of living and studying and taking out loans to go to Yale, they needed to walk around like they owned the place, not like they were squatting on somebody's back porch. We would bring them out of the shadows—which sounds rich coming from me, I bet.

Anyway, that was the plan: we'd get these boys together, we'd get 'em in good shape, put 'em to work in service to somebody else, help 'em find the keys to the rest of the kingdom so they could rob the place blind instead of taking a couple sacks of quarters.

Now we had to actually find them.

Daniel and I took our nets and became fishers of boy-men: calling them over the phone, sitting with them at the same small table at the same crowded coffee shop on the corner of Chapel and College Streets, waving them down from the wide stone steps of Sterling Library. If a prospect was away, we sent him an email and offered a snippet of the Union's mission, just enough to get him on the phone, then into the coffee shop when he was back in New Haven—somewhere close enough for the human element to have the greatest effect. We needed to see his eyes: Was he looking at us or at the floor; was he smiling or yawning; was he taking notes or checking his phone? We needed to mold the message to his untold needs, though it was the same always, as the Message has always been: *follow me.* That most people do not want to lead, we knew. That most who want to lead are not willing to work, we knew. That most who are willing to work cannot endure the suffering that work requires, we knew. What we did not know was how much of their energy and our time people would waste lying about this: that a steady drip of *Let me think about its* and *I'll get back to yous* and *I'm not sures* would prove that *no* is one of the hardest words in the English language to say—this, especially, we did not know. We learned, that summer.

And so the cause depended on the few too blind to have any doubt— me and Daniel—and our friends. Perhaps it has always been this way. Those friends, to be clear, do not commit themselves to the cause. They commit themselves to you. If you are lucky, one of them may be a true believer, a zealot. May be an Elijah. But you'll have to work for it.

When I asked Elijah to join the Union, asked him to create and lead its mentoring program, he said no. Many times. *Got other things to do, Case.* It wasn't because he was afraid to lead or work or suffer. No, he was one who had known suffering, though it's not your business to know it all and not my place to tell it all.

I will say that of all the recruits I hosted in my four years, who visited Yale reluctant to ever come back, Elijah was the most serious. I remember how young he seemed—must have been seventeen then—how he kept close to a boy from Fort Lauderdale, Trevor, who looked to me like some members of the University of Miami football team, with the dreadlocks and strange dance moves, which I saw because I took him and Elijah to a party. Though I missed the recruits' formal dinner, I heard, years later, that at that dinner Elijah's guardian had told Doris *If you all cannot give Elijah everything he needs, please tell us. He can't be let down again.* She had been assured, gave her blessing to the journey, and he came.

I was in touch with Elijah over the summer before he arrived—the language of our messages from that time is so foreign to me now that I wonder where we hid those boys we were back then. And when he showed up in the fall, I watched over him (to the extent that a nineteen-year-old can watch over anybody) as I watched over my other recruits who matriculated, especially those, like Elijah and Trevor, who played my position and were, because of the norms of the sport and whatever ideas I had about being my brother's keeper, in my care. That is why, when Trevor showed up to the first day of football camp with fake gold teeth in his mouth, stood there in broad daylight in the Vanderbilt College courtyard with fake gold teeth in his mouth, surrounded by a horde of prep school boys oohing and aahing at the fake gold teeth in his mouth, I walked over and stood next to him as if I was just taking in the view of whatever he was looking at and said, almost without moving my lips, *Nigga, if you don't take those damn golds out your mouth.* He waited until I walked away to curse me (and take the golds out), waited until I was about to graduate to admit how much he had hated me, how hard I had been on him, and waited until Elijah was gone and we were grown men to say that he loved me like a big brother. While we still have time, let the siblings, real and imagined, find a way to speak to one another.

In the time that I'd been watching Elijah, as we became friends, I saw—or came to believe—that he was a bit like a stray cat who, sensing you near, freezes, back arched, kitten-roar ready. *Don't come any closer.* But if you just stand there and watch him, and don't make any sudden moves, the roar will become a purr, the back will relax. After a few days or months, you may find the cat on your porch every morning, roaring at the mailman. In this way, I suppose, I became a part of *everything he needs* because Elijah saw this same trait in me. Besides, there were few other places to turn. So I stood there, nice and easy, and did not get angry when he said no, like I often did. Just kept on asking and, in time, he joined.

It did not matter, or at least was not discussed, that Elijah wasn't even black. His parents, or their parents, or some other of his kin had come to America from Mexico before Elijah was born. While I have since learned that there are also black Mexicans, Elijah's people were not among them as far as I know. They could have come from Pluto for all I cared—not that I was color-blind, I just felt that I had more in common with Elijah than almost anyone who would more obviously be part of the Union.

By August 2007, we had a loose collection of eager boys, about a dozen, mostly athletes, and a name and good intentions. But if the Union was going to be an institution, it needed real structure, an official leader. And so, as it was with that first inauguration, we went to New York City to decide.

Six or so of us convened in the dim living room of a bulky brick high-rise at the northern edge of Manhattan, might as well go ahead and call it the Bronx. Through the tall windows we could look out at the tops of dark huddled trees and, beyond, at the skyline of the city, lit up then as it always is, to remind us all of what great things the human race can accomplish. I didn't have any interest in looking at any trees or skyscrapers—I was watching the people in the room, which is what you better be doing if you find yourself in a group where something you care about will be decided.

Nobody sat for the few hours we were there, except the host, AJ Hawkins—a small boy, a man in fact (with glasses that gave him the look of a shorter, milk-dud Malcolm X), one of the few upperclassmen I had admired freshman year, not least because it was from him that I first heard the word *diaspora*.

Blackness is global, man, he told me, in a voice that made me believe that he had searched all over the planet to see where blackness was and had returned to tell me all about it—which he did, in the pages of a magazine he founded at Yale. And unlike many of his peers who said words like *diaspora*, AJ didn't make a big fuss about it, didn't walk around in dashikis or change his name or nothing, just wore slim black jeans and spoke softly and laughed like he had found some real joy, calm joy. Here he was—here we were, in his apartment—and as the elder, AJ would break any tie or override any bad decision in his gentle holy way.

Riley Edwards was there and didn't sit, either. Riley was a freshman, a running back whom I had hosted on his visit to Yale—which had not been too far of a journey for him because he was from Mount Vernon, New York, and also because he already attended one of the best high schools in the country. I bet he did not sit for much the same reason he went on to Yale Divinity School and, soon after, launched a decent rap career. He was not yet a preacher or a rapper at that time, but the boy is always father to the man and so he stood and walked around and moved his hands a lot, and because of or despite all this, his classmates listened to what he said—which meant that we, in this room, had to listen.

There were a few others there, a black Greek chorus, not carrying much weight but offering a minor point or question, willing, in the end, to go whichever way the rest went.

And then there was Daniel.

In our two years at Yale, Daniel had fashioned himself into the closest thing we had to a *black and shining prince*. He had the build for it and the bona fides (he was an Omega and also from the same town as the Jackson 5) and the brains: he knew the histories of the programs that had come before us, and many of the people, too. He introduced me to Ella Baker (or tried) and to Paul Robeson, who was his idol. Daniel took to the task of becoming Paul Robeson the way some boys I grew up with tried to *be like Mike*, but with much more success. He played on the varsity football team, of course. He was a star in the black theater ensemble, especially whenever the role called for *Tired Respectable Pre–Civil Rights Negro Father*. He tutored children in Bridgeport, you remember. He knew how to navigate the archives at the Beinecke Rare Book and Manuscript Library before many of us knew they existed. When the idea of the Union first took shape, it was natural for Daniel to be at the helm. He knew this. Everybody else knew it. And though I knew it, too, that did not change the fact that I wanted desperately to be in charge.

I'm going to keep dragging my name through the mud, don't you worry, but I will say that this one desire of mine was not sinister, even if part of it was due to my fear of being subject to anybody's authority. I had come up with (or stolen) most of the ideas that had shaped the Union so far, had worked hard throughout the summer, even as I sabotaged my relationship with River by night, even harder than Daniel Blake himself—and despite the fact that I could be a mean petty queen under all the football pads, I had great respect for Mr. Blake and never stepped on his toes. Besides, he already had so much . . . Couldn't I have this little thing that wasn't even a thing yet and would not be a thing unless the leader, unless *we*, made it so? I could not make that case, though. So I stood and watched and waited.

At some point, Riley—pacing the floor, stabbing the air with his hands like he was fighting some invisible monster—spoke up.

Yo . . . so you're gonna be president of this thing, right?

He was talking to Daniel.

Daniel leaned against the white wall with his long thick-knuckled fingers pressed to the side of his chin. Everyone turned to him like he was the goddamn Queen of Sheba. AJ floated into the living room without notice, before Daniel could respond.

Hey . . . what do you guys think about co-presidents?

He could not have known, poor holy fool, that asking football players what they thought of co-leaders was akin to asking the College of Cardinals whether it made sense to have two popes for a while. We all knew there could be only one, despite the trend at Yale and other colleges to have enough leaders to satisfy everybody's parents and destroy all hope that anything would ever be accomplished.

The room had gone for Daniel, which meant that I would go for Daniel—I have always believed that groups must choose their leaders and that naked grasps for power make folks look bad. But still, I kept my mouth shut, because there is one other thing you must try to do in a group meeting: speak last. Daniel had not yet responded.

You know . . . Daniel let the words ooze out, stretched those giant hands, *I actually think it should be Casey.*

Really? Riley, knife tip at my back.

I mean . . . Casey pushed us not to do that Men of Color Council bullshit in the first place. I think he's the best one to lead this.

That was enough.

Daniel must have known that you can trace most revolutions, even small ones, to a group that includes at least one boy or girl with a vengeful heart and an open mind. Must have known I was that boy. If he had not seen what I was willing to endure to play against Harvard, if he had not read my *we should be America line*, if he had not listened to my rants throughout the summer as we birthed the Union, then he would not have taken his power and put it in my hands. But he had and he did, though I did not know exactly what to do with it. No matter.

> *i made it up*
> *here on this bridge between starshine and clay*

I had no idols. I was not an intellectual. I was not an activist. History did not interest me much, hell it was hard enough to understand what was happening day to day. All I knew for sure was that I didn't know much of nothing. So I watched people. I listened to them, actually listened to understand, listened to what they said and tried to hear what they did not say, too. I was willing to consider almost any notion as long as there was no obvious reason why I should not. (My *obvious reasons*: gut instinct, superstitions, prior experience, sometimes the law.) And I never forgot a thing because I wrote it all down.

You got to, Casey—you got to write it.

Dr. Edward Joyner speaking: a man who looked and sounded like the perfect person to have been Jesse Jackson's press secretary, with the low afro and stadium-announcer voice and the proverbs and the need to touch everybody he met, to tell them something they'd remember. I reread Doc's words more than any others, though I also am reminded of something my daddy used to say when I was a little boy and he was still telling me stuff: *Opinions are like assholes, Scooter. Everybody's got one and they all stink.*

It wasn't until I met with most of Yale's black faculty, hoping to learn from them how to lead the Union, that I realized just how wise my daddy had been. It is also clear that father and son share a tendency to say things that are more extreme than the truth will allow, since some of the opinions I heard were helpful, especially Dr. Joyner's.

Aside from taking me and Daniel for a meal every now and then (he was the only elder to ever feed us; didn't these rich black people know we were hungry?) and buying me a suit for graduation without me even telling him I needed one, Dr. Joyner also gave me the most important advice that I did not listen to: *Fellas*—sitting across from me and Daniel in Mama Mary's, his favorite diner, he unfolded a white napkin and started writing out a few principles—*all this work you're doing, all this work we got to do, is liberation work. Got to be about liberation.* And he gave me the most dangerous advice, which I sopped up like gravy:

You fellas remember this. I tell my son all the time. I say, "Son, the best revenge is excellence."

I had not told Doc how I hungered for revenge, revenge against so many people for so many reasons that I might even have wanted revenge against myself—the hunger was that unfocused. He must have seen it in my eyes or hands or something. Whatever it was, I took that as an endorsement, a green light, a voice that had cried out in the wilderness for years and years for me, and now was at hand. So I led the Union, led these boys who *were* the Union, the most excellent way I knew how: far and without mercy.

Exhibit A: my dear friend Quincy Strickland, the Union's first secretary—well, the second, since the first was fired after two or three weeks. Boy thought he was going to sit up on his phone in our meetings, which apparently was what he did in architecture studio, too, since he was (at least I was told) the best student in the program. *Uh-uh.* Anyway, Quincy was a year behind me, a wiry high-yellow boy from Tulsa, where his family had been during the 1921 race riot led by a white mob that destroyed Negro Wall Street, in the Greenwood section, then the wealthiest black community in America. Judging from his skin and cheekbones, which were just like his mother's, I figure some of his family had been in Oklahoma long before this.

Quincy and I became close, perhaps because we were both from that part of the country where every individual can choose to be either from the South or from the West, perhaps because not many other boys at Yale had the same sneakers he wore, perhaps because nobody else called him *nigga.* It could have also been because, winter break of his freshman year, I had a car and he needed a ride back to Oklahoma.

We hit the road minutes after he submitted his organic chemistry exam and just as a snowstorm slammed New England. Sometime after making it past New York but definitely before we were west of Scranton, Quincy announced that he either had an empty stomach or a full bladder. He asked to stop.

I only stop when the gas tank is empty, Quincy. That's two more hours from now, so you're just gonna have to wait.

What?!? Casey. What the fuck?

We gotta keep moving, man.

Nigga. You better stop this damn car.

I kept driving. Turned up the music.

He handled his business when we stopped for gas. We got back on the road without much more delay, driving through the night across Pennsylvania and Ohio and Indiana, arcing down through all that land I never wanted to see again, down through Saint Louis and the rest of Missouri, stopping only when we were right at fumes. It's nearly twenty-two hours from New Haven to Tulsa, and by the ten-hour mark Quincy had either accepted his fate, grown delirious, or found some pride in his fortitude. He was in a good mood, behind the wheel. I reclined in the passenger seat to doze.

I woke up as we were passing through some unknown town, and spotted a fast food joint approaching on the service road. I had not eaten since we left New Haven.

Pull over at that Wendy's, Quincy.

He signaled to switch lanes and slowed down as we neared the exit. Then at the last minute, he let out a wicked country laugh and slammed the accelerator.

Ha! Naw, bitch. We ain't outta gas yet!

I was too impressed to be angry. He had come so far, so fast.

The next time I woke, it was morning. I was lying almost parallel to the floor of the car, and all I could see was the interior and the view outside the two passenger windows. I realized immediately that I was dead. The sky looked like it had smudged all the ash of the universe over its face, covering the clouds, blotting out the sun, blending in with the charred anorexic trees, which were dead, too, planted there on the banks of the Acheron. While I was sleeping (I told myself), Quincy had crashed the car and what I saw outside was hell. Perhaps you stay in hell forever just the way you died, or at least come in that way.

I looked over at Quincy, who was driving. Dead.

Where are we?

We're almost in Tulsa. You wanna drive?

There had been a bad storm in Oklahoma before we rolled in, he said. It had massacred the landscape.

Nah, you can take us on in.

You should have seen that boy's face when we walked into his mother's house. Part of me wonders whether he was so happy to see her because he had worried through the night that he might never see her again.

Mama! Casey wouldn't let us stop unless we needed gas. We didn't even eat nothing! All that way. Crazy.

His mother looked genuinely horrified but she was so kind that she fixed a meal and let me have some, too.

Wow. Well I'm so glad you guys made it. Thank you for getting him home, Casey.

Glad to, ma'am.

And I was glad. Glad to get back on the road and head to Dallas to rest for a while, since it had been a long fall with the Union and with the 2007 Yale football campaign—the Bulldogs had been on track to have our first perfect season since 1960, to become the first ten-win Yale team since 1905, until we suffered such a shocking loss to Harvard (37–6) in front of 57,248 people in the Yale Bowl that I still have a hard time talking about it.

But more than this, I was glad to show Quincy just what was feasible when he threw out all prior notions of what was plausible. I wonder if our night ride helped him at all during his years in medical school—he became one of the top neurosurgery residents in the country, you know.

I tell you of that ride because an institution is only the shadow of human beings—in the beginning it is nothing but human beings—and my journey to Tulsa with Quincy is different only in form from the rest of my work with the Union in those early days, so that many of the men say to me, today, the same words I said to them again and again a decade ago: *Always go above and beyond the call of duty.* Be first. Be bold. Be perfect. Give your last full measure of devotion. Then give some more. They learned this commandment and kept it well. But it also seems that one of them snitched.

Not long after I returned to New Haven from winter break, Doris invited me to her office. I went gladly, no hat this time.

My dear. I've gotten some reports and I'm concerned. The boys . . . You're just driving them too hard, Casey. Too hard.

I had my notebook but did not bother to open it. Just stared at Doris.

Now, listen, she continued. *I understand. I can be like that sometimes. My way or the highway. Really, I can.*

She flipped her hands over on her desk like she was playing patty-cake alone. Looked at them. Looked back up at me. Smiled.

You know what I'm saying?

Yes I get it . . . but what am I supposed to do?

Ha . . . I don't know! Maybe, you know, try a little tenderness?

I assume that I laughed and agreed so the meeting could end. I know for sure that I didn't take her advice. It's not that I intended to be cruel, to drive them *too* hard. I just believed there should be someone in their corner always shouting and clapping for (or sometimes *at*) them, pushing them even when they did not want to be pushed—felt it my duty to be there and show them a way. I realize now, much too late, that my way *was* too hard, if only because I did not know a thing about tenderness and could only give what I had. No excuse, just a reason.

It did not help that my way seemed to work. I asked Riley many years later why any of them put up with me. *Man, we all just wanted to be the greatest,* he said. And they were. They truly were.

You should have seen them walking around campus in their ties, even the ones they had to borrow, meeting en masse in the nicest rooms on campus, in full view of skittish white students, learning *Robert's Rules of Order* to ratify the Union's constitution, standing out in the cold to collect donations for the New Haven Children's Hospital, raising their right hand to recite the Union's pledge:

As a member of the Yale Black Men's Union, I pledge to uphold the standards of the organization: unity, service, and support. I will commit myself to fostering a true bond with my brothers. I will commit myself to enhancing the lives of those beyond Yale's campus through my service to the community. I will commit myself to providing a helping hand in my brother's time of need and to accepting one in my own.

It was beautiful to see them live up to their commitments.

Even Noah Lockhart, a doctoral student who became my closest advisor, was proud. *Organizations,* he explained, *especially black organizations— are like jazz. If you don't know shit about jazz and you went down to New Orleans and saw a bum playing the trumpet on one corner and Louis Armstrong on another, you wouldn't know the difference. Know what I'm saying? People don't know shit, Casey, so they can't tell serious organizations apart from unserious organizations. You have to be serious. You have to use every opportunity to show others you are serious. Don't nobody wanna do that, man.*

Noah had not wasted a single opportunity since he left Baltimore to enroll at Harvard, a journey that had been quite similar to mine from Dallas to Yale. In four years on the Charles River, he became the most quoted black person in the history of the *Harvard Crimson* and the most successful president of the Harvard Black Men's Forum. Went on to Oxford for a masters, then to Yale for a doctorate (where I tracked him down), and the last time I saw him, one of the Rothschilds interrupted our meal to hug his neck and ask that he accept an offer to come back to Harvard as a professor. We sat in that dim restaurant and looked at each other with a nod and a smile—a nod and smile to all our ancestors, to let them know that we, the race, had produced this cold, cold boy from Baltimore. I didn't need a Rothschild to tell me that, though. Knew it when I first sat with him in the Hall of Graduate Studies like it was his living room—him leisurely eating snacks, reclined in his seat with that smirk he always wore, telling me in a low voice but with no uncertainty that there were three principles I had to keep in mind if I was going to be a real leader:

1. *Manufacture the Momentum:* Always convince others that something big is happening, even if nothing at all has happened yet.
2. *The Illusion of Inclusion:* Make everyone feel like they are helping to decide things, even if you have already decided, which should be the case.
3. *Shame and Fame:* These are the leader's most important tools of coercion, absent money or guns.

I had discovered no obvious reasons why these were not principles by which to live and lead. I had used the first and second to great effect in the early months of the Union. I was eager to test the third, but needed something grander than a meeting or a charity drive. A spectacle, that's what I needed. So as with our alma mater, we stole the best thing our rivals to the north had done and made it our own, at the *inaugural* (we always used this word instead of *first*) Tribute to Black Women.

The Tribute was much more than a way to coerce my members, I promise—though I will admit that I stumbled on the right and noble impulse without trying. When I read a statement such as: *For generations men have come into the world, either instinctively knowing or believing or being taught that since they were men they in one way or another had to be responsible for the women and children, which means the universe.* I did not shout *Patriarchy!* (had never heard the word) nor did I rush to a feminist text (had not read any) or a black feminist text (did not know there was a difference). I just said to myself the same thing Audre Lorde said, in essence, to James Baldwin when he threw this claim at her: *Bullshit.*

My life had been so often saved by women and so often disturbed or at least made uncomfortable by men that I had never been convinced that men should be in charge of anything, let alone the universe or a woman or a child, especially if the child was me. So I believed in the Tribute for much the same reason I believed I should not disappoint Coach Reno when he said *We really need you, Case.*

My personal particulars were also helpful: Since I had no romantic ties to the women at Yale (nor the men, for that matter), I was able to see the relations of black women and black men on campus with a pretty objective eye—enough to see that such relations were not good.

It was not only that so many of the boys did not seem to desire these girls as partners, though that was a real issue that I don't take any blame for and don't want to wade into. It was also that, in the four-hundred-year saga of black people in America, the main storyline has been the Crisis of the Black Man—which made all of us the stars of the drama, made us few who had reached a place like Yale a precious commodity, and made our peers of the other sex, far too often, invisible. And because my only friends outside the football team those first two years had been three girls from three very different corners of the *diaspora*, I had enough data to know that even if 97 percent of these women graduated, at least that percentage of them had an awful hard time—quite often because of my members. The Tribute would be a small remedy.

But beyond (or beneath) all these motives, I pushed for the Tribute to Black Women for the same reason most people host events: to give awards to people I liked.

The chief financial officer at Yale, our Woman of the Year, had offered me and Daniel solid advice, wrote sizable checks, and possessed a smile that still makes me happy when I picture it. Elizabeth Alexander, our Distinguished Alumna, was Riley's mentor as well as his employer, since he babysat her children. The three Rising Trailblazers—young women from the senior class—were friends of Daniel's, which explains, in part, why he got the tap for Skull and Bones instead of me; we will get to that shortly. And these three were, for me, placeholders for the three girls who had been my friends and had gone on to be three brilliant, accomplished young women on campus.

This is how, or why, the sausage of an event is made. You want an event to put your institution on the minds of the people, to convey your values and reflect on them at least for one night, to get luminaries you admire to have a meal with you, and to make your friends feel good. You also, in the spirit of Shame and Fame, want to reward your members for the work that they have done and, in the case of college students, perhaps get them some tail.

Elijah, hardest-working of them all, spoke first. I can't tell you what he said because I don't remember it and I did not write it down. And if it had not been for the *Yale Daily News*, I wouldn't be able to tell you what anybody said, not even Elizabeth Alexander, who spoke that night as she would in less than a year's time at the most important inauguration of the young twenty-first century—spoke like a butterfly who still remembers what happened in the cocoon and can tell it to you, wing-voice a-flutter, so that you feel what it was like in there, too.

Black love is a powerful thing, she said, according to the student reporter who covered the Tribute.

And on this night, love—or whatever the feeling was in the room— indeed seemed powerful, powerful enough to put genuine smiles on the boys and girls, even those who had not won an award; powerful enough to make them speak to each other, hug each other, stand up a little straighter around each other and alone; powerful enough to satisfy another mantra we adopted in that first year of the Union: *We measure success by the lives that we change.*

But love, of course, can't pay for living—so I was eager to give something else a try, like money.

chapter **SEVENTEEN**

There are years that ask questions *and years that answer,* and other years that throw their hands up and say *You figure it out.* 2008 was that kind of year, at least on Wall Street.

I wasn't actually *on* Wall Street, to tell the truth. Hardly anybody was. Of the ten major firms crippling the world at that time, only one operated from the place on everybody's lips: the US headquarters of Deutsche Bank, at 60 Wall Street. Germans.

As for the rest: Goldman Sachs was *close* to Wall Street: at 85 Broad Street in the financial district, though the firm had already decided to move. Credit Suisse was one hour (by foot) due north of Wall Street, on Madison Avenue just west of Madison Square Park, which is almost a mile east of the Garden. Even farther away was Morgan Stanley, nestled in the theater district at 1585 Broadway.

There was Citigroup, at 399 Park Avenue, which no one likely noticed because the firm did not put its name on this building; instead, the Citigroup Center towered across the street, seemingly designed to keep the attention of passersby away from the real action. There was Merrill Lynch, with three offices still open in the city, none of them on Wall Street. There was the United Bank of Switzerland (UBS), which claimed to have an office on Sixth Avenue, in Midtown. But everyone I knew who had the misfortune of working for UBS traveled every morning to Stamford, Connecticut—nearly forty miles from Wall Street. Most elusive of all was Lazard, hidden on the upper floors of Rockefeller Center somewhere between *The Tonight Show* and the observation deck that overlooked the rink where children came to skate at Christmastime.

JPMorgan Chase—which built the most famous house of American finance at 23 Wall Street in 1914, now abandoned—had its headquarters at 270 Park Avenue. One block west, at 383 Madison Avenue, Bear Stearns sat like your neighbor's newspaper, swiped by JPMorgan in March 2008 for 2 dollars per share, down from 150 dollars per share the year before.

That left Lehman Brothers, still alive if not well, at 745 Seventh Avenue, between Forty-Seventh and Forty-Eighth Streets, nearly in the heart of Times Square, figuratively at the heart of the worst economic crisis since the Great Depression, and right next door to the Lace Gentlemen's Club, where a friend took me one night to receive my first and last lap dance, from a kind young woman. This felt much worse than the Crisis, to me.

And while it may seem that these varied addresses are just minor details, if not wholly irrelevant, I have little doubt that the world would have been much better off if it had truly known *where* everybody was, not to mention the *who* and *what* of the matter. But the only thing I know for sure about that time is that nobody seemed to know anything. So we all became like those adults I knew as a child who, instead of saying *Texas Electric cut my lights off,* protested *The devil is busy.* Disaster never strikes in such abstract terms as *the devil* or *Wall Street,* unfortunately. It comes from places we fail to look, from things we fail to name, from people we fail to admit look much like us—*are us.* Me, at least.

In my defense, none of this was my idea at first, either. Let's go back to South Oak Cliff for a moment.

Not long after the tall pale sunken-eyed man from Yale came to watch me run on film, another tall pale man, this one in a suit, came to ask me questions. He was a lawyer, and had been sent by the Dallas Bar Association to find out whether there were any kids at my high school who wanted to practice law when they grew up. You should know that this was a program in spirit and in form just like the Mayor for a Day setup, except for a whole summer and with pay: one student from every public school would be chosen, sent downtown for a special experience and a write-up in the paper, and the city would otherwise continue with its regular programming of letting the children in its public schools waste away.

I sat in that same small conference room next to the principal's office and spoke clearly and laughed whenever the tall pale man laughed, and said something about wanting to help people—Perry Mason and Johnnie Cochran were the only lawyers I knew, though neither personally—and a few days later, I was informed that I would be the envoy from South Oak Cliff.

I was placed at one of the top law firms in the state, Vinson & Elkins, a firm that had been legal counsel to the company *Fortune* magazine had named "America's Most Innovative Company" six years in a row, until it was revealed that this company, Enron, had achieved its historic success through a system of historic fraud. So, months after its final *Fortune* honor, Enron made history yet again as the largest bankruptcy of all time—a record it held until it was surpassed by Lehman Brothers in 2008.

But that summer I knew nothing about Enron and nothing about Lehman Brothers and only slightly more about the law, since the only people who spoke to me were a few legal secretaries and the mail clerk and the two lawyers whose job it was to supervise me. And although one of them let me tag along on the case she was litigating that summer—representing one of the big accounting firms, which had allegedly cheated somebody out of money—I can't tell you much about the particulars. It's not because I signed anything, it's just that I have never been more bored in my life than the few weeks I worked on that case. Aside from the brief spells I left the building to pick up sandwiches for everybody, I spent a good chunk of the trial itself asleep, my head resting against the comfortable walls of the federal courtroom.

I woke up from one of these naps on a late-summer afternoon just as the judge announced the verdict: *not guilty*, which was fine with me, although it never was clear to my untrained legal mind how all that money could have disappeared and nobody was guilty. I didn't ask any questions, though. My days in court were over and I was free to continue my summer internship in peace—left alone all day to browse the internet, to sort file folders in a long cold conference room, to take an hour and a half lunch, which all the lawyers did, too. Because of this stellar performance, they invited me back for the following summer, after I graduated from high school.

But something happened in the short time between the summer of my seventeenth year and that of my eighteenth year. I still looked the same. Still sounded the same. Still wore the same loud clothes—Auntie O worked at Haggar and gave me a nice gold shirt and cuff links. But now, instead of being left alone to browse the internet, instead of sitting alone in that freezing conference room with those manila folders, instead of wandering the tunnels below downtown Dallas en route to Subway, I started receiving an offer that I had no obvious reason to decline: *Hey, Casey, why don't you let me take you to lunch?*

These were not just any old fogies asking, but partners of the firm. All men, all white, all monied, all kindly extending invitations to lunch. And they did not want to join me in the tunnels for a foot-long sandwich. They wanted to take me to Stephan Pyles and Al Biernat's and Mi Cocina. *Get a salad, get an appetizer, get a steak, get some foie gras while you're at it. Have you had foie gras before? No, sir. Well try it! Dessert? Sure.* I'm not complaining, just trying to tell you what it was like to be a whore for the first time. Well, this kind of whore for the first time.

Those men were so nice to me, that food was so delicious, those lunches were so long—these were real blessings being poured down on me, you see? Nothing about me had changed on the outside, so there had to have been some inner change, some light turned on in my soul that these men could see. Or, as was the case, I had just been accepted to Yale.

And they did not want anything in return. The only request these men made of me, typically when joined by a colleague or a wife, was that I tell my *story*.

Casey, why don't you tell Laura your story. Laura, you've gotta hear this.

There I was, nineteen years old, trying to keep the foie gras goo down, unsure at first what these men meant. But if I took too long to tell it, my host would relieve me of the duty—*It must be hard to talk about; mind if I tell Laura?*—and do it himself.

So Casey is from South Dallas—Oak Cliff, right, Casey? (Yes, sir)—really poor neighborhood, as you know. Had a terrible, rough childhood. Both parents—both parents, right, Casey? (Mmhmm)—gone at an early age. Drugs. His grandmother—which grandmother helped raise you, Casey, was it both? (Yes, sir)—both grandmothers took care of him, and I think a sister. And then Casey finishes from South Oak Cliff and is headed off to Yale in the fall. He's even gonna play football for them, for Yale. Can you believe that?

Whether they could believe it or not, audiences seemed to enjoy it a great deal—and the men asked for more lunches and a few coffees (which I still did not drink) and the summer after my freshman year invited me back to Vinson & Elkins for another round of story and lunch and introductions, which, of course, I accepted without hesitation. But the finest lunch in the world could not last all day, so I still spent hours in a little cubicle browsing the internet, waiting for the next invitation. This was not what I had in mind for my halcyon days.

I went back to Yale my sophomore year, clueless as to what I wanted to do with my life. So I asked a senior boy from the football team (the same who'd taken me to Bridgeport and would soon take me to Lace) for advice.

Case, I say you should really try to get into investment banking, man.

What's that, Kev?

Listen . . . it doesn't even matter. Just let me tell you—bankers make like $60,000 right out of school. You should look into it.

I had always dreamed of being rich. Whenever someone offered me that *Money can't buy happiness* crap, I responded, if only in my head, *You clearly have no idea what money is for.* Money may not buy happiness, but it sure as hell can buy you food and some clothes and a ride somewhere— can buy you all those things that, when you don't have them, make you very unhappy and mean. So I decided that I should be an investment banker simply because I did not have any money and none of my people had any money and I wanted to acquire some for them but mostly for myself.

And wouldn't you know it, one of those Vinson & Elkins partners had a dear friend who was an investment banker at the Dallas office of Lehman Brothers, and they arranged for me to spend a summer there in 2007, where I heard an incredible, if prescient, piece of wisdom from my boss's supreme boss, who was beamed into a conference room via a combination of television and the internet: *In the land of the blind,* he said at the end of one morning meeting, *the one-eyed man is king.*

The bankers in Dallas had a vast store of these proverbs, but they did not have $60,000 salaries for twenty-year-olds. Only the bankers at Lehman Brothers headquarters made that kind of money, so at the end of that 2007 summer I realized that if I was going to be rich, I had to make my way to New York City. This, too, was easy enough—a former Yale football player ran recruiting for Lehman's New York office, set up my interviews, and offered me a job for the summer of 2008. A job that, sure enough, came with a $60,000 salary, adjusted for my eight-week stint.

I say all that to say: The American Dream is real. Not that foolishness you hear from politicians—*If you work hard and play by the rules you can do anything, be anybody, in this country.* I'm talking about the *real* American Dream, the way the country actually works: *If you know the right people, they can help you do anything, be anybody, rules and hard work be damned— as long as they like you.* They *do* have to like you, and that takes a good deal of work.

This dream, of course, cannot be extended to three hundred million people and, therefore, cannot be confessed to any. So despite the fact that America is designed from rooter to tooter for most of its citizens— especially those in places like Oak Cliff—to have nothing and achieve nothing, the political version of the American Dream is essential, kids like me are essential: something and/or someone has to keep the steam down. Perhaps that's why this crazy thing happened that I wasn't going to tell you about, since I think I've made my point—but it's one of those stories that will make you want to die all over again if you die without telling, so I'll just tell it real quick.

One summer evening not too long ago, as I stood near the end of a long buffet line in Dallas, I felt a hand rest on my shoulder. I rarely like to be touched without notice so I just stood there a second or two, hoping it might be a phantom sensation, before I glanced back. I saw, then, that the hand belonged to George W. Bush.

For some reason, the 43rd president of the United States had to stand in line for dinner just like normal people, and also like normal people (but unlike me) he did not want to loiter there fondling lint in his pocket and pretending to appreciate the art on the walls, which was his. The president wanted to talk. Fine. So we talked as we moved along the line and put a few rolls and potatoes and, if I remember correctly, a slice of salmon apiece on our plates. The Secret Service or somebody took the president's plate once it was full. They did not take mine, so I held it between myself and the president, who squared up with me before we went to our seats.

Lemme ask you somethin', he said. Scrunched his mouth. *Was your dad around?*

This felt as out of the blue to me then as it may feel to you now. For six or seven minutes, the president and I had run a pretty good gamut of gab—talked about his paintings and his schooldays and his brother Jeb, who was at that time campaigning, poorly, to be the 45th president. Yet after all that, Mr. Bush needed to know—or *wanted* to know, I'm trying not to speculate—whether I had grown up with a father. And since I had mastered the art of giving people exactly what I thought they wanted (which got me into a lot of trouble, not all of it bad), I replied, without even thinking much:

No, sir. Both of my parents were gone by the time I was twelve.

Which, as we know, was not quite true but not entirely untrue, either.

I don't remember what he said right after that but I do know, because there's video evidence, that two years passed and I remained on the president's mind. He was sitting on a stage in Beverly Hills, being interviewed by a gentleman who had also been famous for a long time—first for his success in finance, then for the felonies which had, in part, made the success possible, and, finally, as is the American way, for his good deeds. The man wanted to hear about the president's latest good deed: a program that he and the 42nd president had launched around the time we met. Mr. Bush seized the opportunity to share, with a *check this out* flick of his hand, a case study:

So I'm sitting next to a young African-American kid ... so, uh, I said, What do you do, man? He said, uh—he skips ahead—*I said where you from? He said, Dallas. Where? South Oak Cliff.* The president lowers his voice as he tells this part—*South Oak Cliff's, you know, on the other side of the Trinity River*—then resumes: *I said, Wow, did you go to college? He said, Yeah, I went to Yale*—he does an *aw-shucks* shrug, voice low again: *That's where I happened to go.* Then he looks down, continues. *And I said, Uh, interesting, you know you musta had parents who drove you*—then looks up and out at the audience. *He said, Not at all. My dad died early, my mother's in prison ... but I had an aunt that focused me, plus I was a pretty good football player.* Shrugs again, smirks—*I said, I didn't know Yale cared about football*—then smothers the laugh line: *Anyway, so he goes to Harvard Business School and he applies [to the program].*

Now, when I first heard the president's story, I thought, *Wow that kid is impressive!* Then I realized that the president was talking about *me* and so I felt a bit confused and a little dirty, too. But I was not upset at all. Couldn't be. In our buffet line tete-a-tete I had offered Mr. Bush a vague, compelling story, the kind of story I'd learned to tell at my lunches years before, though shorter and more to the heartbreaking point. And he, being the world-class politician that he is, took that raw material and fashioned an even more pointed and compelling version, so inaccurate that it became a new delicious story of its own, the kind of story a man needs if he's going to keep his subjects from despair or mass unrest or, most of all, from the truth about their society. I imagine that is one reason he became president, and I reckon it is also why so many of the lunch-men and their wives said nice things to me like, *Casey, you are the embodiment of the American Dream!* But it took me many years to realize that, instead of smiling and saying *thank you,* I should have wept.

Anyway, there would be plenty of time for tears. The summer of 2008 was a time for money, though not for all.

On 16 May 2008, three days before I arrived at Lehman, the *New York Times* announced:

People on Wall Street seem to be vanishing overnight.

Perhaps it seemed that way because there was no one on Wall Street to begin with. But aside from the wrong location, this journalist used the wrong word to describe what happened overnight. When I showed up on May 19, there were surely some people missing: over a thousand gone in the past month. But these people had not *vanished*. They had been *fired*—again, not an act of God but of women and of men. Mostly men. Men like Skip McGee.

Good morning, ladies and gentlemen. Welcome to Lehman Brothers.

There were a hundred some-odd summer apprentices planted in the polished cushioned wooden seats of the Lehman Brothers auditorium that first day, all silent, listening to Skip McGee. Someone told me he was the head of the investment banking division, which sounded important. Even better, he sounded like he was from Texas and he looked rich. He was both.

I know there's been a lotta noise—he waved his hands at us as if to sprinkle pixie dust—*out there. But lemme tell ya. The fundamentals of this firm . . . are strong. I been here a long long time, and this i'nt the first time we been knocked down. I promise you it won't be the last time we get back up. I do believe y'all are gonna have a great summer here at the firm.*

And, you know, on the whole, I *did* have a great summer at the firm, if only because I was paid great wads of US dollars just to sit at a desk from seven in the morning to eight or nine or ten at night and do what almost everybody else does at work for much less money: try to avoid actual work, and try to keep your boss from figuring out you don't know what you're doing.

The first objective was hard, sometimes. I was the only intern in our little group; there was always lunch to order or copies to make. Besides, it is impossible to convincingly twiddle your thumbs for thirteen hours.

Toward the end of my time at the firm, a new policy was instituted: we now had to work until nine to get a free ride home in a black town car. So I had to keep up my act for an extra hour from then on.

The second objective was much easier, since nothing I was asked to do seemed too difficult. Consider my first task, assigned by my immediate boss, who couldn't have been more than twenty-four years old:

All right, Casey, so there should be a file on your computer that I've already downloaded. Think the name is CDO Rate Table. You know what a CDO is?

I shook my head.

Got it. Yeah, I didn't know at first, either. It stands for "collateralized debt obligation." Pretty simple. Say you've got one thousand mortgages. They all generate different cash flows with different degrees of risk, right? If you pool all those mortgages together—collateralize them—you can then sell pieces of the pool—we call it an instrument—to investors at different rates, based on the risk of the underlying debt. Make sense?

Ah yep. That sounds cool. (I still don't know exactly how these things worked.)

Great. So every week, I need you to go in this file and follow the instructions to pull fresh data. We've got to keep the table updated for the whole group. Shouldn't take much time.

That day, or thereabout, Lehman Brothers was worth roughly $680 billion, more valuable than all the goods and services produced that year by all the nations of the former Soviet Union, save Russia. $269 billion of those billions were produced by *financial instruments*. Within four months, Lehman Brothers would be dead: purchased by a British bank for $1.35 billion, most of which was paid for the building at 745 Seventh Avenue. But I did not know that then.

I also did not know that, by the end of 2008, thanks in part to those CDOs, 861,644 families would lose their homes to foreclosure; that every American household would lose, on average, $5,800 in income; that the federal monies spent to keep the financial system from collapse—at least to keep my bosses from collapse—would cost each of those households, on average, $2,050; that five and one half million jobs would be lost, or *vanish*. The folks at Pew said all this.

But there was pain that Pew did not record that year, further away from *Main Street*—another term used to describe this crisis without actually understanding it—yet no one pitied the victims.

One morning at 745 Seventh Avenue, my boss's boss, and *his* boss, and their overlords all the way up to the executive suite, were called to meet with the Lehman chief, Dick Fuld. (This is all second- or third-hand, close to gossip, but from a good source: Theodore Roosevelt's great-grandson was a higher-up; his speechwriter sat behind me.) Fuld had an announcement: the firm's senior leaders would now be compensated more with Lehman Brothers stock than with hard cash.

What are we supposed to do with this shit?!

That's all I heard before my boss's boss slammed his office door. He was inside, commiserating with a colleague. I figure it was just setting in that his money, his homes, his retirement, his children's—or his great-grandchildren's—college funds were soon to *vanish*. But again, I did not know this then. And if I had known, I am not sure I would have cared. I had my own concerns, very far from 745 Seventh Avenue. It's only now that I realize how those concerns, which seemed so alien to world events, in fact furnished the most important lesson from my days at Lehman Brothers, the last days of a certain world.

You see, 2008 was a wonderful year in the gay clubs of New York.

Let me follow my own rules. It was a wonderful year at Secret Lounge, over by the West Side Highway; and at Mars 2112 which was just a pop-up party that summer, held in a cavernous basement at Fiftieth Street and Broadway; and at Escuelita, the first club I ever went to and almost the last, since it was vogue night and I had never seen a drag queen, so my fear obscured their magic; and at the G Lounge—at least,

I hear it was a good year there. I was not then (and am not now) a Chelsea kind of boy.

Nearly all these places are now closed. That's New York for you. But 2008 was perhaps the only time in American history when poor black and brown queers were more respected than rich white men. So in the midst of this great fun—and since I had more monies and less free time than ever—I agreed, one Saturday night, to do something I never did: go to Brooklyn. To *Langston's*, which I despised, if only because West Indians terrified me.

My routine that night was the same as always: Get dressed in my remaining pre-Yale clothes. Find one of my fitted caps and my sunglasses. Go to the nearest bodega for chewing gum. Wait for my then-friend to pick me up. Arrive at our destination and wait for him to buy me a drink. Stand on the wall, preferably in a corner. Drink the drink. Stand, drunk. Demur. Refuse all proposals to dance. Refuse most proposals to exchange numbers. Refuse some proposals to lock eyes, thus the sunglasses in the nighttime. Wait for a good song. When it comes, make a lap—more like a figure eight—through the club, to see who is there. See them. Make sure they don't really see me. At Langston's, I tried not to see anybody; somewhere deep down I worried that many West Indians carried pocket machetes.

I definitely did not want to see Victor. *Was that him? It was dark. He was dark. The club was crowded. I'm drunk. Jesus.* My then-friend thought I was ill. I was not ill. I was dead. Oklahoma-storm dead. *Where's-the-money* dead. I cupped my then-friend's ear to tell him I would be outside. I stood outside the door. I paced around the block. I came back for his keys. I sat in the car and cried.

Victor was much more dangerous than a machete-wielding West Indian. He was, for lack of a better phrase (and I don't mean this as an insult), Yale's most prominent queen. Sometimes he was a butch queen, but that distinction made no difference to me. Like most cute queens from Harlem—some of them my friends now—he talked a lot. About every-body's business, especially. Though he talked, he did not lie. And this gave Victor tremendous power, as did the fact that he was incredibly smart and helped a lot of people.

He had only gotten a glimpse of me, sauntering, then scurrying by him in the club. But that was all he needed, all that was required for him to go back to Harlem, back to his friends, back to Yale, and inform the whole world that I was not some *black and shining prince*, but a faggot. I had not yet realized that these things were often one and the same. It had also never crossed my mind that any boy from Yale would be at Langston's, since I assumed they would frequent a place like the G Lounge instead—and since hardly any of them crossed my mind, in that way, in general.

Don't worry . . . I got you, Victor texted.

I did worry. I sat in the car and waited for my then-friend to exit Langston's and drive me home or throw me in the Hudson River or park his car in a garage somewhere and leave me in it, engine running.

You aight, man?

Yeah. I'm cool.

I said nothing else on that long ride back to my friend's house, shades on, the sun beginning to rise, showing its light but not its face as if to say *What more do you want from me?*

It required the best of my eyelids to bar the door against all those tears in that New York dawn doom. I waved goodbye and went to sit in the driv-er's seat of my own car, parked a block away. I dug in my jacket pocket for my cell phone and dialed the only number I knew to dial.

Um . . . Casey? . . . Hellooo?

Micah . . . Mi—I could not speak. Tried to reach through the phone with sobs.

Micah was twenty-six at the time, five years my senior. But he was my elder in many other ways as well, and also my best friend. Some of his elder stature likely came down to him through his grandfather, a pastor in the AME Church, and *his* father, a pastor in the AME Church, and *his* father, also a pastor in the AME Church, back when the AME Church was the finest if not the only institution that black people had established on this continent, or at least in North Carolina. The stature was fortified by the fact that Micah *looked* like an elder. Not that he looked old, which he did not. It's just that some people—with deep obsidian skin, stern voices, rail-thin frames, and narrow fingers that, when they pop you, seem filled with adamantium—make you believe the claim that there were, not long after Adam and Eve, black people: carrying the curse of Ham, perhaps, but carrying the wisdom of the world for sure. And for nearly two decades, going back to his late teens in Atlanta's heyday—where he trained at Morehouse and as a classical violinist before going off to get a PhD—Micah had been shepherding lost confused boys like me into the light of day and of themselves. That is why I called him.

Whoa ... what is going on??

I coughed out the start of the story. He cut me off. Guess I was crying too much.

Uh-uh. Casey. I can't. That was all he said. I knew he meant it. Micah had the rare ability to refuse any inconvenience, even if it might save your life.

Bye, Micah.

Thus betrayed, I pulled myself together for the long drive from the depths of Brooklyn where my then-friend lived, across one of the majestic New York bridges that inspire you to dream or jump, up the West Side Highway to the low Nineties, where I was renting a room big enough for a tiny desk and a twin bed, which touched three of the walls. I lay on that bed on my back, staring at the ceiling, then at my phone. It was five a.m. or so. In the time it took to get from Bay Ridge to Ninetieth and Broadway, I had decided it made sense to call River for help.

He was probably as upset to hear from me as I had been at Micah for hanging up, but I figured he could relate and find a morsel of concern, or at least pretend. Besides, he had called a few months earlier with a crisis of his own, which I don't remember now because I had not been listening closely, had just been glad to hear from him. I bet he also got some pleasure from hearing me cry and talking to me like he was my daddy.

Why did you go to the club, anyway?

I don't know, man. Just something to do. I don't know.

Hmph. Well. Listen. I bet you're gonna be okay. Just get some sleep, aight?

And for the first time since I'd known them, River and Micah agreed on something, and were right. My life was not over, at least in the way I feared. Victor and I became good friends; he never said anything or forced my hand. Neither he nor Micah (I didn't speak to River again for a long time) shamed me for being so invested in a lie, so distraught when it seemed that lie had run its course. Maybe they knew that sometimes a lie is all that holds a life together. All it takes to tear one down, too. For in the end, there is an extraordinary cost for fraud—personal and otherwise. It may be paid this evening, this lifetime, or the next and next, but it must be paid, with dollars or with blood. We don't need evil to destroy the world, after all. A simple lie will do.

As far as I can tell, the Crisis was not much more than this, the end of a well-told and profitable lie; a bill come due. There's no big scandal in that. America was born and raised on much more-inhumane lies, much greater crimes. In fact, of all the things that *do* pay in this country, crime seems to be near the very top of the list. Would rank much higher if we called the things that *should* be crimes by their rightful name.

No, the scandal, if there is one, of the Crisis and the country, is that some folks ate up all the grub of lies and skipped out on the check.

Including me. Once Lehman Brothers was sold in September, I was offered a job at the acquiring firm. A job that came with, of course, a $60,000 salary. I didn't take it, though not for guilt or morals. Just plain common sense: I knew that not a single person who went to work on *Wall Street* at that time would ever be president of the United States. So the money had to wait.

An Interlude for Me

I had a dream that somebody was trying to kill me.

It was a dream I'd had for a while, first when I was twenty-one, back in that summer of 2008. I'd hoped that was the last time, just as I'd hoped all the times after that were the last, just as I hoped this time was, too.

The dream begins in a house, I think. I know that I keep going to the same house, a large wooden house with many windows and wide doors. Each time I go to the house, the doors are open. Somebody has broken in, looking for something, looking for me. I go to the house three or four times in this dream. Each time, I am more frustrated with the house, or with the situation. I can't tell. Each time I go back to the house, it is empty, then someone runs through the door or jumps through a window or drives across the lawn, coming after me. Each time I go back to the house, I feel more afraid.

Next, I am in a bar. A friend I know in real life is there. He orders a drink, though in real life he does not drink. I pull up a barstool next to him, order the same drink he ordered, listen to the bartender tell me about the drink. I feel eyes on me. I look in the far right corner of the bar and see a woman, I do not know her, watching me. All of a sudden, I'm back at the house. It is night.

Everything is fine at the house, quiet. Then a car crashes through the wall. I run.

Next, I am jogging in the middle of a neighborhood street on a cloudy afternoon. I am aware, in the dream, that I do not jog in real life. I am aware that the shoes I have on are not good for jogging. Another boy, a stranger, who does have good running shoes, jogs up beside me, passes me, continues to run in front of me, down the middle of the street. A woman—the woman from the bar, it seems—approaches him, upset. She's asking him questions that sound something like *Why are you so kind now? Who are you hanging with?* He keeps jogging. The woman vanishes. Soon, he is gone, too.

I approach an intersection: a four-lane Main Street, with shops on each side, two lanes going each way, a median with grass and small flowering shrubs. Suddenly, it is dusk.

I jog across the two lanes nearest me, then across the median. It is night again. Just as I'm about to cross the other two lanes, a car makes a U-turn in front of me. The car that crashed through the house? I don't know. I hear the engine vroom behind me. I feel the front of the car crash into my legs, launch me into the air, over the back of the car. I land in the middle of the street.

I can't move one of my legs. I am not paralyzed, just stuck on my butt in the middle of the street, trying to drag myself to the sidewalk, trying to crawl away because I know the car is coming back. I cannot tell if I am crying or saying *whoa* or *oooh*.

A woman, a girl, rushes over from her car, trying to help me. *Are you okay?* she asks. *Somebody's trying to kill me.* I'm dragging myself through the street, trying to get away from her, looking for the car, yelling at her— *Somebody's trying to kill me!* She's trying to grab my hand and get me out of the street. She keeps laughing, cooing *Nobody's trying to kill you. Come on.*

Another car, a van, speeds past her, parks in the street behind her. A man is in front, smiling, looking at people in the back of the van. *This is it.* But they just sit there in the van. I feel a bit relieved, but I stand up and try to limp-run away from the van anyway, away from the girl, who is still following me, reaching for me, trying to help. *Somebody's trying to kill me,* I keep telling her. *Nobody's trying to kill you,* she laughs. *You just got hit by a car. Nobody's trying to kill you. You just got hit by a car. Come on.* Laughing at me like I'm crazy, following after me as I limp away from her, away from the van, looking up and down the street for the car, for the person or people that are after me. *Somebody's trying to kill me! Nobody's trying to kill you.* Suddenly, a man appears from behind her—an older man, with no expression on his face—coming after me, not running, more like speed-walking around the girl, hands out for me, trying to kill me. *No no! No no no no! No no no no no no.* He keeps coming. I can't get away. He's reaching out for me, a knife in his hand, though at first it looks like a white card, like he would just put a white card in my breast pocket. But it's a knife and he's reaching out to put the knife in my chest and I'm yelling *No!* But he doesn't care and the girl won't stop him or is gone and nobody's coming to help. *No! No no no no no no no no!* My *no* won't work he won't stop I feel the knife going into my chest I scream or I moan *No no no! No no no no! No no no* and then I wake up, in the dark, in my bed, screaming *no.*

I lie there in the dark. It takes a few seconds to realize that I am not dead. But I can still feel what it was like to be hit by that car and thrown in the air, what it was like to keep telling that girl somebody was trying to kill me, to be laughed at like I was crazy, to be ambushed by the man with the knife, to have the knife put into my chest, to die in the dream for a moment. I lie there and I can still feel what it was like to be hunted.

I lie there in silence and can still hear the echoes of *no*. I bet the neighbors heard me. That's embarrassing. I feel exhausted, even though I've hardly moved. Feels like I've been electrocuted, or shook somebody real hard for a long time. My arms are tired. I catch my breath.

I lie there in the dark and a few thin streams of tears that seem calm and tired and disappointed run down to the pillow. I have had this dream since I was twenty-one and each time I hope it's the last time. Though not as much as I hoped that first time—a few weeks after I left Lehman Brothers and returned to New Haven to prepare for football season and my future.

I was lying in the floor of a secret society tomb because somehow that was the only place I had to stay. I don't remember what exactly happened in that first dream, besides what happens in all the dreams. I remember, more than anything, a friend shaking me out of my sleep. He seemed frightened, or disgusted.

Yo, Casey! Wake up. Get up, man. You aight??

He shook me awake right as I was about to be killed in the dream. I couldn't tell him what happened, so just looked up from the floor and wiped my eyes.

You were rocking down there, screaming and shit. That was wild, man. Fuck. You sure you aight?

Yeah, I laughed, *yeah I'm good. Just a bad dream or something.*

He looked at me as if I were a freak, which was fair and how I felt myself . . . out of control, with no idea why this had happened or how to stop it from happening again. I began to dread sleep, the *thought* of sleep, knowing that the dream would be there waiting for me. So I tried my best to stay awake. I figured, or I hoped, that if I worked instead of slept, I could keep the dream away. And, you know, I got a lot of stuff done in those waking hours. But here I am, a decade later, still being hunted in my sleep. I still feel the same panic when I wake, the same exhaustion, the same thin stream running down to my pillow. Still hear the echoes of *no.* Still hope that this time is the last time, though now I do not worry that it may come again tonight, or always.

Now I know what I did not know when the dream first came: that my dreams are part of *me,* even the nightmares—and all the waking hours of work in the world cannot erase them. I had to learn the hard way, though.

chapter EIGHTEEN

I am not the best mathematician around but I would estimate that, at any given time, about a quarter of the students at Yale want to be president.

Another quarter hope to work for a president (or prime minister, or the like). A third quarter dream of being imprisoned or martyred or publicly persecuted for opposing a president. My best guess is that the remainder is a mix of boys and girls who enjoy things like playing music and writing poems and making money, or who feel that high politics—which they have possibly seen up close—is beneath them, or who simply want to have a good time and take life as it comes.

This is all unwritten and unspoken. In fact, one of the surest signs that a young person is not fit to be president is if they *tell* you they want to be president. But even if they do not admit it, the germ has to be there, in their minds and behavior, by the time they are twenty-one, so that the first three years at Yale are spent moving toward that moment when the field has thinned and their odds are, more or less, set.

There are some countries where, it seems, all you have to do is go to Yale or Harvard or Oxford or Cambridge—the Ghanaians and Nigerians prefer Harvard; other former colonies, Oxford—and you have a good shot. It requires a bit more in this country (at least it did until very recently), but not much: a graduate degree from whichever school, Yale or Harvard, you did not attend for college; some time abroad or in the military; a dramatic childhood story that is true enough not to be totally false; and a seemingly idyllic personal life. That is why, I suppose, despite only ever wanting for sure to be a truck driver, to make $100,000, and to exact revenge on those who wronged me, the *Hartford Courant*, another fine newspaper, reported in the fall of 2008, *No wonder his Yale teammates voted Gerald the most likely to be elected president of the United States.*

Another thing: it helped to be able to give a good speech.

Here's one for you, the first I delivered in my last year at Yale, to prospective members of the Black Men's Union, who sat before me on a mid-September evening in the same Ray Tompkins House trophy room where my journey had begun years before.

I opened with those famous lines from Ralph Ellison's *Invisible Man*, which I held in my hands:

I am an invisible man. No, I am not a spook like those who haunted Edgar Allan Poe; nor am I one of your Hollywood-movie ectoplasm. I am a man of substance, of flesh and bone, fiber and liquids—and I might even be said to possess a mind. I am invisible, understand, simply because people refuse to see me.

I slowly closed the book. Placed it on a nearby table. Stared out at the audience, silent for an uncomfortably long string of seconds, then began to speak again, slowly, twisting Ellison's words for my own purpose:

If Ralph Ellison were here tonight, after reading that he would urge you to understand that you are by no means invisible. He would look out into this crowd and be encouraged because each and every one of you is more powerful than you can imagine. No matter what people say or think about you, regardless of the doubt you may have about yourself, you can and will be seen.

Because of that fact, it is our duty and pledge to open your eyes to those who remain invisible—those who we see on the streets every day; those who we find in our schools and our homes and, sadly, those who we encounter on this campus. We aim to make ourselves aware of their invisibility, but even more we strive to gain the tools to make them visible again.

It is your responsibility, with the immense talents and opportunities that you have been afforded, to put flesh on their bones and present them to the world as individuals that are just as capable and promising as you and I. You must be the vanguard that expands the boundaries of what is expected of us, and of what we accept from one another. That is what the BMU is about. That is what we are inviting you to join. That is what we are asking you to add to.

So as president, I can promise you that we will do everything in our power to make ourselves better men; to harness the great potential that lies within us and forge a path for a new generation of leaders. Because tonight you have the opportunity to not only join a tradition that can be traced back almost two hundred years—to men like James Pennington and Edward Bouchet—but you also have the opportunity to create a legacy of your own by daring to be great. So with that, I encourage you to come on board, and I echo the words of twentieth-century British author Wyndham Lewis, who said: "We are the first men of a Future that has not materialized. We belong to a 'great age' that has not come." That, ladies and gentlemen, is the BMU.

At least two handfuls of new converts signed the BMU pledge that evening. Even more had packed into this room a year earlier for the Union's first informational meeting and my public debut—a debut that seemed to vindicate Daniel's choice, for those gathered.

This one short speech goes to show why, since the days of Lucifer and Cicero and Christ and Lincoln and Hitler and right on up to today, the speaker, the sorcerer of language, has kept a dangerous hold on the people, always toeing the line between demagogue and liberator, between sophist and prophet. And this kind of rhetoric may also be why, aside from all the work so many members had done over the prior year, one man, Warren Kimbro, said, when we met with him in the fall of 2008, that the Union was *the most radical thing I've seen at Yale since the sixties.*

He would know.

On the night of 19 May 1969, Warren Kimbro was thirty-five years old. He was a member of the New Haven chapter of the Black Panthers, whose national chairman, Bobby Seale, was in town to speak. Mr. Kimbro was not in the crowd but in a basement elsewhere with three other Black Panthers: Lonnie McLucas, George Sams, Jr. (the national Panther field marshal), and nineteen-year-old Alex Rackley, who was tied up.

Mr. Kimbro, Mr. McLucas, and Mr. Sams had kidnapped Mr. Rackley on May 18. They suspected him of being an FBI informant. They interrogated and tortured him for two nights. And in the early hours of 20 May 1969, they drove young Mr. Rackley to the town of Middlefield, Connecticut. Mr. Kimbro shot Mr. Rackley in the head. Mr. McLucas shot him in the chest. They dumped his body in the Coginchaug River, where it was discovered the next day. Perhaps it was around this time that Mr. Kimbro learned that *there are no excuses for committing a crime, but there are reasons.*

Mr. Kimbro, Mr. McLucas, and Mr. Sams were arrested along with six others—they'd be christened the New Haven Nine—including Bobby Seale, who Mr. Sams accused of ordering the killing, and who became, when he went to trial in May 1970, the most polarizing American negro defendant since Nat Turner. Too bad Nat didn't have someone like David Hilliard, the Panthers' chief of staff, on his team. In March 1970, Hilliard had ordered the nation's college students to help free Chairman Bobby— not in the courts, but in the streets:

If you want to break windows, if you want to kill a pig, if you want to burn the courthouse, you will be moving against the symbols of oppression.

The students killed no pigs. They burned no courthouses. But they did break windows. They threw cherry bombs. Gave speeches, made demands, gathered on the New Haven Green—over ten thousand of them—not just students, but Abbie Hoffman and Tom Hayden and Allen Ginsberg, who wrote and read a poem.

They drew the support of Yale president Kingman Brewster, Jr.:

In spite of my insistence on the limits of my official capacity, I personally want to say that I am appalled and ashamed that things should have come to such a pass in this country that I am skeptical of the ability of black revolutionaries to achieve a fair trial anywhere in the United States.

And the scorn of American president Richard Nixon:

My fellow Americans, we live in an age of anarchy, both abroad and at home.... Even here in the United States, great universities are being systematically destroyed.

In the end, the students did not destroy the universities. They did not free Chairman Bobby; a judge did that in 1971 when the case was dismissed. They did not free Warren Kimbro; he confessed and served four years in prison. But the students had *moved* against the symbols of oppression, even if the symbols—or the oppression itself—did not budge. And after the May Day demonstrations at Yale, the symbols of oppression moved against the students, killing four at Kent State on 4 May 1970.

This was not all Mr. Kimbro remembered of the time.

The month after Warren Kimbro shot Alex Rackley, a twenty-three-year-old black drag queen named Marsha P. Johnson shattered a police car windshield outside the Stonewall Inn in Greenwich Village, helping to spark riots that launched the gay liberation movement. Later that fall, three black Yale students completed their siege on the university when they opened the Afro-American Cultural Center, to complement the Black Student Alliance—which one of them, Glenn de Chabert, presided over like (in the words of Henry Louis Gates, then an underclassman) our *black and shining prince*—and the Black Studies program they had designed, the first such department in the country.

It was a strange time to be young and black, in 1969. It was also a strange time to be young and black, though for different reasons, in 2008. I suppose it is always a strange time to be young and black, anywhere in the world.

And while it may seem that Marsha P. Johnson and Glenn de Chabert were very different young black people with different aims and different means, they unite across time in two ways. For one, Ms. Johnson and Mr. de Chabert are both long dead, both mysteriously, both before fifty. I won't say *before their time*, because *Nobody ever died too early or too late; you always die right on time.* Be that as it may, my point is that the movements they gave their lives to could not (or did not) save them.

There was another link that spoke through Mr. Kimbro as we sat with him, even if it was not clear to me then.

Ms. Johnson and Mr. de Chabert, if I've interpreted their lives correctly, wanted to change, or at least subvert, the terms of life for what some folks who think they're being considerate call *marginalized communities.* And all those ass-kickings they got and gave had evolved, in the forty years between their youth and our meeting with Mr. Kimbro, into political agendas shaped by homosexuals trying to convince themselves and others that they were not faggots, and black people trying to convince themselves and others that they were not niggers. What was birthed as a push to declare *We can be free* had grown into a program to insist *We can die for our country like you, and marry one person like you, and even bring a child into this world like you; we can be corporate executives, we can be your good neighbor, we can be president if you let us.* All these possibilities might amount to a lot more than a hill of beans. But compared to liberation, they strike me as sad, provincial concerns.

Yet these were the concerns of the time. So when Warren Kimbro said that the Union was the most radical thing he'd seen at Yale since the 1960s, it did not mean that we were akin to Bobby Seale or Glenn de Chabert. It meant that the bar was low. Incredibly low.

But it was 2008, a year of wonders and wanton language, so meeting this bar was called a *revolution*—especially after November 4.

We cannot quite proceed with business as usual. We have all just ordained a new American Revolution.

Those were the words of Akhil Reed Amar, spoken—shouted, really—from the dais of the Yale Law School auditorium on the morning of 5 November 2008, to us, his Constitutional Law students, many of whom had not slept much the night before; most of whom had just cast their first ballots in a presidential election, for Barack Obama.

Professor Amar was a small man. Reminded you a bit of Gandhi, if Gandhi had long black hair, wore blue blazers, and was an expert on the US constitution instead of nonviolent resistance. But much like Gandhi, much like nearly everyone on the campus and in the country on the morning of November 5, Akhil Amar displayed a surplus of intensity, of energy, of *hope*, in his face and in his hands—which kept clutching the long black locks and covering his mouth—and in his voice, which went from silent to whisper to tremble to shout as he explained what we had just witnessed.

If my class notes can be trusted, the 2008 election was the fifth turning point in presidential history. The first came alongside Jefferson in 1800, when the Federalist Party was swept away; the second in 1860, when Lincoln, with only 40 percent of the popular vote, brought Republicans to power and the country to civil war; the third in 1932, when what was left of Mr. Lincoln's Republican regime was undermined by its response to the Great Depression and overthrown by Franklin D. Roosevelt; and the fourth in 1968, which was a turning point in large part because the office of the presidency, and the country itself, seemed to be on the verge of collapse.

Our situation today is not as bad as the Great Depression or the Alien and Sedition Acts, Professor Amar clarified, *but it is quite serious.*

And so, he explained, what we had witnessed and ordained was not just the election of one man, however historic, but the ushering in of a moment that would decide the future of the country—a future that was bright because of the epic turnout this man had generated (*probably the greatest percentage in history, with more people motivated by hope than by fear*), and the technology this man employed (*the internet has finally been married to political action*), and the generation this man had inspired (*pivot points are often generational elections, and yours will be around for a long time*), and the new coalition this man created (*like Lincoln, Obama has brought the Midwest into his party's fold*).

It was hard to resist the euphoria of that morning, as it had been the night before, when thousands of students gathered on the Old Campus like they hadn't since perhaps May Day 1970, this time not to protest but to hug and cry and toast each other with beers, and to sing for hours all those patriotic songs we sang in elementary school before patriotism went out of style. It was hard to turn away from that scene on the television, the mass of bodies packed into Grant Park—middle-aged white men crying, hundred-year-old black women crying, children crying, Oprah Winfrey crying; some in the crowd unable to speak, able only to stand there in the chilly Chicago night and lean on the shoulder of the stranger beside them and look up at the stage, waiting, waiting for him, for the history that they had helped to make, waiting to see the handsome man who walked out on stage with that broad smile of his, and stood before his people, and spoke to them and to the world:

It's been a long time coming, but tonight, because of what we did on this day, in this election, at this defining moment, change has come to America.

It was hard to resist this message, this man. But it was not impossible. I watched the Grant Park spectacular on television. I listened to the singing outside. I had enough sense and joy to write in my notebook the night of November 4:

BARACK OBAMA
President of the USA
<u>*WOW*</u>

But I did not go to the Old Campus or shed any tears. And though I did not get much sleep, that had little to do with the election. You could say that I resisted for much the same reason Gore Vidal said *Every time a friend succeeds, a piece of me dies.*

Now imagine what happens when it is not a friend but a stranger, and he has not simply succeeded, has not only been chosen to be the most important person on earth, but he has also become the most powerful black person in the history of the human race (depending on where you slot the Egyptians). I voted for the man, I was excited by his election, I grew, in time, to care somewhat deeply for him and to respect him even more. My initial feeling, though, aside from skepticism, was that he had become, just as my father had once been, a considerable inconvenience.

For on the morning of November 5, the *Dallas Morning News*, like every other paper in America, put the new president on its front cover. Headline: *It's History*. It was, of course. This would have been all well and good if the story had not overshadowed, for all time, another story on the front page of the sports section of that morning's paper: mine.

When he left South Oak Cliff for Yale in the fall of 2005, Casey Gerald took with him a valedictorian's standing, a thick coat, his father's genes and the expectations of a community.

An interesting lede, no doubt, since I had taken a relatively thin coat and also had my mother's genes when I left. But the reporter was doing his thing and went on to recount how those expectations—from some, that I would fail; from others, that I would do something special for us all—had *nearly overwhelmed* me.

But Casey couldn't quit, he wrote.

It is fitting, looking back at that Wednesday paper, that Mr. Obama and I were both there, as stories like ours have been so masterfully employed, by us and others, to show that there is never an excuse for anything—for crime, for failure, for sadness, etc. etc. Here was a flawless new president from god knows where, and here was a magical boy from Oak Cliff, Texas.

Casey Gerald didn't drop out, he didn't transfer, he didn't come home. He's started three seasons at cornerback for Yale. He'll graduate in May with a

3.69 grade point average and a degree in political science. A Rhodes Scholar semifinalist, he's been accepted into Harvard's business school. Last week, he found out that . . . he's one of 15 finalists for the Draddy Trophy, presented by the National Football Foundation to college football's top scholar athletes.

None of this was a lie. The whole truth would have been helpful, though, if I had told it then.

I *had* been accepted to Harvard Business School, which, seeing as I knew nothing about business schools when I went to college, was not entirely my idea. And in the years since 2008, I've told so many stories about my motives for applying that I have a hard time seeing through my own propaganda. But I am almost sure it happened this way:

Once I decided that I wanted to be an investment banker, I joined one of the many programs that exist to prepare young black and brown boys and girls—*underrepresented minorities,* they call us—for successful corporate careers. I am not being snarky when I say that the main thrust of these programs is to rid us of any trace of our natural personality. Imagine some combination of *Pygmalion* and *A Clockwork Orange*: boys chastised for wearing the wrong color shirt, forced to cut their braids or afros; girls advised to buy a different shade of lipstick, told to raise their hands at a particular angle, erect. All trained like white-collar circus elephants: format your résumés the same way, use this utensil at that time, mention this topic at the water cooler, sell that ambition in your interview, show the right perspective on whatever hardship you've endured: *I'm very thankful, it made me resilient.* For all my cowardice and complicity, I take some pride in the fact that, though I joined these programs, I was always on the brink of expulsion.

I believe it was someone in such a program who told me about Harvard Business School—that business school was a great place to go, not just to learn about business, but to create *options* for my future; that, of all the business schools, Harvard's was the best. I liked options as much as anybody, and had gone to Yale because everyone said *it* was the best college to attend and that had worked out fine. So when I arrived at Lehman Brothers and was taken to lunch by a Yale alum who had also gone to Harvard Business School, I listened when she suggested that I consider applying myself, through a special application made just for college juniors. I studied a few hours for the entrance exam, wrote my essays while I was at work and asked Doris to review them—which she not only did but went so far as to send them to a friend for further feedback. This friend, I later discovered, was the top business school admissions consultant in the world. So, not long after I gave my *Invisible Man* speech to the Union, I was accepted to the Harvard Business School, thanks, in part, to Doris's tireless, invisible work on my behalf.

But in this new era, it was not enough to attend Harvard Business School, which is why it mattered that the *News* mentioned that I was also a semifinalist for the Rhodes Scholarship.

This had not been my idea, either, but that of the one person perhaps most responsible for the peace that held on May Day 1970: Kurt Schmoke. Mr. Schmoke was a junior on that day, a varsity athlete, a serious scholar, a community leader—and because of these facts and his soothing personality, he was the only student allowed to speak at the official May Day rally, right before Kingman Brewster.

There are a great number of students on campus who are confused and many who are frightened. They don't know what to think. You are our teachers. You are the people we respect. We look to you for guidance and moral leadership. On behalf of my fellow students, I beg you to give it to us.

That mind and mouth earned Mr. Schmoke a Rhodes Scholarship, got him into Harvard Law School, got him elected as the first black mayor of Baltimore, got him a seat on the Yale Corporation, and got him invited to the lunch where I met him, my junior year. He and I and Noah Lockhart had been brought, by Doris, to a closed dining hall, to convince a seventeen-year-old to choose Yale over Harvard.

This wasn't just any seventeen-year-old, I was told. He was the son of the most powerful black executive in America (this was before the Obama situation). Noah was there because of his connection to Harvard and, since he was from Baltimore, to Mr. Schmoke. Mr. Schmoke was there because the seventeen-year-old's father was a longtime friend, from their days together at Harvard Law School. And I was there because Doris had asked me to come, and for the food, and because Kurt Schmoke was something of a legend.

At some point during the conversation, he turned to me: *If you haven't considered Rhodes, you should.*

Six months or so before this lunch, I would not have known what he meant. But I had been watching and listening, and had learned some of the shorthand of this world—*The Hill, The Street, The College, The City, The Acela*; that any number, if it referred to compensation, stood for *thousands*, so that *150* or *60* meant *$150,000* or *$60,000*, not, as had long been the case, *150* or *60*—so I knew what Mr. Schmoke meant when he said *Rhodes*. I knew, for sure, that the Rhodes had very little to do, at least explicitly, with the aspirations of its namesake, Cecil Rhodes: *to form a secret society with but one object, the furtherance of the British Empire and the bringing of the whole uncivilized world under British rule, for the recovery of the United States, for the making the Anglo-Saxon race but one Empire.*

No, the Rhodes, as the most prestigious postgraduate fellowship in the world, was the premier means to separate college wheat from chaff; this is why it mattered so much more than Harvard or Yale alone. Of nearly 20,000 applicants to the Yale College class of 2009, 9.7 percent were accepted. Of nearly 9,000 applicants to the Harvard Business School class of 2014, 13 percent were accepted. By the time you have made it through three years at Yale, these percentages seem depressingly high—after all, there are years when it seems that no one who applies to Harvard Law School is turned away.

And now we had to deal with this new, pure man who had won the most selective fellowship of all: the presidency. There were thirty-four candidates who ran in 2008 under a major party banner and thirty-seven more who appeared on a ballot in at least one state (including Santa Claus, who was a write-in candidate in West Virginia), which meant that the White House had admitted roughly 1.4 percent of people who sought to occupy it. With more than eight hundred American applicants and only thirty-two scholars chosen, the Rhodes was not the narrowest gate, but it was close at 3.7 percent. Those eight hundred, by the way, represented a smaller cohort than the thousands who had been seeking the Rhodes for the past year—they had already been screened and selected by committees at the nation's universities, officially endorsed by a college president or equal, and sent for near-last judgment to sixteen regional committees across the country. These eight hundred were the semifinalists.

Some of those eight hundred boys and girls had been dreaming of the Rhodes since secondary school. Many had pasted *Rhodes* on goal boards in their freshman dorms or, less openly, taken careful steps from their first days on campus, steps that would make them strong candidates. All had spent the past year, at least since fall, securing the best recommenders (past Rhodes Scholars, governors, senators, Nobel laureates, perhaps a beneficiary of foreign aid)—eight letters in total. They had crammed every noble and harrowing detail about their lives into a two-thousand-word personal statement, crafting that statement for months, months during which every course taken needed to produce an A, A– at worst, months during which they worked incredibly hard yet told very few about the work because, as one of the eight hundred, the Rhodes would likely be the first time they attempted something they had a decent chance of failing at.

I was late to the Rhodes train but found no obvious reason why I should *not* apply, so I hopped on anyhow. And the day after the *News* reported that I was among the eight hundred, I received word that I had advanced to the final round—that I was one of another twelve, boys and girls from Texas and Oklahoma (district VIII). Two would be chosen on

November 22 at the end of a two-day interview process, and would join pairs from fifteen other districts, marching two-by-two up into the ark of excellence where thirty-two would live forever.

But that was not all I would have to do to be chosen. I would also have to betray my teammates.

Casey, that is the day of the Harvard game so what happens do you miss it or what??

Doris sent this short panicked question via email on the night of November 6, just after hearing the good news. The Rhodes interview was November 21 and 22, in Houston. The Game was November 22, in Boston. I could not do both.

By the morning of November 7, this choice became the greatest non-spiritual dilemma of my first twenty-one years. It became one of the few pieces of evidence that there was still some good in my heart at that time. And it became the best parable I have to share with anyone who wonders why this bitter earth turns just as it does.

As the *News* reported, I was in my third year as a starter and had not missed a game. I was a member of the most successful class in a generation, a championship team born out of a coup that we led as eighteen- and nineteen-year-old boys—boys who had played through broken bones for each other, who had *been there* for each other when that was about all any of us had on campus. Then there was Tony Reno, who had become the closest thing to a father that I had in my adult life. When I woke up from surgery with those pins in my hand, Coach Reno was the one at the hospital to pick me up, the one who pulled off to the side of the road when I needed to vomit from the anesthesia, who drove me to his home in Massachusetts, where his wife cooked a big pot of pasta and made sure I took my pain medication. In the rush to decry the silly and dangerous aspects of this sport, the critics miss a vital fact: these boys, these coaches, are often not just brutes in tights and screaming maniacs, but *family*—and family does not come easy in America. Or anywhere else, I imagine. So I wanted to play in The Game with my brothers, for the last time.

But I also wanted, though much less, to win the Rhodes. I cannot say that I was eager to go to Oxford or to leave the country at all. Can't say that there were many Rhodes Scholars, aside from William J. Clinton, whom I considered good role models. (Career role models, I mean.) I was fond of the idea that I would always be called a Rhodes Scholar, just like when you win a Super Bowl or an Academy Award and you're forever introduced as *Super Bowl champion Yada Yada* or *Academy Award winner Whoopdee Whoo*. I wanted, and suppose I still do, *to call myself beloved, to feel myself beloved on the earth.* But even if my hunger for praise was nearly as great as my hunger for revenge, that would not have been enough to make me betray my teammates.

The Rhodes was not simply a personal honor, though. That was the problem.

If I am fortunate enough to be selected, it would not just be some personal accolade, I told *USA Today* at the time. *Symbolically . . . it would be an opportunity for my life to serve as an example for those who don't have a sense of hope to try and to dream for something like this.*

When I read this quote and remember that my high school coach told another reporter that there would be a ticker tape parade through the streets of Oak Cliff if I won the Rhodes, I realize that there was yet another reason the *News* put me and Mr. Obama in that same November 5 edition—the same reason Nelson Mandela, who had a decent amount of credibility on the matter, said to the new president: *Your victory has demonstrated that no person anywhere in the world should not dare to dream of wanting to change the world.*

And the same reason it has been said that the presidency is the loneliest job on the planet.

I've never been president, so don't know for sure, but I bet it has less to do with the particulars of the job and a lot more to do with the fact that any president, especially that president, is not just a person but a symbol—and *symbol* is truly the world's loneliest job.

You arrive, by force, as a baby and become a little boy or girl and without much thought, because children don't think about these things, you do something that leads somebody—your mother, your teacher, the lady who runs the candy house—to say *That kid is special.* You pick up, along the way, some honest basic virtues: you get a little angry when something seems unfair; you get a little sad when a dog dies or a friend falls off his bike; you get a little excited when somebody gives you a new task, a new challenge, and you work very hard to do it well, to please them and to see what you can do. If you, like me, are indoctrinated into a religion, you take the religion at its word, enough to adopt some of its mandates as the mandates of your life: feed the hungry, visit the sick, clothe the naked, *help somebody.* This goes on. Perhaps some tragedy befalls you and you wind up wandering around, meeting lots of strangers. You come to depend on their kindness. You come to like them more than many people you already know. At some point, a stranger shows up from another world and finds you, minding your business being special and all, and they say *Why don't you come with me?* And you will go, for the same reasons I have mentioned re: journeys, and you will also go because your people want you to go—for you and for them. So you go. You go off to the new world and realize pretty soon—or you *feel* and don't realize until many years later—that you are in limbo: you can never fully be a part of this new world, but you can't go back to the old world, to your people, because you are now, for them, a symbol of what *they* can be. If you go back that defeats the whole purpose. So you stay. You accept this calling and you try to live up to it. You try to earn the respect of the new world, play by its rules. You try to do some good for the old world, for your people. You may very well do both. But along the way you notice—just like a pebble in your shoe—that though you have won the race, many races, you have lost the people, *your people*, because you are not a person anymore, but a *symbol*. Therefore, you are an illusion. And you are a liar, if only by omission: you have learned so much on your journey that you can't tell the people anything. If you told them what you've seen, how little of it makes any sense, how sad the whole thing is, my lord, a third of the people might revolt, a third might try to kill you, and another third might fall apart, instead of just you. Your silence holds the world together.

I HAVE SOMETHING TO TELL YOU
WHILE THERE IS STILL TIME

If I had known all this in November 2008, I would have played in The Game and moved on with my life. But I didn't know. So when the crisis began on November 6, I believed, enough to tell it to the *New Haven Register*, that this *honestly would be the most difficult decision that I have ever made in my life*.

But then I did not have to make a decision at all. That's where we find the lesson of this parable.

I sought, starting in the early hours of November 7, advice from at least two dozen men and women—aside from coaches and friends, there was a Heisman Trophy winner, an Emmy Award winner, an All-American, a former mayor, and at least nine Rhodes Scholars including Chesa Boudin, who, as the son of convicted domestic terrorists, inspired a professor to tell the *New York Times* on the day he was selected: *Cecil Rhodes . . . would be horrified.*

Out of these varied advisors, two camps had emerged by the morning of November 11: one camp felt that I should forego the Rhodes and play in The Game. It was small, and led by me. The other camp felt that the Rhodes was too important, so I should miss The Game instead. Its leader was, surprisingly, the Yale athletic director, Tom Beckett, a man who in another time might have been a US senator—that coif of silver hair, that booming velvet voice, that ability to please everyone he met by saying exactly what they wanted to hear. He asked me to meet him at Ray Tompkins House on the afternoon of November 11. We sat face-to-face in blue high-backed chairs, in silence, until he spoke.

Casey . . . I know how much Yale football means to you. How much the men of Yale football mean to you. I know—Well, I have to be honest, I don't know. I can't know. *But I certainly can imagine how agonizing this must be. I've talked to Doris. I've talked to Tony and Jack (the head coach). I've thought long and hard about it. I really have.* He sighed. *Casey, you have to go to Houston. You have to go to Houston and when you go there . . . and you sit in that room with those judges . . . and you interview for the Rhodes Scholarship—Casey, you have to know that the men of Yale football are right there with you. As you, your spirit, will be with us on the field against Harvard.*

Tears ran down his face and mine by the time he stopped speaking. *Okay?* he asked. *Okay.* We hugged and I left Ray Tompkins House, walked back across the street, past the Grove Street Cemetery, to my room, resolved.

But by evening, missing The Game felt like the wrong thing to do. I went to sleep still torn. Then, as the morning of November 12 began, a third, tiny, seemingly delusional camp came to the fore: those who believed that I should in fact do both, and who had been working clandestinely to make that which seemed implausible, feasible. I am not sure who its leader was, but its voice was Chesa, the revolutionary son. He had written to me: *i'm totally happy to email the secretary to the rhodes trust in the usa . . . he is in charge of the whole selection process for the US . . . organizes the committees etc.*

The secretary was not a friend of his. Chesa simply figured that he would understand the dilemma, not only due to his long service to the Rhodes Trust but for a more pertinent reason: the secretary had gone to Harvard College and then to Yale Law School. The Game had to mean something to him.

you'll get the rhodes, the game, and the girl, Chesa wrote to me.

As you can guess, I did not get the girl. And not long after I wiped the matter from my eyes on the morning of November 12, it was also clear that, despite Chesa's valiant effort, I would not get the Rhodes *and* The Game with the secretary alone. Before nine a.m., I wrote to my boss from Lehman Brothers, who had become one of my third-camp advisors, since he was a Yale alum (college and law school), a former varsity lacrosse captain, and the least sympathetic son of a bitch I've ever worked for. It also helped that he was not new to crises.

Brian,

People in Yale's administration have tried to work something out, but there's nothing more they can do. It's a pretty tough spot, but I've talked to the coaches and they seem to support whatever I decide.

Thanks,
Casey

Hope wheezed its last few heavy breaths.

But then, sometime between noon and two p.m., a ram appeared in the bush—in the form of an old Texan who, when I finally met him in person, carried a briefcase made of raw-honey-colored ostrich leather, to match his boots. This man was a federal judge in Houston. He was the head of my Rhodes interview committee. Most important: he was an alum of Harvard College and Yale Law School, just like the secretary. His remedy: grant me a special dispensation to interview for the Rhodes on Friday and play in The Game on Saturday.

I wrote to Brian again at 2:19 p.m. *Update ... talked to the judge that's over my region (Harvard ugrad/Yale law) and he said I should play in the game ... so I'm going to do both, thankfully.*

He responded at 2:42: *Good luck with the interview, and with the Harvard game—by the way, you just witnessed one of the intangible benefits of a Yale degree . . . .which will be with you the rest of your life.*

There would not be many witnesses for this miracle, of course. The official word, given to the *New Haven Register* on November 15, was simply: *Casey's problem has been solved.*

The crisis was over.

But a crisis loses much of its power if it is seen only as a single event, as a string of *this-and-that-happen*eds, with narrow causes and personal effects. If it is not also seen as a *symbol.* For however dangerous they may be, symbols—as it has been since the caves—help us to explain ourselves and our world, allow a mortal boy to reach his hand into the distant future and deliver a message: *This is what I saw, what I learned, what you've got to know.*

In the seven days it took to resolve this crisis, and in the nine years after that time, I heard and watched and learned a great deal from the people who turn, or try to turn, the axis of the world. What a wonder it was to behold. To see past their fights in political ads, in boardrooms, in history books—to witness how often they, in fact, want the same things, how they view the world through like-colored lenses, are shaped by schools and jobs and clubs that are the same or nearly, how well they work together to play in a game, to win a fellowship or get into a school, to make a billion and protect those billions, to run a country or save it or ruin it or claim it as their own. I am not complaining, necessarily. Just trying to tell you what I've seen.

And I will also tell you that I am not convinced the world should *not* operate this way—that these happy few should stop coordinating, stop making ways out of no way for one another. All I am saying is that it sure would have been nice to know as a child, down in my forgotten world, that this kind of support was not only possible, not only normal, but expected.

I might have—we all might have—asked for a lot more help and had a lot less trouble. That's all.

In any event, I got the help I needed and I was on my way to Houston.

The *Hartford Courant*, which seemed to be in a rivalry with its New Haven counterpart during this time, set the scene on the morning of November 22:

He has a chance today to win a Rhodes Scholarship and a football game at Harvard. For a Yale man, these are hours of no greater possibility.

Casey Gerald left campus late Thursday [November 20] afternoon for Bradley Airport and a 7:10 p.m. flight through Charlotte that got him into Houston at midnight. There was a luncheon Friday followed by a 25-minute interview with the Rhodes committee that forever could change his life. There was a cocktail reception at 5 p.m., a taxi to the airport for a Houston departure at 8:45 and arrival in Newark at 1 a.m. If all went well, a town car rushed him into Boston about 4:30 this morning.

All went well, through four thirty a.m. There was a knock at my hotel room around seven that morning. I don't remember getting up to answer, but I can still see, in my mind, a man standing in the doorway. Can hear what he said: *Case, let's go. It's time to play.*

Coach Reno had allowed me to sleep past the mandatory wake-up time and through the team breakfast. That was as far as this leeway could go, so here he was, on his maybe sixth cup of coffee, with a Styrofoam container in his hands. *Brought you some waffles. Probably fucking cold by now. You can eat 'em on the bus . . . C'mon.*

The three team buses were already full, waiting for me and Coach Reno in the hotel parking lot, ready to take us on the twenty-minute ride from the outskirts of Boston where the team had spent the night, to Harvard Stadium, for the last time. He and I sat in the front two seats of the bus—me leaning my shoulder on the window, resting the Styrofoam container on the bar that kept us from falling into the entry stairs, scraping dry syrup onto the cardboard waffles. The sun was bright—the light of the sun, that is. I did not see the sun itself. It was hard to believe that light came from a burning star, as cold as it was outside. Hadn't even reached the day's high of ten degrees. For some reason, the light and the cold are the things I remember most about that day—not the rest of the bus ride, or what happened when we arrived at the stadium, or the game itself.

I do remember one television commercial break. It was so cold that I tried to warm myself by jumping in place for thirty seconds. An official walked over to me, a mask covering his face. *Hey, pal . . . you might as well stop. That's not gonna work.* He laughed and walked away.

It did not work.

Nothing seemed to work for the Yale Bulldogs that afternoon, except our defense, which, though it was still one of the best in the country, was made up of many boys like me, who had led the coup as freshmen and had paid the price to keep the land we conquered: achy swollen joints, tingly nerves, headaches, loose tendons, unhealed cracks in bones. We had enjoyed greatly; we had suffered greatly. And here we were, twenty-one years old, most of us. We had reached that holy moment that comes one day, in the second half of your last game, when you stand on the field and slowly turn around and squint out and up at twenty, thirty thousand bodies smashed together in the stands of Harvard Stadium, those stands that tower over you like their Greek inspiration—when what was once a dean, a senator, your freshman roommate, your mother, is now a blot in a great sea of blues and tweeds and fur and crimson. When the noise is so loud and varied that the twenty thousand voices become one voice, a voice you seem to have heard your whole life, a voice you don't pay much attention to anymore; when the cold wind blows across from the Charles River to make your joints ache even more, and the 120 practices and 300 hours of film and 3,000 plays have turned eleven boys into one body, the body of a much older man who looks at himself in the mirror and asks *What am I about to do?* and may not know the answer, and is okay with that. We twelve had reached that moment in this final football game. We were tired. And we knew we were about to lose, which we did. 10–0.

If the internet had not reminded me recently, I would not have thought to mention that this was the 125th edition of the Harvard-Yale game, or that the Crimson, led by one of the Bishop twins, won its second straight Ivy League championship. I did not care much about this at that time. I care even less now.

And if I had not asked one of the other Rhodes finalists to send a message once the selection was made (the Rhodes committee decides immediately after interviews are complete), then I would have headed right to the showers in the visitors' locker room, still in the dark as to my fate. Instead, I went to my travel bag to fetch my phone. There was a message.

Hey Casey, it's Jordan from the Rhodes interview in Houston. Just wanted to let you know we didn't get it. Sorry, man.

I said nothing. Put the phone back in my bag and sat on an old wooden bench between two rows of lockers. For the last time, I cut the matted strips of dingy white tape from my cleats. Pulled down the long thick sweaty socks and threw them in the garbage. Peeled off my tattered neoprene sleeves. A little boy ran into the locker room. *Hey, number 1! Can I have your gloves?* They were already off, on the bench right next to me. *Here you go, buddy.* He skipped away with the gloves on his tiny hands. I unfastened my faded pants. Squeezed the too-tight pads up and over my sore shoulders. The domed crown helmet was already off, visor gone, stadium lights gone, fear gone, opponents gone.

I walked, gingerly, to the showers. The Downing twins, Willy and Tommy, were still there. At least one other player was there, but I can't remember who. We stood under the water, which washed their trickling tears down the drain. *Remember that first day of practice?* Tommy asked. *That fucking fight we had? Jesus we were crazy . . . Seems so long ago.* We all remembered and laughed, then just stood there, silent. It seemed that none of us wanted to leave, for many reasons, perhaps the same. But we had to—not to catch the bus, though; this was the last game, no more bus rides. We had to leave the showers because we were not those wild young boys that we had been. According to another reporter who chronicled the team that day: *Tommy Downing was the Heart of this Yale program . . . Casey Gerald was its Voice.* So we both had to leave the showers for a press conference, where we were joined by another of the twelve, Marvin Matthews, the greatest running back to wear Yale blue in many years. The same reporter said *and Marvin Matthews was its Legs.*

We three sat at a short table, microphones in front of each, folding chairs lined all the way back from the table to the glass wall that overlooked the field. For twenty minutes, for the last time, we played the same old roles. Marvin sat there looking pretty, even with a fractured toe. Tommy began to answer a question, then broke down in tears. I offered an obvious statement—*This is definitely not the way we wanted to end our careers*—to the *Boston Globe.*

Someone asked about the outcome of the Rhodes. It had not been announced yet.

It's been a crazy forty-eight hours, for sure. I should know something soon.

I don't know why I didn't tell them that I lost, that I already knew. Just couldn't say it yet. It seemed that everyone—these reporters, the coaches, my teammates, all of Yale, all of Oak Cliff, the brilliant boy from Baltimore, the revolutionary son, *everybody*—was eager to know, to rejoice. For all my faults, I've always hated letting people down, which is, in many ways, a fault itself. And I had done much more than let folks down. I had gone, in one afternoon, from one of the most celebrated student athletes in America to one of the biggest losers. So I figure I did not tell him or anybody else for hours because I was ashamed and numb and sad. But I cannot say that I was angry—not about losing this final game, and not about losing the Rhodes. I have the sport to thank for that.

You see, I have witnessed or been a part of only one true meritocracy in my thirty years: the game of football. It all goes back to one afternoon at South Oak Cliff, when I walked into the locker room with a request for Coach Price: six senior football players wanted to attend tutoring for our math class—one day a week, we'd need to come late, only one hour late, to practice.

Coach Price leaned back in his swivel chair. He crossed his legs at the ankle. Took off his glasses. Slid his tongue over his front teeth.

Now lemme make sure I heard you right . . . You niggas wanna go to tutoring? Hmph. Okay. Okay. I thought, by his silence, that he supported our request. He sat there with his eyes closed. I stood there, waiting.

Gone on! He shouted, jerking up in his chair, eyes bucked. He slammed a folded newspaper on the ground. *Take your fucking asses to tutoring! One hour. I'll be John Brown. One goddamn hour. Now here we are, six weeks away from the Lancaster game. Six weeks! You walk in my office and say you wanna give up one hour of practice a week. One hour of my practice. For tutoring! Okay. All right. But lemme ask you something. What in the hell do you think them niggas at Lancaster are gonna be doing in that hour, while you're upstairs licking your math teacher's ass? Huh? They ain't gone be in tutoring, I'll tell you that. The niggas are gonna be practicing! Putting in six more hours of practice than you niggas! And with those six extra hours, they gone step right on the field, and they gone drive they feet right up y'all's motherfucking asses. That's what's gone happen. But yeah. Gone on to tutoring. Close my goddamn door.*

None of us went to math tutoring. We went to practice. And we defeated Lancaster, even if we did not drive our feet up their asses. We also, at least I did, came to believe—because we had seen it for ourselves—that you can only get out of the game what you're willing to put into it. *You don't work, you don't eat.*

You learn this lesson so consistently, so painfully, that by the time you arrive at the end of your career, though you may be sad or ashamed, you are not angry after losing a game or anything else that you did not deserve to win, on account of your talent and effort and execution. You accept your fate because it's the one that you earned. This is why I was not upset about the Rhodes.

Before I left Houston, before my interview even ended, I had a solid inkling of what the outcome might be. I was sitting at the head of a long conference table. Seven other judges sat on either side (one sat at the tail, a former senator). The ostrich briefcase judge sat to my left. He asked a question: *Casey, what is the last book you read that didn't have anything to do with race?*

Now, there are two problems with this question.

The first might be obvious: The question is either strange, racist, or lazy. Or all three. It reminds me of a story Toni Morrison told about reading a passage in which Hemingway wrote: *Two men walked toward me. One was Cuban, and one was black.*

What?!? Toni asks, rhetorically and annoyed. *They both could be Cuban. They both could be black.*

Hemingway's sloppy use of language revealed how little, if anything, he knew about race. And here, the judge's question revealed how little, if anything, he knew about not only race, or me, but about *books*—otherwise he would have known that every book ever written, at least in this country, *has something to do* with race.

The second problem with the judge's question is far more interesting. It reveals why the white supremacist mind—by that I only mean the mind that is conditioned to see a book that does not have white characters in it as an inferior book, a café with no white patrons in it as an inferior café, a school with no white children in it as an inferior school, a company with no white employees in it as an inferior company, etc. etc.—why *this* mind is at once and always a half-formed mind. Why its owner is, ultimately, doomed to miss many points, much of the truth, and a few great opportunities— like this one, when the whole story could have been about *my* problem, not his.

If the judge had only asked: *Casey, what was the last book you read?*

I would have given him the same answer: *You know, I would say* A Testament of Hope. *It's a collection of writings by Martin Luther King, and it's really not about race per se—it's about human rights, about all of us, the whole country.*

But he would have been off the hook with me and you and all of history, because the truth was more damning than even the Klan's Grand Wizard could have hoped: I had not read a book at all, at least in full, in all my time at Yale. Just had that copy of *Invisible Man* for a prop . . . found the quote I recited online.

In fact, the last book I know that I finished before this Rhodes interview was either *Black Like Me* or *James and the Giant Peach*, in Ms. Davis's fifth-grade class, both of which I'd read because we had mandatory reading time each day.

Some teacher in middle school had told us to read *Great Expectations*, but you could not have paid me to do that. Or, rather, only paying could have convinced me.

After that, in the eleventh grade, I'm pretty sure I read some of *Animal Farm*—my friends and I loved shouting *Manor Farm!!!* in the hallway. I was going to read *The Scarlet Letter*, but we watched the movie, so there was no need for the book (I felt). *The Bluest Eye* was on the syllabus, but that little girl seemed so sad I just couldn't get through the first bit. At the end of junior year, I passed some special national English test just fine.

Then there was senior year, when I thought I had read enough Joseph Conrad to talk about it in public. But recently I realized that my favorite line, *We're all savages, more or less*, was not in *Heart of Darkness*, as I'd thought, but in *Pygmalion*. So now I have to wonder whether I opened the books or just read the CliffsNotes. At the end of senior year, I passed another national English test and got into Yale.

Once at Yale, I quickly realized that I could either read the assigned books and flunk out, or read just enough to get the point and do my work. I am not even talking about reading for *pleasure*. Who had time to do extra reading? Or time for pleasure, for that matter. Besides, even though I enjoyed some snippets that I read, nothing in any of those books—at eleven, or sixteen, or eighteen, or twenty-one—seemed to have anything inside that I needed to get through life. My days were filled with *surviving*, then *doing*, then supplemented with *listening* and *watching* and, when feasible, a little *sneaking away*. And all this took a great deal of time and energy, taught me more than I could have asked for. I would be nearly twenty-three years old before I discovered, after exhausting my other methods, that books held many keys to my kingdom and, in time, my life. But as of November 22, they were little more than expensive burdens that I had to acquire each semester.

So the judge missed one of the more unbelievable facts he could have learned that day. He still had enough to deem me unworthy of the Rhodes. I did not disagree.

But it seemed that I had reached that stratum of American life where, even when I lost, regardless of *why* I lost, people treated me like I won. Instead of introducing me as a *Rhodes Scholar*, they introduced me as a *Rhodes Scholar Finalist*. Thanks to the then-president of Yale, I learned that this was just as well.

> *Dear Casey,*
>
> *I know that it must be a deep disappointment to lose both The Game and the Rhodes on the same day. But just think about it: it is an amazing accomplishment to be both playing in The Game and interviewing for the Rhodes on the same weekend!! And I want to assure you that it is no disgrace being a losing Rhodes finalist. I was one myself, in a cohort of losing finalists that included, among others, Dick Brodhead (former dean of Yale College, now president of Duke), Jeff Garten (former dean of the*

Yale School of Management), Dan Yergin (Pulitzer Prize winning
author and the world's leading expert on the energy industries),
and Michael Mandelbaum (one of the nation's leading foreign
policy scholars).
    You have a brilliant future ahead of you.

With admiration,
Rick Levin

    I suppose I did have a bright future in front of me, at least for another month. There was still, as the *News* reported on November 5, the Draddy Trophy. After the Rhodes/Game saga, the National Football Foundation decided that I should speak on behalf of the fifteen boys who had been chosen as the best student-athletes in American football, at the College Football Hall of Fame induction ceremony.

    That early December night at the Waldorf Astoria—a hotel that was a lot crappier than I had expected, based on the hoopla—many of my heroes, or folks I had long histories with, sat before me. Tom Beckett had flown Granny and Clarice and Tashia up from Texas. Coach Reno was there. The owner of the Dallas Cowboys was there. Archie Griffin, who played with my daddy at Ohio State and who remains the only person to win the Heisman Trophy twice, was there. My favorite Yale football captain—one of my closest college friends, a Jewish All-American defensive lineman whom Clarice forced to pray—was there. He came to the hotel early to help me practice my speech, which I had finished on the train down from New Haven, inspired by Lincoln's train ride to deliver the Gettysburg Address. If I had read Garry Wills's *Lincoln at Gettysburg* before then, I would have known that Mr. Lincoln did not, in fact, write his speech on the train. But even without reading, I knew that Lincoln had (purportedly) looked to Pericles's funeral oration as a model, so I tried my best to rip off Pericles and Lincoln in these last words that I would speak about the game of football, for many years. Spoke of dreams, and sacrifice, triumph, peril, the whole lot, all in less than three minutes.

So, I closed, *while I cannot do justice to the honor it has been to be a man of Yale football, to play this great game that has given me a chance to rise above any obstacles and dare to be somebody, or to speak in the presence of this august body, I say on behalf of the fourteen other phenomenal men behind me: thank you and God bless.*

And boy, it sure did seem that God had blessed us all. Blessed the people in that Waldorf Astoria ballroom with money and awards. Blessed me, as He blessed His own Son, to walk the earth as a self-same god: Jesus, the lord of light . . . me, the lord of darkness. Both of us to be reviled. One for good reason, and soon.

chapter **N I N E T E E N**

Osiris.

That's what they called me. God of the dead and lord of the under-world. Fitting, since I spent so much time in a tomb.

Its proper name was *the Hall*—not all the secret societies at Yale built or borrowed tombs in which to live. Of the seven oldest, the *landed* societies, two took a different approach: Elihu owned a house with a white picket fence across from the New Haven Green, and Wolf's Head hid itself on York Street, behind that stay-out stone wall with its ivy rash, inside a castle-like compound, shingled and copper-trimmed, with iron bars over most of its narrow windows and a dungeon basement where, some nights, you could hear the seniors howl. At least I could hear them, because I was inside.

I had been inside on the night of initiation, junior spring, though I can't tell you what I saw—there is a reason to keep some of this stuff se-cret, mainly the same reason we want (*I* want) little kids to believe in the tooth fairy and Santa for as long as possible. I don't know when we got so hostile to the idea of magic, you know? So since there will be sixteen ju-niors initiated this year who will see what I saw that night, and sixteen the next and the next, on up to the end of the society, I will leave it to them to see it and tell it if they want.

I had also been inside throughout the summer, once my time at Lehman Brothers ended. I slept there, in the basement, until I had that dream I told you about, after which I stayed awake nights there until the dorms opened in the fall. Then, just like members of every other Yale society, I spent my Thursday nights and Sunday nights there, and many days and nights besides. Wrote my senior essay there. Got drunk there. Saw a mummy there. Told my life story for the first time there—it took about seven hours to tell it, the same amount of time it took to learn that you can tell people a lot of stuff without telling them much of anything. I still don't understand why the societies make twenty-one-year-old boys and girls tell their personal histories to each other. Nobody at that age knows hardly anything about their lives, and all of them are going to lie about much of what they do know, anyway. Maybe that was just me.

I say all this to say that I spent a hell of a lot of time at the Hall my senior year—so much time that I must have lost touch with my responsibilities, since I was the last or nearly last person to know that the Black Men's Union was about to collapse. I assume nobody told me because they could not find me, locked away in my tomb. It's also possible they just wanted to wait until they were sure.

Whatever the case, a week or two after I gave that speech at the Waldorf, the two most important people in the Union were at war with one another. It was much like the conflict that broke out between Jefferson and Hamilton in the later stage of Washington's administration. You read some of that back-and-forth and you'd think the country was founded by a bunch of queens. Probably would have been a better country, if it had. In any event, the Union was facing a Jefferson-Hamilton-style conflict, and one of the other reasons I was the last to know, I bet, was that instead of states' rights and the national bank, the Union's founding fathers were fighting over what every other boy in college seemed to fight over: on the surface, a woman; at the root, pride and honor. So they might have told me last because despite all my meddling in their lives, I had never asked a thing about their romantic situations. Nor did they ask about mine, to my face.

I won't get into the sordid details because it's not even about that. Not about what Daniel did or did not do, not about how Elijah should or should not have *responded* to what Daniel did or did not do. The central question—which I'd really like your help in answering—is this: What matters most, your cause or your friend?

I did not realize that was the question at first.

From what I have on record, around mid-December, the only question on my mind was: *Why can't they leave me out of it?* That's what I asked the rest of the board and our friends, though I did not ask Elijah or Daniel because I had no interest in talking to either of them about it. In addition to enjoying time down in my tomb, I also liked to stay above the fray. Could have stayed there, too, if it had not been for Elijah, who'd become like a little brother, the one who has done everything right—who is, in many ways, *you* but better, with a cleaner heart and a righter spirit. It was this heart and this spirit that made Elijah so committed to the kids we mentored, to the rest of us on the football team, to everyone he did not have a vendetta against. It was also this heart and this spirit that made him see most personal interactions as life-and-death, which explains why, by the time I was informed of the matter, he was a few thoughts away from kicking Daniel's ass. So I had to, finally, intervene.

Now, ever since I had to find a way around believing the Bible word for word, around 1999, I have never believed 100 percent of any story anyone has ever told me. So all I knew after talking to Daniel and Elijah separately was that this situation was much worse than I'd imagined. The one wanted justice. The other wanted . . . I'm still not sure.

And it was no longer a personal feud. Many members of the Union, fifty strong by then, began to fear that if these two elders could come to such a bitter pass, then the Union itself was doomed. Many men and women across the campus, aside from soaking up the scandal of it all, shook their heads at such an early demise of such a hopeful institution. The house was divided and could not stand.

I read somewhere, years later, that *the slow questioning of alternatives before decision is the inner quality of leadership.* If that is true, then I spent six weeks—fall exam period, winter break in Dallas, most of January—*leading*, which also resembled kicking a giant can down the road. By the third week of the new year—right after Dr. King's birthday and Mr. Obama's inauguration, no less—things had only deteriorated. It was time to decide. And since this was the twenty-first century, I did not even have to look anyone in the face when I decided. I simply sent an email. The gist of my message: *Get over it or you're fired.* It was much gentler than that, actually. I said they would be *asked to resign,* if that makes any difference.

Daniel responded the following morning, in a way only he could:

I agree that Elijah and I should talk . . . Should that not happen for whatever reason, I will not be forced into a hasty, and what I deem wholly unjust, decision to resign.

Elijah responded the next day:

I know the mentoring program will not work in the current state if the Union asked me not to be a part of it. Those kids, my kids, listen to me in a way that they will not even do for their parents. I have worked tirelessly on building those relationships so they can trust that I will be there for them. I have never violated that trust. It would then not be in the best interest of the Union to carry on that initiative without me—with those kids without me.

Before either could have a second thought, I declared victory for the Union and wrote to all, three minutes after Elijah's email:

Men,

Elijah and Daniel have agreed to continue doing their jobs. I am disappointed that this situation happened and hope we have

all learned something from it. We must immediately get back
on track.

Casey

We did just that. Elijah grew the mentoring program, gave even more to the kids, implored all Union men to give more, too. Daniel helped prepare the Union for our departure in May, when Riley would become the new president. The only thing I learned was summed up in Doris's message to me: *You did EXACTLY the right thing* she wrote when I shared my message to the Union with her. Some believe that everything a god does is just. But since I ruled in darkness, there was much I did not see.

I did not see the part of Elijah's email that read:

I am forever in debt to those of you who value our relationships outside of this great organization which we have all worked diligently to build and protect. Respect, honesty, loyalty, trust, and sacrifice are things that I will continue to display to you all in our continued friendships.

If I did see it, I did not understand what it meant. Otherwise I might have understood why Elijah stopped speaking to me. He never slacked from his work, never let those kids down. But for the rest of my time at Yale it was as if he had let a river run between us and walked away from the other side.

Or did he stand there, waiting to see if I would swim across?

I ask because there is a memory, hazy, that lingers stubbornly enough to believe it is real: I am leaving the Hall after dark . . . pulling, slowly, the iron handle of the wooden gate, trying not to draw attention. The lock clicks, still loud against the silence on York Street. I turn away from the gate and walk along the high stone wall, toward the empty intersection at York and Elm, watching my feet. It is that time of night when the campus stands desolate, and small sounds echo against the Gothic cliffs, and you feel eerily alone, watched from some high place.

I hear a voice. *That's Mena.* I think of crossing the street before she sees me. I hear a laugh, not hers. I look up. It's Elijah. He is walking at her side, grinning. He turns his head from her and sees me. It looks as if, at once, his mouth loses all power in the muscles that make smiles. Mena looks to where Elijah is looking.

Hey Case! she calls out. I get the sense she's more excited to see what's about to happen than to see me.

Hey!

We begin a game of chicken. A single building between us . . . now a parked car. Elijah slows, falls behind her, stops. He pulls out his phone.

Hey man how you doing? I ask. We're close enough for almost-inside voices.

I'm good, he murmurs, after a glance at me.

Mena and I keep talking, or she talks to me, a minute and a half, maybe. I look over her shoulder at Elijah, standing there, pushing phone buttons, adjusting his bag straps, scraping one foot over a small spot of sidewalk. Mena looks to where I'm looking, then back to me.

I gotta head out, he says to her. *I'll hit you later.*

He walks away, in the direction from which they came.

Case, Mena sighs once Elijah is out of earshot, a pitiful smile on her face, that *do something* look.

I did nothing. Just watched him turn the corner. I thought, and maybe even said, the next move, the next word, ought to be his. It was, in a way.

Casey was supposed to be my brother. He treated me like this was just business, like I didn't mean shit to him.

Quincy passed this message on to me, after speaking to Elijah not long before my graduation. *Lord, he's being dramatic,* I shot back, and truly felt. But I wonder now—not solely out of guilt—whether Elijah was right. I only realized, for example, that he had stood there clutching my right shoulder, celebrating that great victory, many years after the fact— and only then because someone told me about the canvas at the Yale

Bowl. Sure, I had been drugged that day. But what if the drugged me was just the *real* me, unbound? Did I ever truly notice him, my supposed little brother? Did I take him, absentmindedly, selfish-mindedly, for granted? Or did he, all that time, simply not mean much to me? I don't know, if that's the case, why I miss him like I do. Why I wish I'd swum across that river, which I've never, when I think about it, done for anyone. I just don't know.

And when I think of the change that took place in Elijah after the Union was saved, I remember him at seventeen, on his recruiting visit, remember his guardian's warning: *He can't be let down again.* I remember that *don't come any closer* cat, the cat that wound up on the porch every morning—the cat that I had been myself. I remember all the times I was let down by those I trusted most, the scars it caused, the nightmares it sent. I remember all this and think of my question—*What matters most, your friend or your cause?*—and know that I answered it wrong, all wrong. Your friend *is* your cause. Choose him. Every time.

I had not read Forster's "What I Believe," where he writes: *I hate the idea of causes, and if I had to choose between betraying my country and betraying my friend I hope I should have the guts to betray my country.*

If I had read this, *believed this*, perhaps I would have realized that I had the wrong kind of courage, a courage that helped me build an institution, yet a courage that broke my friend's heart—nicked it, at least. Not sure what courage is worth if it can't keep folks alive. But I did not understand that then.

And so I took this courage, the *courage of my convictions*, so to speak, into the last holy war I'd wage at Yale. Let's go back to the Hall.

You should know that the societies at Yale are a bit like the so-called elite colleges in America. We would be just fine if not better without them, yet they loom over the culture and have their own strange ways of dealing with one another. From what I can tell, Harvard people don't think any other school matters. Yale people think that Harvard and Yale matter. Princeton people think that Harvard, Yale, and Princeton matter—and this continues all the way down to some place where some poor student has borrowed $85,000 from a loan shark for an education they could have gotten in high school, all because a flyer calls the college the *Harvard of Chattanooga*. As for the societies: nobody ever turns down Skull and Bones unless they have an extreme moral objection. No one turns down Wolf's Head unless they are tapped for Skull and Bones or (sometimes) Scroll and Key. Hardly anyone turns down Scroll and Key unless they are tapped for (sometimes) Skull and Bones or (sometimes) Wolf's Head— but it is hard to predict the behavior of Scroll and Key taps because they are prone to have both moral objections *and* highly functional personality disorders, mainly because they are often geniuses, in the literal sense of the word.

In any event, there are real differences between these three societies, referred to as the *Big Three*. The differences might seem trivial, but I have come to believe that they represent very different, warring visions of how the (American) society should work. Bones believes that *might makes right*, so each year, each of its fifteen members selects the junior they want to tap, and that junior is tapped unless there is enough of a protest from the group, which is rare. Keys, on the other hand, believes in *meritocracy*, and employs some mix of search, recommendation, DNA tests, MENSA scores, and so forth to find fifteen of the most accomplished members of the junior class to tap. Wolf's Head lands somewhere in the middle, depending on which seniors run the tap process, as I helped do in 2009. That was my first mistake.

My second mistake was taking the Wolf's Head hymn seriously.

The gods of Egypt bid us hail
We're chosen from the best of Yale

To Worship at the Shrine
To Wor-ship at the Shri-ine!

Every Thursday and Sunday night we sang these words and the verses that come after. As you know, I've always looked to song lyrics for vital instruction—and the Wolf's Head hymn's instructions were pretty clear to me: *Choose the best of Yale.* Not a copy editor from the *Daily News.* Not the third-string softball pitcher. Not the tuxedo steamer for the Whiffen-poofs. So the Wolf's Head process was to begin much earlier than the rest, with a list of every member of the junior class. We would divide that list amongst the sixteen of us. We would scour the juniors' online profiles, check into their academic records, question friends and enemies about their character, watch them in action on stage, on the field, *anywhere.* Every week from February to Tap Night in April, we would gather at the Hall. We would sit in the ancient leather chairs that bore our god names and deliberate, sometimes all night, until we had culled, from thirteen hundred of the "best" young people in the world, sixteen of the *best* of the *best.* That is how it was explained to us. So that is what we set out to do, in theory.

But then we began.

The early weeks were perhaps the most important. They revealed each member's approach and, eventually, their agenda. A Wolf who cut his or her friends in the early rounds was seen as impartial. I knew this, and cut many friends. A Wolf who saw a name on the list that he or she did not recognize and, instead of nixing the person, decided to do some extra research—this member was seen as having a thorough, open mind. I knew this, and took a second look at a few strangers. A Wolf who was silent in those early weeks should have been seen as dangerous. This I did not know.

That's the last swimmer we have on the list . . . protested Mighty Mighty Sheshonk sometime in March.

If anybody said anything, it wasn't me. I just lifted my eyes from the list in my lap and stared.

We can't just break tap lines! he continued. *Seriously, guys. Every year— going back for-fucking-ever!—a swimmer is tapped for WHS. I'm not going to be the swimmer that ends the fucking tap line. Don't do this.*

Tap lines had not come up earlier in the process, if I remember correctly. The idea was that one slot would be saved in each delegation for a particular student group or demographic: a guaranteed slot for a junior swimmer, for a junior baseball player, for the women's squash captain, and so on. Many societies had this arrangement. But tap lines violated the principles of our society, of a meritocracy. Besides, we had the votes to kill the swim line. So we did.

Just so you don't think I was out to get Sheshonk—which I was not, yet—let me also point out that I later learned the swim line did not, in fact, go back *for-fucking-ever,* but rather about fifteen or twenty years. I've also learned since then that whenever somebody says *Things have always been this way,* they're lying. And I have learned, just to warn you, that if you call them on the carpet, change their status quo, they'll come after you quick and hard, which is what one god of Egypt did after losing that vote. Our overseers, some committee of alumni, helped put an end to the reforms. No other tap lines were cut.

We entered the final stretch in late March, winnowing down the remaining forty or so candidates. In that time, many members of the delegation found incredible ways to kill the prospects of juniors they did not like, to replace a worthy tap with a friend or to orchestrate a secret exchange of votes. Looking back, it would have been more honest and a hell of a lot less work to just run a direct-tap process and get on with our lives, since many years later, though some of us have excommunicated one another, none of us cares too much, if at all, about who was in what society and why.

Once we settled on a final group of sixteen, there remained only one vital issue to discuss: god names. Sometime after my own initiation, I had discovered that I'd been christened *Osiris* not because the class that tapped me felt that I shared any traits with the lord of the underworld, but simply because I was a black male. Every Osiris going back *for-fucking-ever* (they said, again) had been the black male tap, just as every Isis had been a black female. I was determined to end this. In part, as you could guess, because I was petty. But there was more.

You benefit most from the god name tradition! the god Busiris yelled, pointing out that, since in Egyptian mythology Osiris was the chief god, I was throwing away my own inheritance and ruining the legacy of all who had come before and would come after.

It is true that Glenn de Chabert had been in Wolf's Head. So had Kurt Schmoke. So had Roosevelt Thompson, the last black football player to win the Rhodes, a boy from Little Rock who went on to earn all As (but one) at Yale, a salt-of-earth savant who many (including his boss, then-governor William J. Clinton) believed would someday become the first black US president, until he was killed in an automobile accident on the New Jersey Turnpike just weeks before he received his diploma, in 1984. Roosevelt had been the *best* of Yale—the best of all of us, black or other.

But you could have called Roosevelt *Osiris* or *Buckwheat* or *Winnie the Pooh* and that would not have changed how extraordinary that young man was. And the thought that you would call Roosevelt Leander Thompson or Glenn de Chabert or Kurt Schmoke or *me* by any name other than our own—solely on account of some chromosomes we had nothing to do with—struck me as absurd if not perverse.

Don't do me any favors! I spewed back at Busiris.

I argued that any junior who was the *best* of Yale should know that they were chosen on the merits, not their skin or sex. I proposed that we randomize the god names for the 2009 tap class—just write them on little sheets of notebook paper and pick them out of a hat. But before I proposed anything, I made sure my side (this was not a solo battle) already had the votes. It's possible that the vote was arranged for a time at which Busiris could not be at the Hall, leaving him to lament to the delegation over email—*It seems to me that we are burning traditions because we like the pretty flames.*

He might have been onto something.

You remember how tap works over at Skull and Bones? In essence, each Bonesman and Boneswoman gets the tap they choose. *Unless*— again, this is rare—there are enough objections from other members of the delegation.

I would not have known much about any of this. But one afternoon near Tap Night, a friend from Bones approached me. Our class had just ended and we lingered behind in the small seminar room, since seniors don't ever seem to rush anywhere, especially that close to graduation. So we lounged and laughed for a few minutes, and then he brought up a junior that I knew and liked well enough. Mentioned that Daniel wanted to tap the boy for Bones. Asked if we would tap the boy for Wolf's Head.

Nope, I'm pretty sure he didn't make it to our last few rounds.

Got it. Could you shoot me an email with a little bit of why?

Yeah, sure thing. I'll send it tonight.

The next night, after reading my email, there were enough objections to veto Daniel's tap for Bones, one of his best friends. I heard this from two other Bonesmen, since Daniel did not talk to me about it, or anything else for the rest of senior year, or hardly at all in the years since.

One semester. One wrong answer. One email. Two friends lost. And for what . . . a Union? A tomb?

Remember Lot's wife, I say.

Jesus said it first, in the gospel of Luke, to his disciples: *Remember Lot's wife.*

Lot, in case you haven't read the Bible recently, was a man who set his family down in Sodom, in the midst of a wicked society that God had to destroy (according to Him, in Genesis). But God, being cruel yet still a sap in part, rushed two angels out to Sodom to warn Lot to gather his folks and get out of dodge.

Arise, take thy wife, and thy two daughters, which are here; lest thou be consumed in the iniquity of the city.

Lot heard the angels' warning but delayed. The angels didn't have all day to wait, so they grabbed his hand and his two daughters' hands and his wife's hand and hurried them out of Sodom. The angels shout—*Escape to the mountain! Whatever you do, don't look back!*—just as God starts raining down on Sodom and Gomorrah (I can't figure out how Gomorrah got dragged into this), *brimstone and fire from the Lord out of heaven.* Lot and his folks are running, fleeing all that destruction, kicking up dust while the Lord rains down death. But then, for some reason, Lot's wife looks back. God turns her into a pillar of salt.

Remember Lot's wife, Jesus says.

But I've got a question, Lord: *Why did she look back?*

Did she look back because she didn't want to miss the mayhem, wanted one last glimpse of a city on fire? Did she look back to make sure her people were far enough from danger to breathe a little easy? I'm so nosy and selfish sometimes that those would have likely been my reasons, if I'd been in her shoes. But what if something else was going on with this woman, *Lot's wife*? What if she looked back because she *knew* some of those dead and dying people? What if she could not bear the thought of leaving them all alone to burn alive, even for righteousness' sake? Isn't that possible?

If it is, then the backward glance of this disobedient woman, this act that we are told to remember, may not be a cautionary tale after all: it may be the bravest act in all the Bible, even braver than the act that holds the whole book together, the Crucifixion. We are told that up on Golgotha, on an old rugged cross, Jesus gave His life to save *everybody*, billions and billions of strangers for all time to come. That's a nice thing to do. Made Him famous, that's for sure. But Lot's wife was killed, turned into a pillar of salt, all because she could not turn away from her friends, the *wicked* men of Sodom. And nobody even wrote the woman's name down. Oh, to have the courage of Lot's wife! I surely did not—not yet.

So it came as no surprise and no concern when one of the gods of Egypt, my bet would be Sheshonk, said as a valedictory word on our days at Yale: *I don't know how anybody could believe that Casey Gerald is a good human being.*

That would have hurt, if I had considered it important. I'd stayed up late and worked for many hours over four long years. Had been changed, had been redeemed. Had learned, without reading a single page of Machiavelli, that a *great* man cannot be a *good* man. I'd made my bargain. Yet I had more work to do.

Like almost every other hopeful-great at that time, I had decided to go to Washington to learn how to run the country, or at least to try. But I remembered something Akhil Amar stressed toward the end of his lecture on the morning of November 5:

We are citizens of the world. This election has reverberations around the globe—you need to understand that.

And so, as many greats had done before me, I packed my bags for Paris.

chapter TWENTY

I was not, before you get the wrong idea, like many of my countrymen, some I even admire, who fled to Paris to escape America. I did and do respect anybody who gets up and goes off anywhere, with purpose or not, as long as they don't abandon their basic responsibilities or *me*. And I knew very well, as you know by now, the urge to debauch upon a different world when the one you've got has worn you down. What I *did not* know was enough about my country to feel that I needed to escape the whole thing. Knew (and cared) even less about France—had not begun to drink so much wine or covet Givenchy or read Genet; and had already mastered one foreign language—Standard American English—so it would never have crossed my mind to tuck tail and run to the City of Lights if I could find a city closer to home, someplace in all the 3.5 million raw square miles of America that might have a little room for me.

I also happened to hate the French, though I can't recall exactly why. I'm almost positive it had something to do with the Iraq War. George W. Bush had decided, when I was in high school, that he wanted everybody to go to war, but some important people in France decided that they had no interest in mass murder at that time, and so a few US congressmen, finding this stance unacceptable, proposed that all true patriots change *french fries* to *freedom fries* and *french toast* to *freedom toast* and so on until all nomenclature was for the war. I had no big commitment to the war myself, but I had a hard time believing that good people would draw that much negative attention, so I went along and developed my own personal hatred for the French at the age of sixteen and, since I had not discovered anything to change my mind back to being neutral or in their corner, I still hated the French at twenty-two.

Thankfully, I did not fly to Paris to stay. I just stopped through on my way to Berlin.

I had been sent, by an international diplomacy outfit, to join a delegation of young Americans and Europeans who would spend a summer studying the great human rights crises of the twentieth century, so that we could snuff out any new crises that sparked in the twenty-first. We had been tasked, I guess you could say, with defending Western civilization, whatever that was or is. Fine with me, as *defending Western civilization* seemed to constitute a big chunk of the American president's job, and Berlin seemed to be ground zero—the place where my future predecessors had once sojourned and speechified about the mission, starting with John F. Kennedy. The words he'd spoken more than five decades ago, just months before his death, still ring true enough to help me explain to you my summer in Berlin, and the less than a year I spent in Washington thereafter—and, in some way, the wretched mess that threatens to destroy *the West* at this very moment. I refer to Mr. Kennedy's "Ich bin ein Berliner" speech, delivered in 1963.

I

It was 26 June 1963, to be exact, over 880 days into the thousand days of Camelot, and JFK was still very much alive that afternoon—as were the more than 120,000 West Berliners who gathered in the war-ruined

Rudolph Wilde Platz many hours before he arrived, and who erupted in cries and shouts when he appeared on the steps of City Hall, and who hushed when he approached the microphone and began to speak:

Two thousand years ago, the president declared, after wasting one minute, twenty seconds acknowledging people onstage before declaring again—*Two thousand years ago, the proudest boast was "civis Romanus sum." Today, in the world of freedom, the proudest boast is "Ich bin ein Berliner."*

Those last words—*I am a Berliner*—made Mr. Kennedy's speech famous. But as with many things that lead to fame, the words did not convey what he and the speech were all about. The next lines did:

There are many people in the world who really don't understand, or say they don't, what is the great issue between the free world and the Communist world. Let them come to Berlin.

To understand what he meant, why the crowd cheered after hearing this, you should know that by 26 June 1963, whoever had decided that it was a good idea to split one city among four nations—America, France, Great Britain, and the Soviet Union—must have been either fired or full of regret. The split had devolved into the greatest geopolitical conflict since the last great geopolitical conflict, which also involved these four nations plus Germany, in a slightly different arrangement. I'm no historian, but from what I can tell, America tried to mind its business (and get rich while doing so) until some mix of the Japanese and Winston Churchill convinced Franklin Roosevelt to finally do more to defend the West and assist the battered British Empire, which might have held on a little longer if France had not surrendered so quickly to the German Third Reich, which might have actually lasted a thousand years or at least more than twelve if the Soviets (or Joe Stalin) had not been willing to send ten million soldiers to die, almost as many dead soldiers as every other country in the war combined (yet not as many dead soldiers as murdered Jews and Roma and homosexuals, real and accused, and people with disabilities and Jehovah's Witnesses and asocials and resisters and ordinary citizens living through an extraordinarily terrible time). As *thanks* for their sacrifice, the Soviets were granted the eastern portion of Germany and the eastern portion of Berlin at the end of the war. In the fifteen years between that 1945 accord and Mr. Kennedy's 1960 election, the Soviets, as those who believe in Causes often do, got mad as hell at anybody who did not agree with them, so they began to employ all kinds of tricks to convince their people that Communism was a good idea—going so far as to prevent the people from seeing anything that *was not* Communism, which was clever if sad. But this trick was hard to pull off in a single city shared with three occupying nations that did not like Communism much, so in 1961 the Soviet-created German Democratic Republic hung a barbed-wire partition between their side of Berlin and the other side, the side that represented Western civilization, the side that John F. Kennedy visited on 26 June 1963—a visit that the people in East Berlin could not even see because, by then, the East Germans had replaced the barbed wire with a concrete wall almost twelve feet high. And standing at and near and in towers above the wall were East German soldiers, just waiting for any East Berliner to develop enough unmitigated gall to wave at Jack Kennedy on the other side or to shout *amen* (also *amen* in German) when the American president put words to their muffled lament:

While the wall is the most obvious and vivid demonstration of the failures of the Communist system, for all the world to see, we take no satisfaction in it, for it is . . . an offense not only against history but an offense against humanity, separating families, dividing husbands and wives and brothers and sisters, and dividing a people who wish to be joined together.

If I had been running East Germany at that time, I probably would have wanted to shoot my people, too, instead of letting some slick bastard come to town and give them that kind of ammunition against my scheme. But all the bullets in the world cannot protect an awful idea—and so Mr. Kennedy's short, famous, yet mostly unknown speech joined forces with his actions and twenty-six more years of speeches and action and all the forgotten words and acts of all the people behind the Iron Curtain who preferred to be free, even with the cost being as high as it was, so that on the night of 9 November 1989, Western civilization prevailed and blew its horn so loud that damn near every able-bodied young person east and west of the Berlin Wall rushed to it to dance and kiss and start to tear it down. Kudos to those kids and to President Kennedy and everybody else involved, because twenty years later I showed up to a united, Communist-free (as far as I knew) Berlin in June 2009.

II

There was nothing ruinous about the city when I arrived. It stretched, like Houston, for miles and miles beyond any obvious use for the space, yet unlike that hot humid jumbled mess on the Gulf of Mexico, Berlin was cool and clean and as thought through as perhaps a museum or, better yet, a mausoleum—a city embalmed to preserve the memory of all that its people and the West had endured.

But if in June 1963, the proudest boast had been *Ich bin ein Berliner*, in June 2009, in the world of freedom, the proudest boast was not a slogan or a city, but a man: *Obama*. At least that was the boast when, on my seventh day in Berlin, I went to prison.

I can still see that gruel-gray sky, the concrete walkway, dark and wet, leading to the prison, which stood behind thin white iron bars. It was a stocky building made of bricks, brown and tan; three, four stories high; rows of tiny prison cells inside meant to hold men like Hans-Eberhard Zahn, who had once been a thin young man but was, in 2009, a big old man with thin white hair and long tan fingers, one of which was pointed at my face as I stood on the back wall of the interrogation room.

You resemble Obama! he squealed.

You may not know this, but I do not resemble Barack Obama. I also don't pick fights, especially not behind bars, especially not with old men who are kind enough to take me on a tour of the prison they were held in by the East German secret police, the Stasi. Such was the fate of Hans-Eberhard Zahn.

He had been only twenty-five years old on 13 November 1953, a student at the Free University of Berlin and a minor resister. Once the Stasi picked him up off the street on November 14, he was promoted to *major resister* and *victim* and *hero*, surviving for seven years before release. Five decades later, Hans was still exacting his revenge, informing visitors of all the wrong the Stasi had done.

He shepherded my delegation through the Hohenshönhausen prison, the most notorious of its kind, through the sandpaper-colored hallways down which he had been dragged to his cell and its tiny bed, and to the punishment cell which had only a bucket, and to the interrogation room, which I can't really remember because we went there at the end of the tour, by which point my feet were tired and I was ready to leave. I had not planned to visit to another jail after the last time Clarice walked me into Lew Sterrett to see my daddy, and there was nothing that Mr. Zahn showed me in Hohenshönhausen that made me any more or less interested in keeping people out of jail or away from Communism. Once I'd learned about the wall and all the political prisoners they kept in concentration camps after the war, I was sufficiently opposed to the Communists and to anybody who was into Communist kind of stuff. But then Mr. Zahn said I *resembled Obama*, and for just a moment, I was pleased that the Stasi had gotten ahold of him for a little while.

I was standing behind a tall German boy when Hans pointed at me. The German boy leaned to the side so there would be no confusion. Hans received a clearer view of me, and I of him. His eyes were those of a child who had just seen her first puppy in the window.

Oh . . . okay, I muttered, siphoning all the anger from my voice and into my hands, gripping my book bag straps. *I'll take that as a compliment.*

No, really! Hans was bouncing in his interrogation chair, looking to the rest of the delegation for a witness. *Don't you think so?*

Whether they thought so or not, they grabbed their book bag straps, too, and stared at the floor and the walls away from Hans, and laughed in such a way that laughter may have meant *I'm sorry, Casey,* which would have been nice to hear.

Now that I've grown and have other grudges to tend to, I can give Mr. Zahn, who passed from this world into the next or nowhere in 2013, a break. He had been on the east side of the wall, I assume, on 26 June 1963. But he was free, or out of jail, forty-five years later, on 24 July 2008—the day that Barack Obama, not yet *President* Obama, proved that he had a historic amount of unmitigated gall when he decided to make a campaign stop in Berlin. Shocked the hell out of everybody, including German Chancellor Angela Merkel, who didn't even attend his speech at the Brandenburg Gate, a gate that had come a long way since Napoleon stood under it in 1806 to celebrate his victory over the Prussians—had come so far that it was right back where it started, welcoming a man on the rise. Perhaps Hans had been there to welcome him, too. Or perhaps he had just heard the candidate's words—*People of the world, look at Berlin*—and appreciated the recognition. And if he did not hear the actual speech, Hans likely read *Der Spiegel*'s translation of Mr. Obama's message: *People of the World, Look at Me.* And old man Zahn, poor of sight or of imagination, looked and saw but through a dark man, darkly.

He was not alone. Hans was but one victim—a more advanced, pathetic case, no doubt—of that glaucoma that dimmed the view of all who hoped to truly see the man in question, or others like him. That's something I learned at George Washington's house a while back. I had bussed down to Mount Vernon to check out the place, and to take a photograph with the defense secretary whose job it had been to get us out of Iraq (he provided no update), and to hear from a presidential historian who I assume knew his stuff, since he'd taught the future king of England about Abraham Lincoln many years prior. Anyway, the historian said something that you might like to know: *It takes thirty to forty years to really understand a president and his term.*

Now, if this is true, then you and I are in one awful bind, since Mr. Obama has only just retired, just moseyed off to sunbathe and Jet Ski while the whole goddamn country falls apart or at least is held in the hands of a madman. I don't blame him. But if we need anything right now it is some understanding, and so the best solution I've come up with is based on the hunch I already told you about—that President O was as much a symbol as he was a man, such that, as with every symbol, the best way to talk about *him* (and tell the truth) is to talk about *us* and gamble that a composite sketch of our desires and beliefs will form at least a faint image of him—and if not that, then at least a glimpse of the time that produced him and the world he tried to shape—and if not even that, then at least a decent explanation of why I was in such despair when I left Berlin and moved to Washington, that sister capital, lined similarly with monuments and perfumed similarly with the odor of history though also the stench of ambition, sprawling though not as far and wide, and not as clean, and not as cool.

III

Despair might not be the right word. I still had a great deal of hope for myself if not the world, and whatever the feeling was—frustration, disillusionment, rage—it did not set in immediately, not even when I could not find a job in the new president's administration. I continued my search based on instructions from the most credible person I knew on the matter,

Charles Hill. If you have not heard of him that means he's good at his job: *advisor*. Good enough for Henry Kissinger, good enough for Ronald Reagan and, even though I distrusted both of those men, good enough for me.

Be a special assistant to someone at the top, he nearly whispered from his desk one afternoon toward the end of my senior year. *It's very hard to know how to run something on a big scale if you haven't seen it from the top.*

The *something* was America, of course, and I soon discovered that *the top* was six blocks east and one block north of 1600 Pennsylvania Avenue, at the Center for American Progress, or CAP, which called itself a *think tank* but which *Time* magazine called *Obama's Idea Factory in Washington*. I applied straightaway. Somebody helped secure the job, but what else is new? In my mind I was a real if minor member of the president's *best and brightest*. On my résumé, I was a *special assistant* to one of CAP's founders. The only difference, I should mention, between a *special* assistant and a *regular* assistant, as far as I could tell from my time in Washington, is that the regular assistant wants to help his or her boss succeed at their job. The *special* assistant wants the boss's job. Immediately. Maybe that was just me, though.

I rose early on my first day and rode the bus to a nondescript building at Tenth and H Street Northwest. Elevator to the tenth floor, across the small lobby, through the spotless glass door, and finally to my desk, more like a shelf built into the wall, where I found a seven-hundred-page book: *Change for America: A Progressive Blueprint for the 44th President*, which I did not read and did not have to, since the words on the pages were already on their way to becoming laws. Turns out that Washington was not too different from South Oak Cliff High School—ruled on the surface by people with *authority*, ruled in fact by people with *power*—people, often, in the shadows. Each representative answered to more than seven hundred thousand constituents. Each senator answered to the residents of an entire state. The president answered, in theory, to the whole country. Yet there were powerful people in Washington who answered, it seemed, to no one.

And if that wasn't delicious enough, I was invited at once to do something many in Washington wait their whole lives to do: work for a Kennedy.

She was a *Shriver*, technically. No matter. Especially since the Shrivers, at least Sargent Shriver, Maria's father—chairman of the *Yale Daily News*, founder of the Peace Corps, czar of Lyndon Baines Johnson's War on Poverty, which, if it did nothing else, provided the welfare that helped me and my sister pay rent and take long hot showers and buy a Christmas tree— meant a great deal to me. To be a Kennedy was one thing. But to be a Kennedy *and* a Shriver was almost too much—*she* was almost too much, Maria Owings Shriver.

I had never in my life seen a woman who looked as completely rich as Maria Shriver did that Saturday morning when she walked through CAP's glass door. She did not open the door herself, that I remember (though I don't believe I opened it for her), and if she removed her floor-length mink coat, then she did it with such ease, such *insouciance*, that it seemed to carefully remove itself from her shoulders all on its own. Installed on one of her fingers was a diamond ring that reminded me of those Ring Pops we wore as kids, except that it was an actual diamond and not a blue ball of high fructose corn syrup. She was a brilliant gesticulator, as anybody with jewels that nice should be, and so she gesticulated a great deal as she traipsed down the hallway, guffawing as I've only ever heard unstoppably rich people guffaw, especially rich and beautiful people, as she was, a gleeful taut piece of history, traipsing down the hallway to the corner office where my boss would brief her and John Podesta, CAP's don, for their appearance the following day on *Meet the Press*, which was at that time the most important forum in politics, since no one seemed to take the Senate chambers seriously anymore, preferring instead the reach and glamour of television.

Their purpose: to promote a new report, aptly named *The Shriver Report: A Woman's Nation Changes Everything*, that chronicled all the ways that America had become a *woman's nation*, and everything that, as a result, had changed or would be changing soon. It was true that, for the first time, over half the workers in America were women. But despite our deepest hopes, it was and remains unclear whether the nation *belonged* to women and whether it had changed much for the better, if at all. I read the report anyhow to know what was to come, and also because the only special assistants who succeed in Washington are those who are prepared— those who know where everything is and who everybody is, those who watch and listen and write it all down.

You hear that, Casey?

The voice of Maria Shriver. I glanced up from my briefing book and saw her, turned around in her back-supporting office chair, diamond ring hanging over the side, deep-set eyes staring at me on the couch. She had been testing different talking points for *Meet the Press*, searching for the best message to persuade men that they should care about a woman's nation, that they should encourage their wives' and girlfriends' desires to work, and look after the children every now and then and, generally, get their boots off women's backs for the first time in human history. The message had been found: *Guys, hello! It'll get you more sex!*

Ms. Shriver wanted me to understand this point. I nodded and laughed since she was Maria Shriver and all but, of course, there were a few problems with her advice. Most obviously there was my stomach-sickness at the thought of touching a woman in that way. Beyond this, though, was the general point that I had taken a vow of celibacy for my time in Washington. If I was going to be president I needed to prove, if only to myself, that I had near-supernatural self-control and near-saintly personal values. Again, it was a very different time. (Let me add that I would have been flawless in my attempt, had it not been for one jezebel who connived his way, just by being gorgeous and persistent, back to my apartment a month or two before I left Washington to continue down my path to destruction.)

Maria Shriver was marvelous on *Meet the Press*—she had the face and mind for television, which I don't mean as an insult—and if our first exchange was, at base, a misunderstanding, then it was just a foretaste of my time in Washington.

You see, there were many people in the world who really did not understand, or said they didn't, what the great issue was between the liberals and the conservatives of that era. They should have gone to Berlin, as President Kennedy had demanded and as I did. It was there, on two consecutive days, that I witnessed *liberal values* in their purest form, at least pure enough for me to understand why, as I tell you this story, liberal values are under siege across all that is called *the West*—which is now defended most vehemently, funny enough, by the Germans. Here, I present the recently unearthed thoughts of twenty-two-year-old me, in part because I must (or *want to*) seize every opportunity to show that, though Casey Gerald was not a *good* person, he was not the Antichrist that he was prophesied to be from birth. Besides, in the years since he had these thoughts, the man he became had other thoughts, some better, some worse, about that summer in Berlin. Those new thoughts would only get in the way. So here he is, at the end of the first day in question.

DAY 13 · BERLIN (6.17)

-The Day that Tipped the Scale-

Trying to summarize today is not very easy, because there is a conflation of feelings & experiences that produces a general sense of anger.

Today's topic: Race/Ethnicity . . . Does Race Matter in Germany Today? The more important question in my mind is: Does Race Matter (Anywhere) Today? My answer is more clear today than it has ever [been] before: <u>YES</u>

During our discussion . . . the issue of affirmative action comes up. Camille, a French girl who has studied in the States for 7 years raises her hand and starts her dreaded oration:

I know I'm going to be unpopular after this. But, just playing devil's advocate: I'm not a racist, but I don't think stopping/ suspecting/arresting someone is racist if the people are more likely to be criminal based on stats. I worked at a federal court in the States, and all of the criminals were black or hispanic. And I saw a black lawyer and thought—"oh, that's weird."—But anyway, I don't think it's racist to suspect people if statistically they are more likely to be criminal anyway.

Of course, I was thoroughly disgusted and couldn't hold my piece [sic]. First, I had to tell her not to "play devil's advocate" for something you don't believe. If you didn't believe it, you wouldn't have said it. Secondly, at the very least your comment and viewpoint is mentally lazy and/or ignorant. But in this case, it is also racist. If you assume that someone will play a certain role—especially one that is inferior/socially deviant, just because of their race or the color of their skin, then your actions are racist. Point blank. If you want to racially profile in the name of probability for your job, then you can do that but you must accept the fact that your actions are racist. You can't have your cake and eat it too in this case.

To make matters worse, it was just as disgusting to see how people coddled her after this incident. In my opinion, they didn't want to believe that even someone in [this human rights fellowship] could be racist. At worst, they agreed w/ her secretly but didn't want to say anything out loud.

Today was one of the few, if only, times that I felt overwhelmed as a black man. Everyone in this program looks to me for the "black answer" or uses me as the "black example" . . . that's though [sic] on its own. Throw in the fact that I'm about the only black guy in Berlin, and now to be reminded that at the end of the day, even "humanitarians" are mentally painting black people as inferior/criminal/etc. They've probably broken more laws than I have!!

Short of crying, I vented for a good while. Being a black American is something else, man.

You might like to know that since that day in Berlin, Camille went on to receive a public policy degree from the Harvard Kennedy School of Government and a law degree from the Harvard Law School. She also spent some time at the World Trade Organization and the United Nations and the World Bank. It is quite possible that she has changed since 17 June 2009—at the very least she has tickled nearly every lever of power that the West has to offer. In return, the West has offered her to you and to me, as an example if not a sacrificial lamb. I hold no brief for her, either way—nor for the other high-minded Europeans in that small lecture hall who consoled her, nor for the German chaperone who chastised me for not taking the time to hear Camille out and offer my personal experience for her edification. I hold no brief for them—nor for all the liberal leaders in Washington who seemed to have a terribly hard time finding nonwhite liberals to hire for their think tanks and aid organizations and other people-saving outfits, not to mention nonwhite liberal neighbors and friends—though they did, to their credit, have an easier time finding a colored au pair or a clean articulate colored person to vote for as long as the candidate said things like:

I am the son of a black man from Kenya and a white woman from Kansas. I was raised with the help of a white grandfather who survived a Depression to serve in Patton's Army during World War II and a white grandmother who worked on a bomber assembly line at Fort Leavenworth while he was overseas. I've gone to some of the best schools in America and lived in one of the world's poorest nations. I am married to a black American who carries within her the blood of slaves and slave-owners—an inheritance we pass on to our two precious daughters. I have brothers, sisters, nieces, nephews, uncles and cousins, of every race and every hue, scattered across three continents . . .

Which translates to: I AM NOT A NIGGER.

And I hold no brief for myself at twenty-two. I was such a budding jingo that I could only conclude: *Being a black American is something else, man.* I had not read Fanon, I had not learned of James's *Black Jacobins*, I had not watched Sembène's *Black Girl*, or considered why the Turkish Muslim woman in my delegation seemed equally upset at Camille, or wondered why the two young Arab men who sold me that croque monsieur outside the Louvre seemed so thrilled to see me, so eager to shout the proudest boast, themselves—*Barack Obama!!!*—which is all they could say to me, since I spoke no French nor Arabic and they spoke no other English than that man's name. I had not realized, you see, that there was hardly any place in *the West* where *the Nigger*—black or Arab, poor or not—does not have a hard time. And the primary if not only difference between the liberals and the *illiberals* on this issue is that the American *alt-right* and France's *National Front* and Germany's *National Democratic Party* (I haven't been to England, so will leave them out of this) will try their best to kill you quickly or keep you out of the West altogether, whereas the liberals will write elaborate pamphlets about your condition while doing little to change it and even less to come in contact with it—or with *you*, for that matter.

The good thing—well, the sad thing, but a helpful thing since we have other things to get to—is that there is so much evidence that the West would like to rid itself of its niggers that I don't have to drone on about it. Even if I should, I don't want to, because I am not convinced that this is the chief threat facing this neck of the woods. Racism, after all, has been good to the West—and if not good, then at least *central*. Even if we want to strike Hitler's reliance on the American eugenics movement from the record, it is a bit more difficult to strike the generations of Africans who were shipped to the New World, over 10 million of whom survived the Middle Passage to live and work in bondage for the sugar and cotton and tobacco etc. etc. that made the West rich, or the untold millions who were subjected to colonial rule and the Western ideals of men like Cecil Rhodes. Yes, white supremacy—again, by this I only mean a belief, even subconscious, that non-"white" persons are inferior—seems to be as fundamental to the West as free votes and free trade. I have nothing to share that will change this fact.

But there is a problem more interesting, and perhaps more solvable, that I noticed in the liberal leaders of the West. Let's go back to Berlin, for day two.

DAY 14 · BERLIN (6.18)

Yesterday's near meltdown was juxtaposed w/ today's visit to a school in Westhafen (northern area of Berlin.)

The German education system is scary: start school at 6 yrs old and at 10 yrs old (some places at 12) you are separated by your perceived level of academic prowess → Realschule, Hauptschule, and Gymnasium. The gist of the story is that only those students in Gymnasium can go to college. Period.

The students in the middle school sometimes have extra years of technical or vocational training, but mostly kids have to go out & try to find a job or "apprenticeship"! That is easier said than done. It goes w/o saying that most of these kids have migration backgrounds, are poorer, and have more difficult life conditions (unemployed/absent parents, etc.). From 10-12 years old, they are pegged to either have free (mostly) higher education, or have no higher education at all. 10 yrs old. Frightening. The headmaster told us that typically only a handful of students (less than) end up going to gymnasium.

The highlight of my trip so far was this visit—I taught 8 young men (and some [program] fellows) how to play football. This was the first time I've ever taught someone the game from scratch. To say the least, everybody was pretty bad @ first. Falling while backpedaling, running crazy routes, looking generally unathletic ☺. There was one kid, Tom, who actually showed a bit of promise. He was a quick learner, a good athlete, and a nice kid.

After I felt that people had some clue about playing offense & defence [sic], I sensed that they wanted to actually get after it, so we went outside. The playing surface was tiny—probably 10-15 yds long, 20-25 yrds wide, and we started the "game" w/ 8 v. 8. What commenced was frantic running into, around and away from one another until a ball was snatched from the air or allowed to fall helplessly to the ground. Playing to 28, we reduced the team size to 4 v. 4—only the kids were playing against each other.

As folks cheered on, [two fellows] tried to give the kids plays to run (most of which were unsuccessful). They did score, and the game was eventually tied at 21. [One fellow] wisely told me to arrange the game so that it would end in a 21-21 tie (we were running out of time so only one team would have a shot @ 28). I agreed, but apparently the kids were thinking otherwise.

Tom & his teammates devised some whacky hook & lateral play that we all thought would fail. Only problem? It worked & Tom cruised into the endzone to give his team a 28-21 victory. Everyone was sweaty and happy, especially the kids, who had found a new admiration for the game (and for their coach— "Coach Casey" as they called me). Hopefully I was able to be a good coach about larger lessons—mostly selflessness, which I find to be one of the ultimate requirements of football & life.

The only downside to this story was that I had to leave the kids, probably never to see them again. Seeing as though they won't be in university most likely, they will probably never have the same opportunities that I've been blessed with. It really pisses me off to think about that because I felt their humanity, even though we couldn't verbally communicate. There will always be times that I think about them.

Times like now. If you think I was sick on Halloween 1992 when Granny made it clear that there would be no candy or joy for the two men on her porch, just imagine how I seethed when I discovered that there would be no *future* for my nigga Tom and his buddies—unless you call *being left behind* a future—all on account of somebody who thought they were so brilliant that they could tell which ten-year-olds deserved some education and which ones did not, all without ever meeting them. I bet they never let Tom design a play, or break the rules, or score a touchdown of his own volition, or smile that snaggletooth smile in his dingy T-shirt and be happy and on top of the world for a few minutes, did they? Man, I want to weep for Tom and his buddies, just thinking about it, I want to punch one of those brilliant Germans right in the goddamn face, I wanna know how Tom's doing these days.

And Tom was not black or Arab. He was an *organic* German boy of fourteen, as were a few of the boys who helped him finagle his way into the end zone; just as some of the kids I saw in the banlieue of Paris were not Congolese or Algerian but might have been pure-blood Huguenots for all I knew; just as Elijah did not trace his people back to a plantation in Alabama but to some town in Mexico. I say all this to say that though I did not know much at twenty-two, I knew *my people* when I saw them, even if they did not speak my language or come from my block or share my color. And I knew—or I felt certain enough to call it *knowledge*—that day in Berlin what I went on to realize at the Center for American Progress, every time I wrote another report or did more analysis on the computer or sat through another expert lecture—yes, I knew that the world, or *the West*, or just my corner of it, was shaped by ideas so perfectly designed that they left little space for *people*. I suppose it was believed that, somehow, all the issues that plagued the human race could be contained or controlled or at least understood without having to be troubled by interacting with human beings at all. That has never worked and never will.

Now before I get too comfortable on my high horse, let me say that these discoveries were not what led me to despair. I had not gone to Washington to end racism or, primarily, to fight for *my people* in America or anywhere else. I went to Washington to find power—to find people who had it and who knew how to use it, to move things, to move *people*, to take a clever idea and turn it into history. I could do without goodness or even brilliance. What I could not do without was *action*.

And if there is one thing that angered me most during my time in Washington—not just me but many of my friends who also dreamed of being great men and women and who, almost to a person, quit the capital before the end of Mr. Obama's first term—it was that, compared to what we expected, nothing seemed to be happening. We all had changed the course of our lives to follow if not worship the least dramatic messiah in the history of the world—a man who campaigned in the style of Revelation but who governed more like a book of the Bible from which no one ever preached a sermon. Nahum or something.

I did not have words to describe Mr. Obama's style until I read a 1986 *New Yorker* article by Frances FitzGerald that traced the gay rights movement in San Francisco, the rise of the Castro and, with it, the rise of Harvey Milk. FitzGerald recounts the events leading up to and beyond Mr. Milk's assassination in San Francisco City Hall, minutes after Mayor George Moscone was also assassinated—a tragedy that came just eight days after the mass suicide (more accurately, mass murder) at Jonestown, Guyana, where over 900 men, women, and children, many of them San Franciscans, under the direction of Jim Jones, drank cyanide-laced Kool-Aid and perished. Left to respond to the most public assassinations in the history of the city and the largest murder-suicide of its kind in modern times was Dianne Feinstein, who had been president of the board of supervisors and became mayor after the tragedy and then the senior senator from the state of California. FitzGerald wrote:

Dianne Feinstein made a sustained and masterly effort to defuse the tensions. She urged no prosecutions, reassured everyone, and talked endlessly, soothingly, never making a point. The city that had gone through the assassinations of its mayor and a supervisor, the Jonestown suicides (the Reverend Jim Jones had a church in San Francisco), and the rioting seemed grateful for the sheer prosiness of her response.

That is almost exactly how I would describe Mr. Obama's approach then and later, as I witnessed it when we headlined an event together in Texas. *Together* is a bit too strong, sorry. They put my name in small font under his on the tickets everybody received, and even made me go through all the extra background checks just so I could share the greenroom area with him—which did not happen because the president went to eat tacos beforehand and showed up late. I don't blame him for that, either. I finished my talk and sat in the audience to listen to his and, sitting there, was reminded all over just how thoughtful, decent, charming, and longwindedly boring our 44th president could be. Again, as with Dianne Feinstein, this was perhaps exactly what we needed. But it was a far cry from what I and many others expected from the next John F. Kennedy.

These expectations, I eventually realized, were also based on a big misunderstanding. Turns out John F. Kennedy was not *the* John F. Kennedy, himself. If I had been interested in research at that time, I might have found the first draft of his Berlin speech, which includes the following paragraph:

I cannot lead you to believe that this will all happen quickly or easily. I cannot lead you to believe that . . . rebellion is a solution, when that would endanger all you have built. Nor can I tell you that the situation is improved by private, provocative actions expressing your anger and deep frustrations against the Wall.

I understand why he or somebody else drew a big line through this section. People really cannot stand it when you tell them the truth, which is why our greatest presidents have also been amongst the greatest liars of their generation. But I sure wish President Kennedy left that passage in, because it took me many years to learn that not much happened in the Kennedy administration, either, at least not as much as I thought, not with all the vigor I'd thought. And that most of the great ideas that Mr. Kennedy spoke about were ultimately put into action by Lyndon Baines Johnson, one of the most effective and morally depraved presidents of all time.

I should have apologized to LBJ's granddaughter for giving JFK all her old-old man's credit when I rode with her to his Hill Country ranch a few years ago, but I'm a big fan of letting bygones be bygones, whenever I'm the guilty party.

Anyway, I did not know at the time that *not getting much done* was also a big part of running the country, so I added *laggards* to the list of epithets I had for the liberal elite. And, having found my final straw, so to speak, and having an open mind, as I did, and knowing so many rich old men who had been trying to influence me since the summer before I went to Yale, I decided to consider being a Republican.

IV

This lasted all of one morning, thanks to my daddy.

I'm not sure that I spoke to him during my time in Washington, but I did speak to a man I met through him—or, rather, through Rod Gerald. The man had been a major champion of Ohio State football and an early supporter of my eighteen-year-old future father. Aside from finding Daddy a job when we fled Dallas for Columbus six months after I was born, and making sure we were never evicted while we lived there, and sending me a computer and coat my freshman year of college—all this without me ever seeing him in person after my fourth year of life, that I can remember—he also offered immediate aid, as a rabid conservative and owner of Prescott Bush's former summer home, when I called about my possible conversion.

He sent me to the best evangelist he knew: a short, beyond-middle-aged Ohioan with a resilient head of gray hair, who spoke calmly but with the intensity of a man who would consider murdering for his beliefs, though the messiness of the exercise would keep him from following through. He was on the board of the American Conservative Union, and invited me to join him at the most important event in the world of the right, the Conservative Political Action Conference, one Saturday morning in February 2010.

I left my Capitol Hill apartment and took the metro out of Washington proper into suburban Maryland, to a Marriott hotel where ten thousand conservative activists and leaders had pilgrimaged for what National Public Radio called, in 2017, *equal parts political rally, conservative boot camp, recruiting tool, trade show and merchandise mart, Beltway celebrity watch party, and this year . . . a celebration*—though on the February 2010 morning I attended, CPAC was the epicenter of resistance to Barack Hussein Obama (they made sure to say his middle name as much as possible).

Some in the Marriott were my peers—at least, they were about my age, judging from their faces and haircuts, though I did not know a single person in my generation, until that day, who carried posters of Ronald Reagan. Somebody else showed up in or changed into an oversized furry elephant costume. A small regiment of grown men wore antique military uniforms. Away from these masses, on a balcony, behind a glass wall that might have been bulletproof, were a few dozen elderly men in suits and dames in gowns, one of whom was the woman who had funded Charlie Wilson's war.[1] She and her fellow grandees were nice enough to give me their word that I would not be harmed while in attendance, and so I tramped back down the stairs to the ballroom floor, where the day's main speaker, a lanky blonde, had just stepped to the podium.

---

1. A 1980s covert CIA operation, supported by Texas Congressman Charlie Wilson, aimed at helping jihadists defeat the Soviets in Afghanistan; an operation, you might have guessed, that muddied our moral high ground in Afghanistan two decades later.

What a difference a year makes she purred with a wry smile.

The crowd, as soon as the speaker released these words, hooted and whistled and *yeaah*ed and stomped and clapped and kept on going for a period of time that seemed disproportionate to the gravity of the line, to me.

This time last year the Republican party, according to the media, was finished, dead, moribund. It was the beginning of the Democrats' thousand-year reich. But this year we have a new governor in Virginia, new governor in New Jersey. Scott Brown has taken Teddy Kennedy's old seat . . .

She did have a point, you know. Not that I was glad about any of these events. But I like an underdog story as much as anybody and so I didn't take much issue with the jubilation, even if I did not join in it myself, standing as I was at the very back of the ballroom, straining to see the podium over a man's tricornered hat.

Polls show that less than fifty percent of Americans approve of the job President Obama is doing. The best thing most respondents could say about him was that he was one of the least dangerous people they know named Hussein. Even Obama's staunchest supporters are starting to leave . . . Last week Michelle Obama demanded to see a copy of his birth certificate.

This was a reference to a theory involving the 44th president, ginned up most forcefully, if you can believe it, by the 45th president—that Barack Obama was not only a Muslim, but a *foreign-born* Muslim, birthed in Kenya and therefore constitutionally barred from being president of the United States. The hoots and whistles and *yeaah*s and claps came back. The speaker breezed through the requisite comments about William Clinton's personal scandals, which the crowd also enjoyed despite having heard them for nearly twenty years by that point. There was new material, though.

The liberal elites keep telling us that they know what's best for us but you know we keep finding out that these liberal elites, the smart people, are kind of creepy—first we had ACORN on tape counseling people on how to bring underage prostitutes from El Salvador into the country. Then we got Obama's "safe schools czar," Kevin Jennings, whose apparent raison d'etre is to introduce homosexuality to grade school children. Jennings's idea of a good sixth grade field trip is to take the kids to the Tony Awards.

The crowd erupted in laughter.

He's even written the introduction to a book titled Queering Elementary Education.

No, no! some members of the crowd cried. The speaker took a short break from her gay-bashing to denounce Mr. Obama's efforts to fix the economy (*failed*), to end the war on terror (*treasonous*), to save the environment (*counterproductive*), and to get people healthcare (*socialist*). The crowd was interested enough in these issues, but had calmed from their earlier fever pitch. The speaker went back to what seemed to work best.

CNN calls them—she was referring to opponents of Obamacare, the president's healthcare bill—"*tea baggers," which is the gayest term I've ever heard on CNN, other than "Anderson Cooper."*

This line drew the longest mix of applause, whistles, shouts, and laughs of the day—you can see for yourself, on the internet. Once the crowd recovered, the speaker sped through a few other issues and brought her address to a close.

Thanks for being here, she said. *Keith Olbermann*—another cable news anchor—*is a girl,* she threw in. *God bless America.* And then once more— *And remember: Keith Olbermann is a girl*—before *I'll take questions now.*

I didn't ask any questions, nor did I count, but it felt to me that many of those ten thousand CPAC attendees had just experienced something marvelous, based on how much noise they made, how they clapped above their heads rather than right in front of their chests, how they did that whistle that I can never accomplish, where you put your fingers in the sides of your mouth and the noise goes real high. Maybe that's just what they always did. But it sure seemed that this woman's message had touched them in a special way. Touched me, too: in less than fifteen minutes, this speech, along with the proceedings that preceded it, had convinced me that there was a roughly zero percent chance that I would ever be a Republican. Between *an open mind* and *a fool*, the line is thin. I have not crossed it.

Liberals might have been hypocrites, might have been out of touch. But conservatives—at least those ten thousand I encountered—seemed terrifying, even deranged.

You might be similarly terrified to know that, less than a decade later, those ten thousand conservative activists—some of whom were leading a newly formed group called the Tea Party, a few of whom were allegedly spitting on congressmen and definitely hanging Barack Obama in effigy—took over the Republican party and, in short order, the White House and, to some degree, the country. And to the extent that America still leads the West as I tell you this story, these Americans for Freedom have thrown much of the known world into chaos. All the while, the liberals who were in charge at that time are still more or less in charge, which means that the main opposition to fascism in America is a cohort of dedicated people with good intentions and able minds yet little clue how any of this could have happened. And to make their lives more difficult, great numbers of citizens in the West have taken to mass hysteria, to strange votes and street protests. If they have not stopped working (though many have done that, too, possibly against their will, since even more jobs have *vanished* since '08), then they have surely stopped *believing* in certain things or at least in certain people and have said, in essence, to their would-be leaders: *The jig is up.* Life comes at you fast when you're not paying attention.

I was not a prophet, but thanks in part to my mother and father I knew when the folks in charge were not looking out for me. And since I learned early on at Yale that I knew nothing, and found that my best remedy was to listen and to watch, I also learned how to quickly tell whether those I watched and listened to knew anything themselves—which helped save a lot of time while I was in Washington, but also meant that by spring 2010 I had exhausted my most trusted tactics. I had no known tools or living people to turn to and so I turned at last, in desperation, to books.

V

It took me just a little while to discover why anyone who's ever wanted to keep the people deaf dumb and blind kept them first and most importantly from the written word. My lord.

I soon found my first poet, Walt Whitman, because of that Levi's commercial with those beautiful young people kissing and wrestling and switching jeans in the dressing room, and standing smiling in rainstorms, and running through fields with sticks and flags, and jumping off little statues in the daytime, and doing cartwheels in the night while fireworks explode overhead while some man with a reedy voice recites *Pioneers! O Pioneers!* in the background. I found my first philosophers, Camus and Emerson, though it was hard at first to remember the difference between the *existentialists* and the *transcendentalists*. Since then, I've learned that Camus did not consider himself an existentialist (he and Sartre ended like me and Daniel, in a way) and Emerson, at least the Emerson I read, was very different from Thoreau, who I did not care for if only because I don't like nature very much. So it turns out I did not fall in love with existentialism or transcendentalism, but with Camus and Emerson—this would have been helpful to know, since labels caused me so much misery at that time. I also found my first novel since *James and the Giant Peach*. This caused some trouble, too. *On the Road* was so original (everything I read was original because I hadn't read nothing) and thrilling that all my fantasies of being a truck driver came back and I had to force them out of my mind again by remembering how Auntie O looked at me the first time I shared my desire to live on the road. It also helped to remember that I was trying to be president and could not admit to the people that *I had nothing to offer anybody except my own confusion.*

And this, being president, was no longer just my teammates' idea. It was mine. I wanted to be president and I was going to do whatever it took, because it was worth it.

The presidency would be the ultimate sign of excellence and thus the ultimate revenge. Nobody would call me by my name or any other smart-ass moniker; they would only call me Mr. President unless I told them otherwise and in the meantime I would be leading the world, wouldn't answer to anybody ever again, wouldn't take shit from nobody, would leave behind all my troubles and take on new troubles, nice troubles, like peace in Israel and sending people into outer space and curing disease. I would be the most loved person on the face of the planet—hell, people I never even met would love me would hang out of windows when I walked by would remember the day they shook my hand. I would also be the most hated person in the world but the people who hated me wouldn't get close to me and so what if they did—if I died being president ooh I would die for big old causes I would die for freeing slaves I would die for investigating Fidel Castro I would die and it would be a grand affair and people would cry when I left for a change instead of me crying for them because nobody leaves a man once he's president, even when he's dead. If I died as president that would be fine they wouldn't find me tied up on the floor, there would be hundreds of people around as soon as I expired and thousands more soon after that and then they'd make me a statue—I would want one far away from Lincoln I don't want that bastard stealing my visitors and I wouldn't want to be close to Jefferson either because I don't like the son of a bitch. I would like to be near the Washington Monument because it's tall and unadorned and Washington was first and I would be last because if I died as president I'd make my final order to end the country just shut down the whole thing party's over folks gotta leave America I'm dead you're dead it's all dead. And at the very least nobody—*nobody*—would be indifferent about me nobody would ever forget that I existed nobody would forget to pick me up from school nobody would forget my birthday—shit my birthday might be a national holiday it might be a global holiday by the time I finished helping people or at least ruling the world.

But first I had to be president, which did not seem impossible. So I stopped reading novels and started reading books that would help me with my job. And so I was glad to also find, right around this time, my first bookstore.

Seeing as though I had so few monies, I should have gone to the DC Public Library, but ever since my time at Yale, libraries had overwhelmed me. There were eleven million volumes of books in the Sterling Library, floors and floors of books that you had to ride creaky elevators to reach and walk down spooky corridors to peruse and interpret varied alphanumeric schemes to find and have your Yale ID to swipe you in and out and hand to the authorities behind the desk who would stare at you like you were buying condoms in the drug store. On top of all that you had to open your bag and let some nosy officer snoop through your belongings just to get back into the light of day and *then*, even if you had not stolen a thing from the library, you still would be at risk of fines and investigations and failing to graduate from Yale, all on account of one book that nobody had even asked about for seventy years.

And don't make the mistake of thinking you're too good for the library, thinking you were going to walk into the big chain campus bookstore like you owned the place. Ha. Soon as I stepped through the door they were always trying to sell me other stuff aside from books, which I already didn't have the money for in and of themselves. I surely had no extra coin for tote bags and umbrellas and cups of coffee and croissants, which looked nice and all but were so expensive, just like the books, which were never on sale, at least not at a steep enough discount so that I could afford them without worrying about my other Life Expenses. No, I did not go to the big chain campus bookstore, either. Now, let me say, as a recovering ex-politician, that the libraries and chain bookstores of America have my full unqualified support. I'm just trying to explain how I felt at that time and why I was so grateful to discover Capitol Hill Books down the street from my Washington apartment, just a ten-minute walk to Eastern Market, with that adult-sized American flag hanging over the narrow wooden door that, once you entered through and got your allergies under control, welcomed you to a paradise full of first-rate books at second-hand prices.

The incredible thing about little bookstores like Capitol Hill Books is that the people inside—often wonderfully strange boys and girls, even if they now reside in the bodies of adults or the elderly—don't seem to take orders from some honcho in an office somewhere who wants to tell them what to sell or how much for, or what labels to put on the shelves—or to buy new shelves to replace the old ones that are leaning, threatening to crush people like me who were turning to books to be saved, not killed. These little bookstore people go through the trouble of asking themselves *What do the books on this shelf really have to say to somebody???* and then they take a marker and write the answer, their answer, on a slice of cardboard and tape it to the shelf. Sometimes, as in a little Canadian bookstore I recently visited, the book people seem to just throw all the books in a pile on the floor and say, as did the year 2008: *You figure this shit out . . .* which is fine with me, now that I know what I'm doing and reading is not such a desperate act. But at twenty-three I was an eager novice, so I'm glad that whoever owned Capitol Hill Books took the time to write *U.S. Presidency* on their slice of cardboard and tape it to the bookcase on the far-right wall of that pulp jungle, the bookcase that I mazed my way to, where I immediately saw it, saw *him*, on the tattered cover of a much-passed-down book: Theodore Roosevelt.

I want to cry when I think of Theodore Roosevelt (though for a different reason than why I wanna cry for Tom and his buddies), and I actually did when I finished the third volume of Edmund Morris's biography of him, *Colonel Roosevelt*, at the end of which my hero died, which should not have surprised me as much as it did. I was and remain a slow reader, so it took me almost a year to get to Teddy's death (took him sixty to get there himself) after meeting him in the first volume, *The Rise of Theodore Roosevelt*, which was, aside from the Bible, the most important collection of words I had yet encountered. Once I followed Mr. Roosevelt from his birth to his ascendancy to the presidency, thanks to William McKinley getting himself killed, becoming the youngest man ever to hold the office—once I plodded through those 780 pages, 814 if you count the epilogue that describes the day (1 January 1907) when Theodore Roosevelt shook 8,150 hands at the White House for New Year's (still a record), once I closed the pages of that book, I no longer considered any man or woman alive to be great, especially not me, and I immediately, almost as if I had been struck down on my own road to Damascus, decided to press toward a new mark: his.

There was nothing particularly compelling, to me, about the young Teddy—a bookish pampered snob, for the most part. I prefer my heroes and my lovers to have some tragedy befall them. But then TR turned twenty-three and things got interesting.

On 14 February 1884, at three o'clock in the morning in the Roosevelt home at 6 West Fifty-Seventh Street in New York City, Theodore Roosevelt's mother died of typhoid fever. She was forty-nine. Upstairs in the same home, eleven hours later at two o'clock in the afternoon, his wife, Alice, died of kidney disease. She had given birth to their first child two days earlier. Morris writes:

Roosevelt drew a large cross in his diary for 14 February 1884, and wrote beneath: "The light has gone out of my life."

This was the Theodore Roosevelt that moved me—the one who lived in darkness, who did not sleep and chose instead to work, to strive, to read at least one book a night, remembering it all the next day, who *spent himself* in so many worthy causes that he was hailed *the greatest moral force of the age* by King Edward VII of England. He was also denounced as *the most dangerous man of the age* by Woodrow Wilson, perhaps the most advanced white supremacist ever to occupy the White House, not to mention the most self-righteous dealer of subterfuge since Thomas Jefferson. And most vitally for me it was said by Henry Adams that Theodore Roosevelt had *the quality that medieval theology assigned to God—he was pure act.* Of course it is now believed that Mr. Roosevelt was a manic-depressive, but I did not know this at the time and I'm not sure it would have made a difference. I'd found the greatest leader in the history of America, at least for the kind of thing I was trying to lead.

And so I also found the sadness Julius Caesar found at the close of one of his successful campaigns, which I read about in another Capitol Hill Books discovery, *The Lives of the Twelve Caesars*, by Suetonius. He wrote:

[Julius Caesar] came to Gades, where he noticed a statue of Alexander the Great in the temple of Hercules. At the sight of it he drew a deep sigh, as one displeased with his own shortcomings, in that he had as yet performed no memorable act, whereas at his age Alexander had already conquered the whole world.

I felt the same way when I discovered the life and legacy of Theodore Roosevelt. If I was going to make up for lost time, still have a chance to meet his standard and mount the world, then I would need more than inspiration. I would need instruction. Thanks to my still-strong obsession with John F. Kennedy and my belief, at the time, that I should read only books that had won a Pulitzer Prize, just to be safe, I found exactly what I was searching for: *The Making of the President, 1960.* In the pages of this book, which explained exactly what the title promised, I learned a vital lesson: *Long service in Washington at the court of power decisions causes men to forget that power rises ultimately from beyond the Potomac.*

And by the time I read this line and all the others in that manual, it was clear what my next move would be. I had to go back home.

chapter TWENTY-ONE

Just like the good old days, home tried to kill me. Ice this time—icicle daggers on the roof, ice crust on the lawn, dirty slush on the sidewalk, black ice, sneaky on the road.

I don't care how bad the roads are, I told myself that January morning, *I'm getting the hell out of this house.*

Five months had passed since I'd returned to Dallas with nothing but my bags and my plans. Five months of those plans foiled. Five months of kissing ass. Five months of less money than the no-money I already possessed. Five months of nights on Granny's couch—one sheet, one blanket, one pillow, a few roaches, a lot of noise. I had to leave and could so did, in the middle of an ice storm.

Little did I know, the house was less dangerous than the roads, and the roads were less dangerous than the idea that was on my mind, that had been placed there by the one man who remained from my time at Vinson & Elkins, perhaps the only of those men who grew to see me as something other than a human trinket. Yet he was still eager to buy me a meal and offer advice and, when I had clearly failed in my homecoming quest, convinced a friend to hire me even though I had no skills and no experience that Neiman Marcus could use, though I used Mr. Marcus's money to get my own apartment and off the couch. And even this had not been enough generosity for him, for Jeff Chapman, the quiet man with the gentle smile and University of Iowa degree to go along with his Iowa City baby pictures and all the stories of the Iowa State Fair and similar niceties of midwestern life, which obscured the truth about this man, which I sensed in him and, perhaps, he sensed in me when we first met: He would slice your throat to get what he wanted. Not that things ever got that desperate, his mind being weapon enough. In any event, Jeff was the best listener I'd ever met, which meant he spent a great deal of time asking questions, which also meant that, if you weren't paying attention, he could ask you something that you might answer and regret. Such a question he asked me on my twenty-fourth birthday, in a plush leather booth at the Dallas Ritz-Carlton.

Have you ever thought about running for Congress?

I had not, I promise. In part because if the vice presidency *isn't worth a warm bucket of piss*, then a seat in the US Congress did not seem worth a metaphor. More importantly, all I wanted to do, all I had come home to Dallas from Washington to do, was start a little program, fight for one lil ole bitty cause.

My hope is to help Mayor Leppert create an initiative to make service easier, more visible, and more effective. This bold action will allow Dallas to join the ranks of over one hundred cities across the country—including every other major city in Texas—that have put volunteerism at the core of citizenship.

In other words, I hoped to get more citizens to work for free on behalf of the common good—which still strikes me as a decent idea . . . perhaps because, as you might have guessed, it wasn't mine. National service, as it was called, was as old as Sargent Shriver, older even, and this particular version of it had begun a few years prior in New York City, led by an alum of Wolf's Head, who told me everything I needed to know to plant it and myself, in Dallas.

And though I had been informed that ours was now a woman's nation, I knew that yet and still, in Dallas, the root question of politics is always: *Who's the man to see?* So I went to see *the Men* with my idea. These men did not mingle at coffee shops, or even at Al Biernat's or the Ritz. They ruled from perches like the Petroleum Club, on the thirty-ninth and fortieth floors of Chase Tower in downtown Dallas. *Petroleum* as in oil: black oil money for white oil men, since membership was limited to white men as late as the 1980s.

A member of the Petroleum Club had to be one of the most important men in the oil business (or, later, an equally important industry)—which meant the most important men in Texas and, as long as Texas was still a global oil capital, some of the most important men in the world. I didn't have any interest in oil or these men, but I needed them to have some interest in my idea, or at least enough interest in *me* to support the idea anyhow. So I went to the Petroleum Club and ignored the dismay on the faces of its patrons upon my entrance. Two, three, four months of this, all captured in one day: a lunch with a man amongst men, one of the members whose table other members paid tribute to, whose name shall remain unsaid because I can't remember it off the top of my head and I'd rather not dig up the notes in my files.

We sat side by side (I never sit across from a person if I can avoid it) at a table for four—me with my idea in my head and on sheets of paper, with everything else exactly where it was supposed to be, according to the rules I'd learned. He, as I imagine his Southern planter forebears might have done, sat with a long white linen napkin draped from his shirt collar, gray wavy hair lightly pomaded to one side, his fingers thick with the extra gristle of a diet rich in US dollars, one baled with a wedding band, another with a ring from the University of Texas.

Now, son, tell me about your idear.

I got to talking—man, I believed in this idea so much, had facts and figures and timelines and everything—and when I finished, I handed him a folder that contained, in writing, all that I envisioned and had just said. I waited for some support. A word.

Well . . . that sure does sound interesting— Before he could go on he started coughing . . . Coughed so long, so violently, that now I wonder whether that was a sign of power for a certain generation: a man starts coughing in the middle of a sentence and the more power he's got the longer his audience is willing to sit there and watch salad and butter roll chunks fly out of his mouth. *Pardon me. Now, I'm not sure I can help you here but let me give you some advice. You should always carry a letter of introduction when you're meeting with somebody. People need to know who sent you. You understand?*

Yes, sir. I'll be sure to do that, I said, as I wrote his advice in my notebook.

Fuck you, I thought, as I added Mr. Man to my list.

You see, I had not stopped reading after Suetonius described Julius Caesar's despair re: Alexander the Great. I read all the way up to page twenty-three, where Suetonius records the famous boast—*I came, I saw, I conquered*—which was the last thing I underlined. But between the despair and the conquest was all the trouble Roman aristocrats gave young Julius, blocking his path to any real power, trying, for example, to stymie his agrarian reforms with the ancient equivalent of a filibuster: announcing "adverse omens."

Business—in the Roman Senate—*could be interrupted or postponed by the announcement of an auger or a magistrate that he had seen a flash of lightning or some other adverse sign.*

Julius got fed up with these charades and so, before long, found a clever solution:

Marcus Cato, who tried to delay proceedings, was dragged from the House by a Lictor at Caesar's command and taken off to prison.

It is fair to say Mr. Caesar took this a bit too far but it is also fair to say his tactics proved effective, at least until they got him killed. I intended to go just far enough with the Petroleum Club men and so I kept my list and garnered, at the cost of all those meetings, wisdom that I was also getting from our modern-day Suetonius, Robert Caro, in his biography of Robert Moses, who seemed so much like myself at the time, not only because he had graduated from Yale a century before me, after also having a miserable start in New Haven. He hadn't fared much better than I had, upon entering the real world:

Robert Moses was the optimist of optimists, the reformer of reformers, the idealist of idealists. So great a nuisance did he make of himself that in 1918 Tammany Hall decided it had to crush him. It did so with efficiency....

When the curtain rose on the next act of Moses' life, idealism was gone from the stage. In its place was an understanding that ... an idea was no good without power behind it, power to make people adopt it, power to reward them when they did, power to crush them when they didn't.

How, exactly, do you crush the people in power? In Caesar's day you could throw them in jail or kill them. We had, for better or worse, come a long way since then. So I learned—was forced to learn—another lesson from the 1960 presidential campaign and accepted that *only the people, voting at the polls, give a man true power in American government.* Only the people could give me the power that I needed. Jeff's question came shortly after I had taken this as truth. And once he told me that the former mayor of Dallas had yelled *Who the fuck does Casey think he is?!* when Jeff ran the idea by him—Well, at that point I figured I'd better hurry up and get to Congress so I could issue this mayor a nice little congressional subpoena so he'd know exactly who I was, or give a big speech attacking him—*something.* In any event, this congressional thing was looking pretty nice, especially since my path to people power would not lead me through just any old people: they would be *my people.*

Confined to Dallas County, the 30th Congressional District stretches from Dallas Love Field southeast into downtown Dallas. It then dips south to take in some suburbs, such as Lancaster, where many black families have relocated after leaving the city. Black residents account for 37 percent of the population—the highest percentage in any Texas district—and 41 percent of residents are Hispanic . . . In 2008, the 30th—the only Democratic district in the Dallas-Fort Worth area—gave Barack Obama 82 percent of its presidential vote, his highest percentage statewide.

If my people had been that eager to give Barack Obama all that power, I figured they would be willing to grant the same or nearly to their son his doppelgänger, even though I had gone to considerable lengths, at least in my head, to distance myself from him, just as I had once done with my father. But if it was bad to be known for so long as little more than the son of Rod Gerald, I could only imagine how bad it would have been to be known as the son of some bum or to not be known at all. The same was true with being considered the next Barack Obama or the next Anybody Else, for that matter. When you strike at a king, you must kill him, sure. But in order to even strike, you've got to be damn close, close enough to stand in the glow of that Great Figure but not so close that the people can't see *you.*

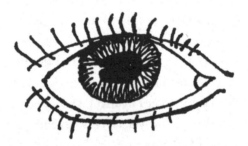

I knew only one person who understood this paradox, who had studied power and those who held it. The person in question had such a burning desire to hold power himself that his eyes—protected behind unframed glasses and often strands of blonde hair—never rested on anyone unimportant, if at all, and he snickered sometimes when no joke had been told, as if some vital part of his designs had been revealed. On more than two occasions he had been seen slashing a conductor's baton through the air—on top of office tables; in Washington Square Park—to conduct heard and unheard symphonies as he would, with hope and patience, one day conduct the world. He was a young man, but one with enough energy, genius, moral objections, and personality disorders to make him the quintessential, if not some day the greatest, member of Scroll and Key. We'll call him Franklin.

Franklin and I had not known each other at Yale, only *of* each other, but we had both gone to a lunch senior year to meet Ted Sorensen, John F. Kennedy's former advisor and speechwriter. This took place the same day my Rhodes/Game crisis came to a head, so I didn't have time to shoot the shit with anybody, Kennedy aide or not. Franklin had time. Moxie, too. He pressed his way into a private audience with Mr. Sorensen and asked one question: What does it take to be a great presidential speechwriter?

Mr. Sorensen, palsied after a recent stroke, responded: *Easy . . . Find a great president.*

By January 2011, it seemed that I had become Franklin's man. For my birthday, he sent a personalized astrology reading: *CASEY GERALD, Destined for Greatness*

This astrological combination indicates an ambitious nature and an incli-nation to seek the limelight of leadership . . . You are at ease in situations in which it is necessary to conform to authority and discipline . . . The key to a more harmonious existence lies in tempering your self-assertive and egotistical tendencies . . .

In response to the universe's call to temper my egotistical tendencies, I informed Franklin that I was going to run for Congress. He replied:

Casey,

Went to Shriver's funeral yesterday. Was five feet from Steve Wonder, fifteen from Bill, Oprah, Bono and Muhammad Ali. There is absolutely no daylight I can see between the outlooks and even experiences of you and Sarge Shriver. I am now at your service to do whatever thinking you need me to. What are the big questions?

—F

There were many questions at this exploratory stage of a campaign: how to recruit a team, how to raise one to two million dollars, whom to talk to and when, what policies to support and denounce and why. But the big question at any stage of any campaign is always the same big question: *How do I win the people?* I knew this and so did Franklin, who had a particular gift for winning people (of their own free will, for now). He sent a homework assignment: *I would love to see from you what the THREE BIG IDEAS are that you want EVERYONE who thinks of YOU to remember WITHIN TEN SECONDS.*

I gave him one: *I'm running so that we may dream again.* Which, in his hands, became a slogan:

CASEY GERALD

We Can Dream Again

And a bludgeon: *Almost finishes for Obama what he started but didn't follow through on—Yes We Can—which is, if you think about it for two seconds, meaningless beyond inspiring hope. Your message says yes we can DREAM again . . . which is to say, there's actually substance in what you're saying!*

Except that there was not. I would present my campaign treatise to prove the point but I won't waste your time, for if you've seen any political ad recently, you've heard at least 90 percent of what I planned to tell the people and you will also understand what I mean when I tell you that Casey Gerald the candidate suffered from a condition known to plague many if not most politicians: he was full of shit. Perhaps not a complete fraud, but so void of substance that it is difficult to view him as an actual human being. And this, in fact, was the point—the more substance a campaign carried, the more likely it was to be a *losing* campaign. The absolute worst kind of substance was the candidate's substance. It only got in the way of the people's substance and thus could be fatal—which is why, I suppose, a United States senator (a serious, liberal senator) stressed in 2008: *The message you've got to send, more than any other message, is that Barack Obama is just like us.* That effort became the gold standard of modern politics if not modern life—which also seems to demand that we each do whatever it takes to be able to look back at the end of our days and say, with peace and satisfaction, *I was just like everybody else.* This draws the candidate and the common citizen into risky delusions and great lies—and so it drew me, as the campaign became a real possibility, into a corner.

Seems to me the key issue in his District is going to be easy: convincing people that he's a leader they can trust. Especially given the recent scandals . . . He basically needs to have people say they trust him over, and over, and over again. That he's honest over and over again.

This was wisdom from one of the country's top congressional campaign strategists, sent through a friend from my Washington days, who was, at that time, what we will call a *senior White House official.* The campaign would have to raise millions of dollars, earn thousands of votes, knock on hundreds of doors and shake even more hands, survive dozens of weeks to reach a final victory—yet all of it would boil down to one issue, one contrast: *trust us, not them.*

This was not a moral issue for Casey Gerald, the candidate. It was an issue of strategy. And so he—I—had been crafting a strategy to make the people trust me. It was informed by my boy Jack Kennedy, who delivered a speech during his 1960 campaign, in Houston, to convince the people that he was not in bed, so to speak, with the pope. It was also informed by Barack Obama the candidate, who delivered his own speech at Philadelphia, in

2008, to convince the people that he was not in bed with radical blacks like Reverend Jeremiah Wright and, more broadly, was not in any way a nigger. My own speech, to be delivered in Dallas sometime in 2011 or 2012, would have to convince the people that though I had, technically, been in bed with men, I was not then, nor had I ever been, a faggot. I was just like *them*—and despite any sense of what might await me in the life to come, they could trust me in the current one.

A miracle of this magnitude would take more time than your garden-variety sort, so I started early, in January, and enlisted my most gifted advisor, Micah. I will share our conversation with you almost verbatim so that you know there was much more to him than his cruelty, and more importantly, so that you know it is often queers who stand, invisible, between the bad world we have and the worse world we could have. You should also know that twenty-four-year-old me still preferred to avoid face-to-face communication and so, in this case, resorted to an online chat.

> ME: so how abt this
> maybe i should just put it out there
> on my own terms
> as a period of experimentation that i went through to find xyz
> and cope w/ xyz
> a period of experimentation that also delved into prescription medicine and liquor
>
> MICAH: i think this will require a phone convo
>
> ME: lool
> well it doesn't have to be asap
> bc i just thought of it late last night on the plane

MICAH: yea, it sounds like a late thought lol
that i don't think i could adequately engage via chat
i see a feasibility so far re: putting it out there on your own
terms
but it's the explanation that i'd have to hear more directly

ME: yea
i kinda feel that the only winning way (in the long term) is to
put it out there on my own terms

MICAH: I agree
absolutely
and i think u, with being who you are, could put it out there
on your own terms
which might also be new terms
that require a person to judge from within, and not from a
external judgement of a person from their specific association w/a certain group
and not in an attempt to break any barriers, but just to be ur
fucking self

ME: right
so i think b/w us, we can craft a really good piece/platform
if i run, it has to be done
bc worse than the risk of putting it out there in a big way
is the risk of being seen as a sham
in a huge scandal
i just couldn't stand that

MICAH: and also, there are just many, many factors here
a black male

recognizably normative

college athlete

leader

scholar

saying something that exposes a truth, but a truth that is
based on his own convictions

and forcing others, regardless of how they want to categorize
or view, to take into consideration a possibility

that they never have to face in the public eye, except outside
of scandal

ME: exactly

i refuse to be scandalized

that's just so low

the impt thing is for it to be the second big hit

the first big hit has to be all casey gerald as he is known

the ideas

the energy

blah blah

then casey gerald puts out a little deal on a new generation of
americans—op-ed to essay length

then casey gerald puts out a piece on his sexual experiences
and what it means for him and for america

with a sentence here and there abt prescription drug use

and alcohol—drinking alone in the room and such

really driving home the psychosocial

"my mental maturity was lightyears ahead of my emotional
maturity, so i struck out for love and affection wherever i
could find it"

MICAH: right

ME: we need to start drafting this

MICAH: right

Micah seemed to have reached a point of fatigue and/or disgust, but his home training prevented him from being anything other than respectful, even in the presence of a monster. I took his respect to mean that I had a damn solid strategy, so focused on other matters until, by early March, the campaign was one decision (mine) away from being a go. I could not make that decision without ensuring that the message was battle ready, and there was only one way to know—*test it*—and only one test audience that came to mind: Brenda Cox.

I have tried to find some complex reason as to why Cox serves the role that she does—the person I and many other young people before and after me have run to in crisis. But the more I thought about it the more I came to the conclusion that there was nothing to conclude. Nothing complex, at least. The woman is just *there*. Whenever you need her. Whenever you don't need her. Before you ask her to be there. After you don't want her to be there anymore. She can be a real son of a bitch, I'll tell you that, and I would advise you to never cross her because she is willing to excommunicate absolutely anyone from her life—even more willing than *me* or anyone else I've heard of. Until such time, and though she will fuss and nag and cajole and talk louder than necessary and longer than necessary and tease you when you make a simple mistake—*Boy, you don't have not one lick of common sense*—and get all up in your business when it has nothing to do with her, she will be there, in your worst moment, ready to listen, even to your worst idea, which I drove to her house to share.

It was night. Her red front door was visible in the dark, as was the low-slung white house, though no weeds were visible in the yard, that night or any day, as was the case for most lawns in this neighborhood full of decades-old three-bedroom homes owned by people, families even, who did not make much noise unless the Dallas Cowboys were playing—and even then, not much. The house was empty, save her. She stood in the kitchen. I sat in a barstool across from her, leaning on the island, getting the message together in my head. I cannot remember whether my voice quavered because I was nervous or because I believed that quavering was the tone this performance required—I was, after all, confiding that years of psychological distress had caused me to turn, from sixteen to twenty-two, to the arms of strangers, of *men*, to love in sordid places. A troubled young man I had been, as are we all, and so on.

Cox sighed. Smirked. Turned to the cabinet and pulled down two wine glasses. Opened the refrigerator and grabbed a bottle of white wine from the door. Slid open a drawer and picked up a corkscrew. All this took about six years to accomplish. She didn't say anything. I didn't say anything. She placed a glass in front of me. One in front of her. Poured. Poured. We had never before had a drink together, that I remember.

I already knew you were gay, boy. She laughed. *I was just wondering when you were going to tell me.*

Standard straight person drivel. But Brenda Cox is not the standard straight person.

I figured when you were in high school— Boy, you never had any girls, and that was odd. But then Tashia came over here . . . It was late one night I didn't know what was wrong . . . Maybe you were a sophomore or junior. She had walked in your room and your computer was up and she saw something, can't even remember . . . whatever. That girl rushed over here all worked up and she say "Ms. Cox Ms. Cox what should I do???" And I said well, girl, just leave him alone. Just leave him alone he'll be okay he'll say something whenever he's ready. She took a long sip of wine. *Oh! Then she called me after the prom. Hmph! Couldn't find your ass . . . and she calls me when you come back, talking about you went to some college party in Carson. I said okay, Tashia. All right,*

girl. But I got off that phone and said to myself, Bullshit. Ain't nothing in Car-
son but a nigga.

She launched that loud country laugh and drew another sip. This is the
other element of Cox's magic: she is, often at precisely the right moment,
rude and inappropriate. I wonder if I looked, to her, as foolish as I felt, or as
relieved as I also felt. Sometimes the weight of lies is not apparent until
somebody snatches the lie sack from you. In its place was not *the truth*, per
se, but I wasn't there for that, just *the message*, which I now had. *Gay*. Simple enough. Cox was sure to warn me that the people were not going to be
as open to this as I'd imagined. I was sure to remind her that they might be
open to *me* and, besides, that this is what campaigns were for: to open the
minds of the people.

So what are you gonna do, boy?

Dunno. I've gotta talk to this guy who might manage the campaign,
tonight.

It was a fifteen-minute drive from Cox's house, probably less since
there were few cars on I-35 leaving Oak Cliff, driving north toward the
beautiful if garish Dallas skyline. I made it to my apartment, on the edge of
downtown in what was once and still is, despite the marketing, skid row,
and carried my phone and notebook to the kitchen table, to call *this guy*.
He had come recommended by Franklin, who hardly recommended anybody who was still alive. *You should get Jonas Stein to work on your cam-*
paign when the time is right. You seem to share a lot of ideals and he's the best
researcher and get-things-done guy I know.

The time had become right. We had already synced our ideals. He had
already gotten things done and begun to research. We now had one call to
make a final decision and this was it and he was ready, as intense and Boston as always, even at this late hour.

Okay, my friend. Let's get down to it. Your story is incredible ... Don't have to say that again. You know I've gotta ask, just to get it out of the way—is there anything I need to know? Gotta tell me before I quit my fucking job, ha.

Well ... you should know that I'm gay.

I had never said this before, for many reasons, most bad, but one being that it seemed strange to call myself with pride something most had called me, since childhood, with scorn. This was the message, though, so my personal feelings were not relevant.

Hmm, I see, he said, as if he had found a shiny penny or a dead baby bird on the ground. *I'm glad you told me. Of course it doesn't make my job any easier ... I mean, you are in Texas, ha! ... But it's not impossible. Not impossible.*

We held the phone. I said nothing.

But, Casey ... tell me this ... I mean ... how are you gonna feel when somebody—say, at a rally, you know ... calls you a faggot? And ... I mean ... let's just be real, okay? You do understand that somebody might want to, you know, physically harm you? I sure hope not. But ... it could happen, you know? Are you really ready for this? That's all I'm asking.

I cannot remember saying anything in response to Jonas's questions. I know we didn't stay on the phone much longer. I know that I went to lie in bed because I can still see twenty-four-year-old me on top of the sheets in the dark with his computer. I know that I sent Jonas a message around midnight:

It's a bit like that last stanza of dover beach, huh?

For the world, which seems to lie before us like a land of dreams,

So various, so beautiful, so new,

Hath really neither joy, nor love, nor help for pain;

And we are here as on a darkling plain

Swept with confused alarms of struggle and flight,

Where ignorant armies clash by night

I am not sure where or when I learned this poem. Nor was I sure, when

I first recalled this night, why the words that came to me would be so hopeless. After all, the boy I was at that time would have leapt, despite his fears, at the chance to be harmed—with luck, assassinated—to sacrifice everything, even life, for a cause, a cause greater than himself. There was something shocking, however—not that there *should* have been, but there was—in the notion that he might be harmed, killed even, for nothing more than *being himself,* which he had not even tried to do in the first place. Not only had this thought never crossed his mind, but it was heresy. Not plausible. My silence on the phone with Jonas was due, most of all (as far as I can tell), to this shock, this new information. But the shock began to fade not long after we hung up. Was gone by the time I sent that message.

I lay there in the dark, on top of my bedsheets. What happened next had never happened before, and rather than rely on my memory of that first time, I will recount a similar, recent episode—one that took place not long after I began to tell you this story. I had gone to New York to celebrate Micah's thirty-fifth birthday. We went out, had some drinks, a good time. We walked back to his apartment—stumbled back, really— and before I entered his front door I felt sick. Too much to drink. Too much of a good time. I scurried to the toilet, put my hands around the bowl and my head above it, sent my drinks and my good time into the bowl. I kept vigil there, kept retching. This went on for a few minutes, maybe ten, I don't know. Micah appeared at the bathroom—*You all right? C'mon, drink some water*—and knelt on the floor next to me. I pulled myself into the doorway and took the glass of water. Drank most of it. Placed the glass on the parquet floor, then laid my head on the floor next to the glass. All of a sudden, I began to cry. Micah thought I was laughing at first and so he laughed, too. Then he noticed that I was not laughing, I was crying—though I did not know and still don't know *why*; it had been a great time and it was his birthday—and I could not stop. I cried so hard, with such abandon, it would have been embarrassing if I had thought about it, but I could not really think of anything. And for some reason—again, I did not really have a reason—I began to mumble, to confess . . . to myself or to Micah or nobody in particular, *I'm sorry, I just don't want to be here. I don't want to be here.* Micah didn't say anything but *It's all right, okay okay, it's okay* and patted my back until I began to whimper and then sighed and lay there on the floor until he helped me up and into bed to sleep.

I still don't understand why that happened—maybe just so I could tell you more precisely what I did and how I felt there in my bed after I sent Jonas that message, and the next day when I woke up crying and brushed my teeth crying and drove to work and sat in the parking lot to cry and closed my office door to cry and locked myself in a bathroom stall to cry and drove back home after work to lie again in bed in the dark and cry and wish that I was dead.

I cannot say that I wanted to commit suicide, if only because I was, perhaps more than anything, a coward. An unprepared coward at that. No gun, no razor blades, no sharp steak knives. My balcony was too low. Cheap belts would break. And what if I did have these instruments and still failed, I wondered. I thought of pills, which would have been decent if no one caught me in time to pump my stomach. But where could I find that many pills, and what kind of pills, anyway? I suppose I was too lazy to kill myself. All I wanted to do, really, was fall asleep and be dead. I did not want to *die.* That required effort. I simply did not want to live. I did not want to be here, in this world.

That, too, was odd. I had done so much to earn this world, to *win* this world and fit into it. Began early, somewhere around nap time, from what I can remember. It was wrong to stay awake while everyone else took a nap, so I took a dozen ruler strikes in my palm instead. And though I did not go to sleep, I did not bother anybody, either. Stayed real quiet and wrote my words in the dark and walked softly, on my tiptoes, which I always did, just didn't want dirt on my feet, but this bothered people who then bothered me and so I concentrated, and at some point, I could walk, most of the time, on my heels, like a normal person. I wanted very much to be a normal person. Those heels, *Shon's* heels, had been a problem, too, and once she yelled at me I never played with them again; and once my sister tried to take my notebook I never drew a dress again, didn't even think about them, really. I did what I was supposed to do, and did not do what I was *not* supposed to do—at least that's what I tried to do. Even in the nighttime, while I slept, when they said I moved around too much, I tried to stop moving and quickly learned to lie still for six or seven hours through the night, could lie real still for however long I needed to, even when I had a cold, when my cough was keeping people up, and they said I'd have to sleep on the couch if I could not stop my coughing; I tried and sure enough, I could stop that, too. Well, actually, I could not stop coughing all the way, but I did learn to cough so soft, so low, that no one hardly noticed. I could stay so quiet that no one had to hear me if they did not want to hear me. And when they *did* want to hear me, when they wanted me to speak, I learned to speak so they could hear exactly what I said. *Enunciate!* they told me, and that's exactly what I did. I spoke loud and clear and when they warned me that I fidgeted, which was not okay, I stood real still and kept my hands still, too, unless it was the right time to move them, with purpose. It took some work to speak and stay still and move my hands with purpose—to hold those hands like a real man, not behind my head like I was getting arrested, not limp-wrist like a little girl. I already *sounded* like a girl, of course, but that was just my voice nobody told me how to fix so I did it on my own, or tried, or waited, and soon enough I sounded like a man or nearly, and that was good, it seemed. Everything was good, all good. I took it all in stride, or silence, whatever. I saved my tears for bathroom faucets. I worked the muscles of my face so it looked as if I smiled. I was good to the program. Whatever the program was, I was good to it. Tried to be, at least. I kept my ass low and kept my eyes open and ran for my life, I really did, just kept on running, threw my hats away and switched my jeans and changed my voice again so nobody needed a translator on the practice field. Fixed my résumé and bought new dress shirts and acted like a lawyer, like a banker, did that well enough, learned my story, *told* my story, got the right perspective on it all, I was grateful, I *moved on*, I got over it—stayed up late, ran away from men in nightmares, worked to be the best and brightest, be the president, be somebody AT THE TOP. It had taken nearly every day to turn the boy that I had been into the man that I became, a dead man.

That, in the final analysis, or my best analysis now, is what I realized that night: I had strived to win this world and won my death instead. Perhaps my tears were simply grief and I was not without all hope but tired . . . exhausted after a long journey in the wrong direction. You wonder why the world seems always headed in the wrong direction, too. In part, because young men like Casey Gerald set out to rule it.

And so I am glad *that* Casey Gerald died that night and the days thereafter—that he realized he was *already* dead, had been dead for a long time, had confused the most important words of all: *life* and *death*.

I, whatever he became, am escaped alone to tell thee. I planned to tell my friend, too. I just ran out of time.

I was sitting alone on my couch, in a house that I rented in Texas to escape New York, or the life I had lived there, which we'll get to, and to tell you this story. It was night, quiet outside and in. The light of one lamp, in the corner, shone on me and the couch and the book I was reading. My phone rang—Riley. I didn't answer. He sent a message: *Give me a call. Very important.* I closed the book and called. He told me to sit down. I was already sitting down. He told me that Elijah was gone.

I closed my eyes, though I'm not sure why or for how long. We sat there—I sat there . . . don't know what Riley was doing besides not talking—quiet, for what seemed like a long time. I have tried to find a way to tell you how I felt there on the couch, holding my phone. All I know is that I hope you never feel it and I'm sorry if you have. At some point I remembered that I was the elder, so I said something. Not sure what. I know we said *I love you* for the first time, before we hung up the phone. Think we meant it, though I bet *I love you* stood for many things we would have said if we had known what to say. I called Trevor, in California, that night. Or maybe the next morning, I really can't remember which. He was the last person Elijah texted, was Elijah's best friend, had just seen him, laughed with him, the weekend prior. Some things had not changed since they were seventeen, though so much had changed for both of them, for all of us, since we had met as boys those years ago. One being that we did not try to keep from crying with each other anymore.

Doris called the next day. I'd never heard her cry, either. She wanted to know what went wrong, what it all meant, what did I think. I thought she should have the answers, not me. I didn't even have good questions. I did know one thing, or thought I knew it, which I told her: The way we were taught to be men, to be human beings even, was a dead end. I knew this to be true because I had learned it for myself and was trying to write it all down. I had found a witness in the book I was reading when Riley called, a book by José Muñoz, who is also gone but left his words.

This world is not enough, he wrote. A world that subdues us, mutilates us, makes us operate on *straight* time, which can only be *death* time for many, makes us strangers to ourselves so that we can be recognizable to others, acceptable to others, normal to others. A world that pressures us to say at all times, at any cost, *It's only getting better.* That is the last message Elijah sent to me, a month before Riley called. I'd wished him happy birthday. He turned twenty-eight that day.

He had written a year before, an unexpected message, a thank-you note:

Casey,

I know that I told you how glad I am that we reconnected last year. But I just want to take a moment to say thank you for everything you are and everything you have done for me . . . I look up to a few people. You are one of them. I know you aren't perfect, but I really do aspire to be at least half the man you are. Keep doing your thing! If you ever need anything, I don't have much, but it's yours.

Best,

Elijah

If I had understood then what I understood by the time Riley called, I would have told him not to do that, or at least made sure he understood what the whole man looked like. How cracked up it was, how *okay* it was to be cracked up. I am not God so will not say it would have changed a thing. All I know is that Elijah was the bravest boy I ever met, and he deserved a better world, a better path, than the one he was given. The one that I helped give to him. I drove him, drove them all, to be first, be bold, be perfect—*be the greatest.* What I did not do was drive them to be whole, to be free. Did not teach them that the best revenge was freedom. Did not know it for myself, in time.

Elijah's memorial was the following week, in Saint Louis. I was already scheduled to be in Norway, to give some speech. Couldn't cancel, or *didn't,* in part because I remembered what Clarice told me when Papa's sister died: *Aunt Ruby ain't gonna be at the funeral what you coming all the way here for?* I also didn't want to see my friend like that. The night before the service, I met that beautiful Norwegian, the one I mentioned. Forgot that there was sadness in the world, just thought of mermaids and magic for a little while. Considered seeing him again the day of, but all I seemed able to do was lie in bed and watch *Forrest Gump* and cry. That seemed to be enough. The boys—the *men*—didn't need me anymore. Trevor delivered a wonderful eulogy and sent the text to me after. Riley released an album and dedicated it to Elijah. Quincy called before he went into the operating room to perform a brain surgery. They were now the ones checking on me, figuring out what to do, finding their own ways to say goodbye, to remember.

It took me some time to find the right words, and even then, they were not mine, but his. Elijah came all the way from the other side, to that diner in my dream, to tell me what to say:

We did a lot of things that we wouldn't advise anybody we loved to do.

I hope you understand.

PART FOUR

And God said, Let there be light: and there was light.

Genesis 1:3

chapter TWENTY-TWO

If only it were that easy.

This world *is not* enough. It *is*, as far as I know, the only one we've got. So. Here we are: *up shit's creek*, together. All I have to offer, all this story aims to be, is the paddle that I made—am still making, to tell you the truth. It is hard to build a thing that's strong enough to get you where you need to go. Hard to find some light in all the dark. To be better than you been. Damn hard. But not impossible. The thing is to get started.

Once I reached my dead end in Dallas, I decided to leave home, never to return again. Fled to New York City, just as outcasts have always done, and was there until I ran out of money and so did what folks have always done when they can't stay somewhere any longer: left. Would have been in trouble if I hadn't had a damn good Get Out of Jail Free card, so to speak, and so fled again, to Harvard, since I had no better place to go. And the nation's oldest seat of higher learning reminded me so much of the Facilities that I finally, eons after Charlie Brown let me sit inside his spaceship, went out on the road instead of doing something *respectable* with my *education*.

Not that I wandered, mescalined, solitary through America. In fact, three likewise educated friends and I drove town to town, working for free with local citizens, *on behalf of the common good*, which I hate to say was in bad shape. We travelled many thousand miles across the country—down to New Orleans, which had come through that Great Flood, and Detroit, which I'd heard had *drowned in a drip*, and out west to Little Big Horn and Montana, where I feared an old tanned cowboy was about to shoot me, until he put two dollars' worth of quarters in my hand and wished me luck in Vegas, where I was headed once I left his town. So much of what I saw, as I had long suspected, was so real, so compelling, that I truly hope we get to chat about it all one day. For now I will just share the most important thing I learned: You can't stay on the road forever. Can't keep fleeing. Turns out that even if you never find the courage to look back, the stuff you fled comes looking after *you*. This, too, I learned the hard way.

One summer morning, on break from my travels, I sat at a small wooden table in a friend's New York apartment and, for no apparent reason, began to cry. By now I know you may think I'm a big crybaby, but I really wasn't up until that morning. From twelve or so on, the older I got the less I cried, except for a few brief and extraordinary occasions, which you know about. So it was a real surprise to just roll out of bed and weep when nothing seemed to be too wrong. But the tears kept on falling and I tucked my head into the pocket of my elbow, resting on the table, and let them fall.

I'm so alone, I whispered.

That also made no sense, I thought, since there were so many things and people swarmed around me at the time. Just that week, I'd spoken with half a million or so people, through a television camera at Rockefeller Center; one of the morning news shows wanted to discuss the things I'd seen out on the road. A few weeks after that, some man I'd never met before informed me that he would soon put my picture on the cover of his magazine. Sure enough, he did. And not long after *that*, a few thousand people crowded into an auditorium, hours early, to see me—or, rather, to see the president, who was coming on stage after me. I don't want to give the impression that I was famous or anything. I wasn't. All I'm trying to say is that I was not *so* alone and that I didn't have a great idea why I started crying that morning in New York. So I pulled myself together and went on about my day, for many days. Moved into my own cramped, overpriced apartment near my favorite Brooklyn neighborhood, Fort Greene, with its brownstones that I couldn't afford but which were still so beautiful to stare at and into as I walked underneath the flowered trees that lined the narrow streets.

My first afternoon there, I passed an old black woman, huddled with a young white girl on the sidewalk. They seemed to know each other. The old black woman said to the young white girl as I walked by: *And she didn't even speak! I said oh no that is not how you treat people in a real neighborhood.*

The young white girl nodded. I smiled, kept on walking, kept on see-ing scenes like that around Fort Greene and thought of all the women I had known like that old woman, way back when.

The children of Fort Greene also made me think of how things used to be, sometimes. They came in many colors, just like the old women, in shades of brown like mine, darker, lighter. And so many of them seemed so happy, joy spilling over—had little skateboards, and wild afros, and some even lugged the same plastic book bags we wore back in the nineties. But what struck me most about so many of these boys and girls was that they did not walk the streets alone. I'd come out of a coffee shop and find myself behind a little boy racing to grab his father's hand, held out at a perfect height for the boy to clasp, and the two would enter Fort Greene Park, where the man pushed the child on a swing. And, more than once, I saw boys climbing subway steps behind their mothers—and the mother would grab the little boy's hand and help him hop up the last step or two, and they'd laugh at each other, *with* each other, and walk on to where they had agreed to go that afternoon. It was an incredible, marvelous thing to see, really. But for some reason, every time I walked behind them, my eyes began to burn, and wetness would gather in the rim of my sunglasses, which I wore to protect myself from UV rays, of course, but also because I never knew when I would see a little boy with his mother or father, walking into Fort Greene Park to swing, hopping up the subway stairs, and feel as if I had seen the saddest thing I ever saw, which made no sense, since I had seen much sadder things.

More and more it seemed my tears were not connected to my brain, as if an edict had been passed, an inviolable law, demanding that all the tears inside of all the people be released. At least inside of me. And just like that, there was a little puddle around my feet or on my pillow when I woke up from that same old dream in the middle of the night, which also came more nights than before.

I hid no big secrets any longer. I waged no wars with God; we were working things out. I'd lost my appetite for revenge, my lust for glory—though I backslid every now and then. Yet here I was, still hunted in my sleep and, more and more, my waking hours. What fresh dead end was this?

And if that was not bad enough, the world seemed at a dead end, too. For example, one weeklong stretch of summer went as follows:

On a Tuesday night in July, two cops in Baton Rouge pinned a black man to the ground outside a convenience store and shot him six times, to death. The following day, a cop in Minneapolis shot a black man in the side—also to death—as the man reached for his driver's license. Two days later, a black man stood on the roof of a building in downtown Dallas and shot five cops with a sniper rifle while they guarded a protest, organized to lament the events in Baton Rouge and Minneapolis. The sniper then barricaded himself in a parking garage, informed interrogators that he'd planted bombs throughout downtown, and was, shortly after the bomb search began, blown up himself, by a police robot. My sister was trapped in one of those buildings that night. A friend—or lover; it's complicated—was thrown in jail down in Louisiana for marching against it all. This was, in kind, a typical week: some cornucopia of national catastrophe and private crisis.

Things did not improve.

Britain quit Europe, which might be finished once again. The North Pole was well on its way to melting into a giant swimming pool. I met a beautiful Palestinian on my pilgrimage to Jerusalem; as soon as I left, his friends were killed in a dustup near the Western Wall; he fled to live in exile: this is not a parable. The Klan came back in full force, membership quite young, all or nearly cheering for the 45th president, whom the FBI feared was in cahoots with the Russians. So did I. California almost burned beyond the ground.

See the world. Savor it. Soon, what will it be? That is a question for the prophet.

My question at the time was simply: *What is wrong with me?* Ever wonder that? If so, my final admonition is this: *Stop.* Drop whatever's in your hand. Leave your basket in the aisle. Retrace your steps out the door. Find the crack. Try to find its source, understand its reason, excuse or not. Try. That is all I knew to do.

With little thought and far less warning, I left New York. *Disappeared,* you could say. I rented a little house in Austin, where I had no kin and few acquaintances. Wanted to be all by myself for a while, to hear my own voice(s) and, maybe, hear the voice of God. See if I could patch my cracks up, at least find out how they came to be. Everything that I have told you in this story is the result of my investigation. I was putting it all on paper, making my little paddle. Then I got that call from Riley. Then Elijah came to see me in my dream. Now he helps me make the paddle, since I did not get to him in time.

I have a radio. It picks up only two stations: Life and Death. I turn the death off, now that I know the sound. The diddy bop of death. I sit in silence if I have to.

———

I have a photograph. The family stands together in a lush green field with leaves at their feet and trees behind them. Daddy. Mama. Sister-girl. There's the little boy again. His arms *were* airplane wings. That *was* a twinkle in his eyes. God has confirmed that he was born that way: a small brown moon with joy for craters. I look at the photograph each night before I go to bed.

I wake past midnight and tiptoe into the kitchen of the world. Reach for the switch and brace myself for what's to come: a million little roaches of disaster, scurrying across the newspaper countertops, taunting, tempting me to fetch a shoe, douse them with a poison mist. I turn off the lights. I lie back down. I rest. Did you know that roaches were around before the dinosaurs? There's a message.

I have not given up.

I set out to find that little boy, somewhere in the rubble. I had no search-and-rescue animals. No flashlight. All I had were words. These words became the bread-crumb trail that led me back to him. He was there! Found him sitting all alone on a rock in the woods with a rain-soaked sack tied to a stick. Wounded. Not dead. *C'mon, boy.* He took my hand, or I took his, whatever. We walked back home. We made home up from scratch. Decided not to buy a Christmas tree this year. He teaches me what joy is. I teach him—no, we learn together—how to live. All that time spent learning how to die. How to run. Now I'm right back where I started.

Perhaps it's fitting, then, that I received another message shortly after Riley's call.

Is your ass in Austin? I'm in Carson the next two days.

It was River.

Five years had passed since I'd last seen him, sometime around my dead end, before I left for New York City. Spring, it might have been. I'm not sure. I do know that I drove to Carson and that we spent a day or two together, and of that day or two I remember only enough to warn you: never spend the night with someone who hates you with just cause. It was agreed, without an uttered word, that we would never see each other again. So much for that. Time heals no wounds, but you do start missing people after a while. Besides, only God has the wild card of destruction in His deck. The rest of us are stuck with the same old cards. And so, of course, I went to pick him up.

Made the hour-long drive north and on through those same dark streets, the same long strips of dimmed shopping centers, same small shadowed churches, the 7-Eleven, the old high school, the park, the same few hills—to the same boy. Now a *man*, I guess, as was I, though I still felt like a boy most days.

I parked in front this time. "How Does It Feel" had been playing on repeat, only because I was trying to tell you about the song and had to make sure I didn't miss anything important. I turned it off once he knocked on the passenger window.

Hey.

Hey, River.

Same greeting as so long ago. Same feeling, once he sat down, that a whole universe had been crammed into a single car. Off we went.

I didn't drive fast because I was no longer in a hurry to get places, and I did not want the cops to blow my brains out like they seemed so fond of doing at the time, and I did not know where we were headed. The sun had just gone down.

Have you seen Moonlight? I asked, thinking that the movies would be an easy way to kill a few hours.

Yeah. The NAACP had a screening out in LA, so I hit that up.

I laughed.

What?

You went to something with the NAACP?

Uh, yeah. I'm a member.

Since when?

I'd heard this laugh of his before, the one halfway between amusement and anger.

Since I was in high school, Casey. Like, since I was seventeen.

You lying. I met you when you were nineteen. Pretty sure I would have known if you were going around with the NAACP.

Whatever. You never wanted to see me in a positive light. Your fault if you didn't know.

Well, damn. My bad.

I had, with time, learned to de-escalate.

We continued down the highway, nothing on the radio. He told me about his life in Los Angeles, about a trip to Rotterdam to see his ailing grandfather, where he'd caught a cold that he still had. For some stretches we were quiet and that was fine.

You wanna come with me to IKEA? I asked. *Need to find a plant for my house.* I had not owned a plant or any living thing since my dog was put to sleep in '97. Actually, I bought two beta fish in '98 or thereabouts, housed them in the same tank so I could watch them rip flesh off each other until they both were dead.

He snickered. *You know they say don't go to IKEA unless you want to end up in a fight.*

Who is they?

Don't remember. Read it somewhere. Said that couples always fight when they go to IKEA.

I looked over. He was staring out the window.

Pretty sure we won't have that problem.

True.

We arrived at the sprawling furniture depot. Strolled through the aisles, under the copious lights—industrial-strength fluorescent tubes, den lamps, vanity mirrors—pushing a cart. He said the California sun made his room a hotbox from morning on, so we loitered among the window curtains for a while. When we reached the plant department, I realized I didn't know a goddamn thing about plants. I confess to you that I had also learned how much better people feel when they feel needed. *Which one should I get?* He suggested a tall, treelike situation. *Majesty palm,* it was called, perhaps because it resembled those homemade fans Cleopatra's servants used back in the day. In any event, it was under twenty dollars and required little maintenance. We were done in half an hour.

You hungry? I asked, truly hungry and also out of ideas.

Nah, not right now. Probably be starving by time you get somewhere, though.

And he was, or so he claimed, when we walked into the restaurant, on the ground floor of a once-abandoned power plant. The waitress sat us at a table in the center of everything. That was fine.

I'll get whatever you get, River said. When the dishes came, he closed his eyes. When he opened them, I was still watching.

What?

Never seen you pray before.

What you mean? I've always prayed.

Never saw it . . . Who you pray to?

Huh? To God. I mean, I stopped going to church a long time ago. Doesn't mean I don't believe in God, though. Just talk to Him on my own. Works for me.

Hmph . . . I feel you. Didn't know.

Clearly.

———

River's cold had gotten worse by the time we settled into my living room. I brought him a warm face towel, which didn't do much good. Brought a glass of bourbon, which didn't do much good, either. Brought some medicine, which he reminded me was not supposed to mix with alcohol.

Why don't you just go to bed? I suggested. And so we did.

Lying there felt like cooking a dish you've cooked many times, except with new ingredients. Or cooking a new dish with the same ingredients you've always had. I don't cook much, hell. What I'm trying to say is that I've rarely felt so awkward doing something I'd already done before. Perhaps that's why, when the room went dark, a quiet laugh escaped.

Are you staring at me? he asked, in all seriousness.

Um, no. I really wasn't. *This is just funny.*

As hell. Welp . . . good night.

Night.

When I woke the next morning, he was already propped up, reading the news on his phone. I saw, in the morning light, that there were bags under his eyes—just a little puffiness, enough to prove that he had lived more life than he had when we last saw each other, as had I. He was still beautiful, maybe more, with life under his eyes. Can't say that about everybody.

You like breakfast tacos? I asked.

Man, my mom used to make those all the time. Which meant yes, I figured.

Cool. Be right back. I slipped on a pair of jeans and grabbed my car keys. Returned with a paper bag. He looked inside.

I thought you were gonna cook.

Boy, I'm not your mama.

A smirk on River's face.

Damn it's almost twelve, he said. *I better shower.*

While he bathed I made my bed, having recently read that people who make their beds every morning are happier. When I finished I felt about the same as I had before, which was fine, and found River in my living room packing his suitcase, naked. I brought up the newly elected president, not knowing what else to talk about.

Is he saying "big league" or "bigly"? I asked, referring to the president-elect's abnormal use of the English language. *I hope it's "bigly" . . . Kinda like that word.*

Yeah. That sounds like a word you would like.

I had been walking away when he said this. I stopped, turned around.

What you mean by that?

You know, River said, *it's just different . . . quirky.*

Oh.

I took a few deep breaths, per the meditation guide I had begun to use. All the rage that had suddenly appeared left just as quickly.

You ready?

Think so.

It was a jean jacket afternoon outside, the weekend after Thanksgiving, leaves already separated from lonely branches. The sun shone pale enough behind a veil of clouds that you had to scan the golden sky to find the thing itself. I wore my shades until we pulled up to the airport terminal.

You're not getting out? River asked when I reached over to hug him.

Oh yeah. I hadn't planned on it.

He sat his suitcase next to my car and we did the whole curbside good-bye thing.

You were actually nice, he said. I was surprised.

Hmph . . . maybe we should just have a reset, you know?

A reset?

Yeah. We'll talk about it.

He laughed. *Aight.*

You better run.

From the airport I drove to a nursery in search of soil and a new pot, then home to transfer my plant. Sent River a picture of the final product. *I sure hope this works.*

Don't worry, he responded, from a tarmac in Los Angeles. *It should be harder to kill it than to keep it alive.*

I followed the instructions. Poured water in the soil and let it drain through to a nice ceramic dish. Opened my living room blinds so the light could shine in. Watched the plant grow.

Days later, I watched a long green leaf immolate, shrivel, collapse to the floor. No alarm. Watched another leaf and then a branch begin to wither. Tried to prune. Less light. More water. Tried less water and more light. Watched the plant stop growing.

By New Year's Eve, the plant was dead.

I carried its brown body to the backyard and laid it down in an empty garden patch. Last time I checked it was mixed in with the dirt. I still don't know what I did wrong but I will try again, someday. Promise.

To my mother, my father, and my sister.
I hope this book is worth a part of all we have endured.

GRATITUDE

To write this book meant to walk, nearly blind, toward an unknown destination that I knew I had to reach yet also knew I *could not* reach without the grace of God. Each day, God took my hand and led me toward the destination, helped me get a little rest at night, woke me up the next morning ready—or at least, *willing*—to go on. Never was I left to walk alone. My editor, Becky Saletan; my agent, Lynn Nesbit; my friends Brenda, Matthew, and Paula-Raye—walked beside me. They picked me up each time I fell, pushed me when I did not want to move, had the guts to warn me if I started walking in the wrong direction. We made it.

I am grateful for the grace of God.

CREDITS

6   *Not infrequently ending in death*: Gilbert Millstein, "Books of the Times" review of Jack Kerouac's *On the Road, The New York Times*, September 5, 1957, http://www.nytimes.com/books/97/09/07 /home/kerouac-roadglowing.html.

12   *As a high school quarterback growing up in South Dallas*: Laura Miller, "Broken Bodies, Broken Dreams," *Dallas Life*, June 22, 1986.

103 *"Oh butter!" cried Jessie*: Gertrude Chandler Warner, *The Boxcar Children Bookshelf*, Box edition (Park Ridge, Illinois: Albert Whitman & Company, 2010).

111 *the war may not have brought a great deal of bloodshed to Texas*: Elizabeth Hayes Turner, "Juneteenth: Emancipation and Memory" in *Lone Star Pasts: Memory and History in Texas*, eds. Gregg Cantrell and Elizabeth Hayes Turner (College Station, Texas: Texas A&M University Press, 2006).

118 *I wish to hear more about this god whose name is Love*: E. M. Forster, *The Life to Come, and Other Short Stories* (New York: W. W. Norton & Company, 1987).

183 *when the gods have ceased to be and the Christ has not yet come*: Gustave Flaubert, from a letter quoted in Marguerite Yourcenar's "Reflections on the Composition of *Memoirs of Hadrian*," *Memoirs of Hadrian*, trans. Grace Flick (New York: Farrar Straus & Giroux, 2005), pp. 319–20.

218 *placed into the dipper and poured back down on the world*: Little Richard interview on Jimi Hendrix for 1973 documentary *Jimi Hendrix*, produced by Joe Boyd, John Head, and Gary Weis, https://www .youtube.com/watch?v=MHlRa-RPjWE.

223 *How does it feel to be a problem?*: W. E. B. Du Bois, *The Souls of Black Folk* (New York: Random House, 2005).

228 *laugh and eat well and grow strong*: From "I, Too" by Langston Hughes, https://www.poetryfoundation .org/poems/47558/i-too.

228 *One must wait until evening to see how splendid the day has been*: attributed to Sophocles, *Antigone*.

230 *We had then to discuss / Whither or where we might travel*: Louise Glück, "Parable," in *Faithful and Virtuous Night* (New York: Farrar Straus & Giroux, 2014).

236 *black and shining prince*: Ossie Davis, eulogy for Malcolm X, February 27, 1965, http://malcolmx.com /eulogy/.

238 *i made it up / here on this bridge*: Lucille Clifton, "won't you celebrate with me," in *Book of Light* (Port Townsend, Washington: Copper Canyon Press, 1993).

245 *For generations men have come into the world*: James Baldwin, in conversation with Audre Lorde, originally published in *Essence* in 1984, http://theculture.forharriet.com/2014/03/revolutionary -hope-conversation-between.html#axzz56LaQFsUL.

249 *There are years that ask questions and years that answer*: Zora Neale Hurston, *Their Eyes Were Watching God: A Novel* (New York: Harper Collins, 2009).

272 *I am an invisible man*: Ralph Ellison, *Invisible Man* (New York: Vintage International, 1980).

275 *My fellow Americans, we live in an age of anarchy*: President Richard M. Nixon, address to the nation announcing the invasion of Cambodia, April 30, 1970, http://www.presidency.ucsb.edu/ws/?pid= 2490.

276 *Nobody ever died too early or too late; you always die right on time*: Clarice Gerald.

278 *It's been a long time coming, but tonight, because of what we did*: Barack Obama, Grant Park Victory Speech, November 4, 2008, http://www.americanrhetoric.com/speeches/convention2008 /barackobamavictoryspeech.htm.

282 *to form a secret society with but one object*: Will of Cecil Rhodes, http://pages.uoregon.edu/kimball /Rhodes-Confession.htm.

285 *to call myself beloved, to feel myself beloved on the earth*: Raymond Carver, "Late Fragment," from *A New Path to the Waterfall* (New York: Atlantic Monthly Press, 1989).

317 *Two thousand years ago*: President John F. Kennedy, remarks at Rudolph Wilde Platz Berlin, June 26, 1963, https://jfklibrary.org/Asset-Viewer/oEX2uqSQGEGIdTYgd_JL_Q.aspx.

342 *I had nothing to offer anybody except my own confusion*: Jack Kerouac, *On the Road: The Original Scroll*. (London: Penguin Classics, 2008).

346 *Roosevelt drew a large cross in his diary*: Edmund Morris, *The Rise of Theodore Roosevelt* (New York: Random House, 2001).

346 *[Julius Caesar] came to Gades*: Suetonius and Joseph Gavorse, *The Lives of the Twelve Caesars* (New York: Modern Library, 1931).

347 *Long service in Washington at the court of power*: Theodore H. White, *The Making of the President, 1960* (New York: Harper Perennial, 2009).

350 *isn't worth a warm bucket of piss*: Attributed to John "Cactus Jack" Nance Garner, https://www.politico .com/gallery/2012/08/11-insults-about-being-vice-president/000342-004455.html.

351 *Who's the man to see?*: Theodore H. White, *The Making of the President, 1960*.

352 *Business—in the Roman Senate—could be interrupted or postponed*: *The Lives of the Twelve Caesars*.

353 *Robert Moses was the optimist of optimists*: Robert Caro, *The Power Broker: Robert Moses and the Fall of New York* (New York: Vintage Books, 1975).

353 *only the people, voting at the polls*: Theodore H. White, *The Making of the President, 1960*.

369 *This world is not enough*: José Esteban Muñoz, *Cruising Utopia: The Then and There of Queer Futurity* (New York: New York University Press, 2009).